MARY SHELLEY

CRITICAL ISSUES

Published

Mary Shelley	*Graham Allen*
Jane Austen	*Darryl Jones*
George Eliot	*Pauline Nestor*
Virginia Woolf	*Linden Peach*
Charlotte Brontë	*Carl Plasa*
Charles Dickens	*Lyn Pykett*
Joseph Conrad	*Allan H. Simmons*
John Donne	*Richard Sugg*
Henry James	*Jeremy Tambling*
John Keats	*John Whale*
William Wordsworth	*John Williams*

In preparation

D. H. Lawrence	*Rick Rylance*
Thomas Hardy	*Julian Wolfreys*

Critical Issues Series
Series Standing Order
ISBN 1–4039–2158–X hardcover
ISBN 1–4039–2159–8 paperback
(*outside North America only*)

You can receive future titles in this series as they are published by placing a standing order. Please contact your bookseller or, in case of difficulty, write to us at the address below with your name and address, the title of the series and the ISBN quoted above.

Customer Services Department, Macmillan Distribution Ltd,
Houndmills, Basingstoke, Hampshire RG21 6XS, England

Critical Issues

Mary Shelley

Graham Allen

First published 2008 by
PALGRAVE MACMILLAN
Houndmills, Basingstoke, Hampshire RG21 6XS and
175 Fifth Avenue, New York, N.Y. 10010
Companies and representatives throughout the world

PALGRAVE MACMILLAN is the global academic imprint of the Palgrave Macmillan division of St. Martin's Press, LLC and of Palgrave Macmillan Ltd. Macmillan® is a registered trademark in the United States, United Kingdom and other countries. Palgrave is a registered trademark in the European Union and other countries.

ISBN 13: 978–0–230–01908–9 hardback
ISBN 10: 0–230–01908–0 hardback
ISBN 13: 978–0–230–01909–6 paperback
ISBN 10: 0–230–01909–9 paperback

This book is printed on paper suitable for recycling and made from fully managed and sustained forest sources.

A catalogue record for this book is available from the British Library.

A catalogue record for this book is available from the Library of Congress.

10   9   8   7   6   5   4   3   2   1
17   16   15   14   13   12   11   10   09   08

Printed and bound in China

Contents

Acknowledgements   vii

Texts and Abbreviations   ix

Introduction   1

1   *Frankenstein; Or, The Modern Prometheus*   17

2   *Matilda*   41

3   *Valperga: Or, The Life and Adventures of Castruccio, Prince of Lucca*   64

4   *The Last Man*   90

5   *The Fortunes of Perkin Warbeck*   117

6   *Lodore*   138

7   *Falkner, A Novel*   160

Afterword: Beyond the Novels   179

Notes   182

Bibliography   204

Index   219

For my mother, Daphne A. Allen,
and Betty T. Bennett, i.m.

Acknowledgements

I would like to thank Professor Nora Crook for all her help, friendship, and guidance over the years; I would also like to thank Professor Timothy Webb for similar gifts. What I owe you both goes far beyond this book. Some of the book was researched during sabbatical leave granted by UCC, for which I am thankful. I would like to thank all those students who have joined with me in exploring Mary Shelley's work down the years. I would also like to thank the following people (with apologies to all those left unnamed): Gary Baker, Bruce Barker-Benfield, Susan Burke-Trehy, James Carney, Pamela Clemit, Siobhán Ní Chonaill, Siobhan Collins, Keith Crook, David Duff, Anne Fitzgerald, Carrie Griffin, Paul Hegarty, Darryl Jones, Forbes Morlock, Éamonn Ó'Carragáin, Mary O'Connell, Michelle O'Connell, John W. Phillips, Roy Sellars, John W. Phillips, Ruth Webb, Lisa Vargo, Sarah Wood. I am extremely grateful for the professionalism and intelligence of all those involved in Palgrave's Critical Issues series, and would like to thank in particular Martin Coyle, Felicity Noble and Sonya Barker. My most enduring thanks must go to Bernie, Dani and Chrissie. Thank you for all your help, support, belief and love.

- Shelley, Mary Wollstonecraft. The Letters of Mary Wollstonecraft Shelley, Volume 2: "Treading in unknown paths". pp. 4, 95, 122, 124, 139, 177, 178, 185, 196, 261, 262, 267, 285. © 1983 The Johns Hopkins University Press. Reprinted with permission of The Johns Hopkins University Press.

Every effort has been made to trace the copyright holders but if any have been inadvertently overlooked the publishers will be pleased to make the necessary arrangement at the first opportunity.

Texts and Abbreviations

I. MARY WOLLSTONECRAFT SHELLEY

References to Mary Shelley's works are to these editions:

L *The Letters of Mary Wollstonecraft Shelley*, ed. Betty T. Bennett, 3 Vols (Baltimore and London: The Johns Hopkins University Press, 1980–88).

J *The Journals of Mary Shelley*, ed. Paula R. Feldman and Diana Scott-Kilvert (Baltimore and London: The Johns Hopkins University Press, 1987; reprinted 1995).

Shelley Novels *The Novels and Selected Works of Mary Shelley*, Gen. Eds Nora Crook with Pamela Clemit, Consulting Ed. Betty T. Bennett, 8 Vols (London: Pickering and Chatto, 1996).

FN *The Frankenstein Notebooks. A Facsimile Edition of Mary Shelley's Manuscript Novel, 1816–17 (With Alterations in the Hand of Percy Bysshe Shelley) as it Survives in Draft and Fair Copy Deposited by Lord Abinger in the Bodleian Library, Oxford (Dep. c. 477/1 and Dep. c. 534/1–2)*, 2 Vols, ed. Charles E. Robinson, *Manuscripts of the Younger Romantics*, Vol. IX (New York and London: Garland Publishing, Inc., 1996).

LL *Mary Shelley's Literary Lives and Other Writings*, 4 Vols. Ed. Nora Crook (London: Pickering and Chatto, 2002).

Individual Text Abbreviations

All texts from *The Novels and Selected Works of Mary Shelley*, Gen. Eds Nora Crook with Pamela Clemit, 8 Vols (London: Pickering and Chatto, 1996).

F   *Frankenstein; or The Modern Prometheus.* Ed. Nora Crook. Intro. Betty T. Bennett.

Fal   *Falkner, A Novel.* Ed. Pamela Clemit.

LM   *The Last Man.* Ed. Jane Blumberg, with Nora Crook.

Lod   *Lodore.* Ed. Fiona Stafford.

M   *Matilda.* Ed. Pamela Clemit, in Shelley, Novels, II, pp.1–67.

PW   *The Fortunes of Perkin Warbeck, A Romance.* Ed. Douchet Devin Fischer.

R   *Rambles in Germany and Italy in 1840, 1842 and 1843.* Ed. Jeanne Moskal, in Shelley, Novels, VIII, 61–386.

V   *Valperga: Or, The Life and Adventures of Castruccio, Prince of Lucca.* Ed. Nora Crook.

II.   PERCY BYSSHE SHELLEY

Letters of Percy Bysshe Shelley   *The Letters of Percy Bysshe Shelley*, 2 Vols, ed. Frederick L. Jones (Oxford: Clarendon Press, 1964).

Shelley's Prose   *Shelley's Prose or The Trumpet of a Prophecy*, ed. David Lee Clark, Revised Edn (London: Fourth Estate, 1988).

Shelley's Poetry and Prose   *Shelley's Poetry and Prose*, eds Donald H. Reiman and Sharon B. Powers (New York and London: W. W. Norton, 1977).

Shelley, *Poems I*   *The Poems of Shelley, Volume I: 1804–1817*, eds Geoffrey Matthews and Kelvin Everest (London and New York: Longman, 1989).

Shelley, *Poems II*   *The Poems of Shelley, Volume II: 1817–1819*, eds Kelvin Everest and Geoffrey Matthews (London and New York: Longman, 1989).

III. WILLIAM GODWIN

Godwin, *Novels Collected Novels and Memoirs of William Godwin*, 8 Vols, Gen. Ed. Mark Philp (London: William Pickering, 1992).

Godwin, *Political Political and Philosophical Writings of William Godwin*, 7 Vols, Gen. Ed. Mark Philp (London: William Pickering, 1993).

IV. MARY WOLLSTONECRAFT

Wollstonecraft, *Works The Works of Mary Wollstonecraft*, Gen. Eds Janet Todd and Marilyn Butler, 7 Vols (London: William Pickering, 1989).

V. ESSAY COLLECTIONS

Companion The Cambridge Companion to Mary Shelley, ed. Esther Schor (Cambridge: Cambridge University Press, 2003).

Endurance The Endurance of 'Frankenstein': Essays on Mary Shelley's Novel, eds George Levine and U. C. Knoepflmacher (Berkeley and Los Angeles: University of California Press, 1979).

Fictions Mary Shelley's Fictions: From 'Frankenstein' to 'Falkner', ed. Michael-Eberle-Sinatra, intro. Nora Crook (London: Macmillan, 2000).

Iconoclastic Iconoclastic Depatures: Mary Shelley after 'Frankenstein', eds Syndy M. Conger, Frederick S. Frank and Gregory O'Dea (Madison, Teaneck: Fairleigh Dickinson University Press, 1997).

Other The Other Mary Shelley: Beyond 'Frankenstein', eds Audrey A. Fisch, Anne K. Mellor and Esther H. Schor (New York and Oxford: Oxford University Press, 1993).

Times Mary Shelley in Her Times, eds Betty T. Bennett and Stuart Curran (Baltimore and London: The Johns Hopkins University Press, 2000).

Introduction

I. THE 'WIFE OF SHELLEY'

Mary Shelley lived a dramatic and extraordinarily 'readable' life, and lived it amongst some of the most remarkable writers and thinkers of her age. It is little wonder that biography has played such a significant role in the academic and the popular response to her work. Biography, however, has also served to mis-shape and misrepresent Shelley's place within her famous radical circle and within Romanticism in general. During the nineteenth and then the twentieth century, debates about her role in the 'life' of P. B. Shelley came to obscure her achievements as a writer. They also helped to produce a depoliticized and domesticated image of Shelley as a devoted if, in some versions, unworthy 'wife' to P. B. Shelley. This image increasingly served a narrative account of her writings which marks out her first novel, *Frankenstein*, as the product less of her own genius than of the inspiring influence of those (P. B. Shelley, Byron) around her, and also presents us with a steady decline in literary achievement after the premature deaths of those canonical male poets. The *return* to Mary Shelley which has been gathering apace in the last thirty years or so necessarily confronts the issue of biography, its influence on literary history, the presence of biographical trends within the work of a writer like Shelley, and its persistence within the critical reception of her work.[1] The fundamental aim of this book is to present a reading of all of Shelley's major fictional works without reverting to the kinds of biographical modes of reading and interpretation which have so significantly marginalized women's writing over the past two hundred years. As we will see, such an aim does not mean that we will be able to avoid discussing Shelley's life when we engage with her writings. What is required is a degree of self-consciousness about the complex relation between life and art, a degree of self-consciousness that Shelley possessed to an intense degree.

Before we can begin to register the complexities involved in Shelley's fiction, we need to return to the manner in which her reputation was shaped in the nineteenth and twentieth centuries. Only when we understand the manner in which her writing and life have been misread and transformed will we be in a position to attempt *the return to Mary Shelley*. A useful guide to the reception history of Shelley comes in the last chapter of Emily W. Sunstein's biography.[2] Sunstein writes that Shelley 'is a striking example of a posthumous reputation bent out of shape by admirers and, more lastingly, by traducers.'[3] Sunstein is referring, at least in part, to the manner in which the Shelleys' remaining child, Percy Florence Shelley, and more importantly still his wife, Lady Jane Shelley, took control of the huge amount of manuscripts, letters and other texts left by the Shelleys and used them to cement what was already a considerable revision of P. B. Shelley's life and work. Percy Florence and Lady Shelley initially entrusted Thomas Jefferson Hogg, one of P. B. Shelley's earliest friends, to write the *Life* of the poet. Dissatisfied with the first two volumes of Hogg's life of the poet, they ordered him to hand back their papers and published, the following year, an edited (and indeed censored) version of these manuscripts in *Shelley Memorials*. They eventually commissioned the writing of the life of Godwin, P. B. Shelley and of Mary Shelley, in that order, each one conforming to their sanitized version of the Shelleys' life together in an increasingly distant 'Romantic' past.[4] Percy Florence and especially Lady Shelley are important players in a Victorian process whereby P. B. Shelley, and by association Shelley herself, were 'white-washed' of their former political radicality and social notoriety.[5]

Her Romantic and Victorian biographers tended to treat Shelley as a figure whose undoubted talents were sacrificed for the historical, literary and social good of supporting the great poet when he was alive and then, after his death, under the most inauspicious of situations, gradually bringing his full canon of poetic and prose works to the attention of the world. This is, for example, how Florence Marshall treats her. After hundreds of detailed, scholarly pages, Marshall presents us with a Mary Shelley whose value is embodied by and in the 'wife of Shelley' role, registered in her 'beauty of character.'[6] This 'beauty of character' (displaying the essentially 'female' virtues of fidelity, self-sacrifice, devotion, deferment to male intellect) is the direct product of the Romantic and Victorian cult of what Mary Poovey describes as *The Proper Lady and the Woman Writer*.[7]

Betty T. Bennett has written about what she calls the 'angelizing' of P. B. Shelley and of Shelley.[8] She writes: 'Mary Shelley became a posthumous pawn in the biographical wars over who had owned P. B. Shelley's heart while he still lived.'[9] The immediate reference here is to Leigh Hunt's initial refusal to hand over to Shelley the sacred 'relic' of P. B. Shelley's heart, which had remained strangely resistant to the flames during the poet's cremation.[10] The wider reference is to the series of biographies of P. B. Shelley which his friends and associates (Hunt, Thomas Medwin, Thomas Jefferson Hogg, Thomas Love Peacock, Edward John Trelawny, and others) wrote, mainly after Mary Shelley's death. While she was alive, Mary Shelley had to contend with a series of pressures which forced her to defer such publications while remaining convinced that only she could do the job in the appropriate manner. P. B. Shelley's father, Sir Timothy Shelley, wishing to see his son's radical legacy expunged from the public record, banned Shelley from bringing his son's works or name before the public after she had published *Posthumous Poems of P. B. Shelley* in 1824. The *Posthumous Poems* had sold three hundred of its five hundred copies in only a few months, before Sir Timothy recalled the remaining number for destruction. Given that she was dependent on Sir Timothy for financial support (not only for her remaining child, but also to support her invariably insolvent father and step-mother), Shelley was forced to concede. Sir Timothy, in 1824, was in his seventies and, unsurprisingly, Shelley believed that this ban on bringing her husband's life and work before the public would not last too long. Sir Timothy lived until his early nineties, however, and only granted permission for an edition of P. B. Shelley's poetry and prose in 1838.[11]

The issue of P. B. Shelley's biography involved a series of extremely controversial subjects, which need to be borne in mind when we examine the way in which Shelley attempted to control, and was herself ultimately controlled by, the fate of the poet's name and reputation. When at the age of sixteen she eloped with the twenty-one year old P. B. Shelley, along with her step-sister Jane (Claire) Clairmont, she, and indeed none of the parties involved, could have known quite how far-reaching and devastating the consequences of their actions would be. Mary and Claire's father, William Godwin, author of the *Memoirs* of her mother's unconventional, even at times scandalous life, already had enough experience to have tempered his earlier belief that if the truth is conveyed simply and understandably it must be believed (Godwin, Novels, vol. 1, pp.85–141). The reception of his *Memoirs* of Mary Wollstonecraft's life and work had been very far from the ideal of the inevitable acceptance of the truth. When Godwin's daughter and step-daughter ran away from home with an older, married poet, it must have seemed as if history were repeating itself; this time, however, Godwin, burdened with a family and irresolvable financial problems, was in no humour to brave the world with unfashionable and unconventional truths. In October 1816, only two years after Mary, accompanied by Claire, eloped with P. B. Shelley, Wollstonecraft's first child, Fanny Imlay, the illegitimate product of her liaison with the rakish Gilbert Imlay, had committed suicide, abandoned, as she felt, by her step-sisters. Godwin's response seems to have been entirely motivated by a desire to keep the event from the public eye. In December of that same year, P. B. Shelley's first wife, Harriet Shelley, drowned herself in the Serpentine. The following year Claire gave birth to her own, illegitimate child by Byron, Allegra.

By the time of P. B. Shelley's death in 1822 Allegra, along with three of Mary's and Percy's own children, had died. The family losses did not end there, however. Earlier in March 1817, P. B. Shelley, in a Chancery Court session, had been denied custody of his two children (Ianthe and Charles) by his first wife, Harriet. The court, because of P. B. Shelley's abandonment of his wife for the then Mary Godwin, and because of his atheistical beliefs, as evidenced in his poem *Queen Mab* (1813), publicly decreed that P. B. Shelley was an unfit person to father his own children. The children were ordered to be 'brought up at his expense by a provincial clergyman in accordance with the doctrines of the Church of England.'[12]

Much of what Bennett calls the 'biographical wars' which accelerated apace in the nineteenth century stem from the scandal of that court case, along with the issue of whether P. B. Shelley had abandoned Harriet, or whether, as some suggested, she had been unfaithful to him. But they are also the direct product of a series of public scandals, many if not all of which were sparked off by the unheeding enthusiasm of the young rebels in their earliest years together.[13] Claire's brief dalliance with Byron was to dominate the rest of her life, as she attempted to hold back rumours of the past and make her living as a professional governess.[14] In 1816, however, as the three elopers plus Byron assembled by the shores of Lake Geneva, rumours from a set of international travellers were filtering back to England that the impecunious Godwin had sold or 'prostituted' his two daughters in a 'League of Incest' to P. B. Shelley and Byron. Such public scandals are novel, perhaps, to the young and enthusiastic; they are something else to a lone widow, struggling to find sufficient money to raise her remaining child in a manner appropriate to his destined station in life, haunted by those that have been loved (some completely, some not enough) and lost, and whose personal ambitions, along with those for her lost husband's work, were continually thwarted by a reactionary, monarchical parent (Sir Timothy) who simply refused to die.

There is, then, a desire in the decades following P. B. Shelley's death, as Bennett has suggested, to wash the poet and his second 'wife' clean from the 'sins' of the past. It is a desire which is massively complicated by the conflicting perspectives different readers took of the main players within the Shelleys' circle: Harriet Shelley, Claire Clairmont, Mary and Percy themselves, Godwin, Byron, the Hunts, Trelawny, and so on. That Mary Shelley's own role was to contribute to the gradual 'angelizing' of P. B. Shelley is hardly surprising when one looks at her later life, let alone the melancholic grip his absence played in her private life (as demonstrated by her journals). It was something, as Bennett suggests, that did great harm to Shelley's own reputation as a serious novelist and intellectual.[15] It also brought her considerable criticism from carriers of the flame, such as Edward John Trelawny. Trelawny was the person who had arranged for the cremation of the poet's body on the beach at Viareggio, near Pisa, and had heroically snatched his heart from the flames during his cremation. In his 1878 rewriting of *Recollections of the Last Days of Shelley and Byron* (1858), now entitled *Records of Shelley, Byron, and the Author*, the ageing Trelawny painted Mary Shelley as someone who, unlike himself, could not stay faithful to the radical charge of P. B. Shelley's vision, once the poet himself had drowned off the coast of Italy in 1822. Trelawny's 'Mary Shelley' is a 'back-sliding' disappointment.[16] But, then, so in many ways is Mrs Marshall's. As Bennett puts it, discussing Trelawny's responsibility in the Victorian production of an 'angelic', domesticated and conservative Mary: 'In their intense desire to clear Mary Shelley of immoral behaviour, they obliterated her inherently unconventional character that had given rise to her actions and her writing.'[17]

It appears that whether nineteenth-century biographers were positively or negatively minded with regard to Mary Shelley, they ended up down-grading her intellectual achievements, figuring her as a woman more interesting for her life than for her work, more significant for whom she had touched than for any 'touch' she might have had herself. Having already had a romantic relationship with Mary Shelley's step-sister, Claire Clairmont,[18] Trelawny appears to have asked Mary Shelley to marry him in the same year she had seen his *Adventures of a Younger Son* into publication (see L, II, 138–40).[19] Mary's playful and yet melancholic response is striking for a consideration of her fate as 'wife of Shelley':

> & with all this do you think that I shall marry? – Never – neither you nor any body else – Mary Shelley shall be written on my tomb – and why? I cannot tell – except that it is so pretty a name that tho' I were to preach to myself for years, I never should have the heart to get rid of it. (L, II, 139)

Was Mary's attachment to her surname due to her 'feminine' devotion to her god-like husband, or was it due to her authorial pride in her public name and the works that were associated with it? How far does her fondness and, it must be said, tight grip on her name, stem from a social accommodation to the role of 'wife', and how far does it stem from the public recognition (positive and negative) which had been drawn, by 1831, to and around that name? It is as 'the Author of *Frankenstein*' that Shelley published her novels and we need to attend to how the attachment to that famous novel affected her reputation and reception as a novelist.

II.   'THE AUTHOR OF *FRANKENSTEIN*'

That Shelley published *Frankenstein* when she was twenty years of age is a great irony when considering the manner in which her life and work have been received. Relegated to being the 'wife of Shelley', or the 'daughter of Godwin and Wollstonecraft', or even 'the acquaintance of Byron', Shelley's first fictional publication presented the world with a novel which has sold more copies and enjoyed more readers than anything produced by her illustrious circle. It is *Frankenstein* that has become the defining text of

Regency Romanticism.[20] Despite this, it is remarkable that one of the landmark texts in the recent reappraisal of Shelley's life and work seeks in its title and its contents to distance itself from this overwhelmingly popular and influential novel. In their introduction to *The Other Mary Shelley: Beyond 'Frankenstein'*, Fisch, Mellor and Schor refer to the wave of feminist interest in the novel in the 1980s. This professional and institutional interest in *Frankenstein*, a move which carried the novel out of the realm of popular culture and into the classroom, making it one of the most frequently 'set' texts on university and school curricula, had, they argued, something of a negative aspect, confirming Shelley's overall 'marginality' in the canon of Romanticism and 'throwing her salient and central voice to the edges of Romantic discourse.'[21] I will discuss the recent canonical fate of Shelley in the next section. Before we get on to that, however, we need to consider how the two figurations we are dealing with ('wife of Shelley' and 'Author of *Frankenstein*') interact and, in many ways, consolidate each other. Why do Shelley's contemporary critics want to get 'beyond *Frankenstein*'? Why is the authorial tag 'Author of *Frankenstein*', under which Shelley published her five other novels, seen as a burden and a problem?

That *Frankenstein* created a considerable critical impact when it was first published in 1818 and that the novel was published anonymously are two very well known facts. Sir Walter Scott, who reviewed the novel very positively, mistakenly believed, like others, that the novel had been written by P. B. Shelley himself.[22] However, as Charles E. Robinson has demonstrated, suggestions as to the real authorship of the novel (in the shape of Godwin's daughter) came as early as a review in *The British Critic* in April 1818 (FN, p.xciv). What is very evident from its earliest reviews, however, is that the novel's dedication to Godwin, added to its universally recognized 'power' as a novel, pulled Shelley's first novel into the political maelstrom created by the conservative reviewers' reaction to second-generation Romantic poetry, in particular to the works of Byron, P. B. Shelley, Keats, Leigh Hunt and their 'Cockney School'. That the novel actually belongs to this public sphere of ideological warfare, and that it deliberately interpolates itself into such a publicly contested sphere, is perhaps the strongest critical and historical argument made about *Frankenstein* over the past three decades. As William St Clair writes: 'Like all the books written by members of the Godwin and Shelley families, *Frankenstein* had a political and ethical purpose.'[23] John Wilson Croker's much anthologized review in the Tory *Quarterly Review* (January 1818) is an example of how virulent the 'war of ideas' could get in Britain in the 1810s.[24] Croker states that the novel 'is piously dedicated to Mr. Godwin' and that it contains 'a tissue of horrible and disgusting absurdity'.[25]

There are various things we need to note about such responses. The first is that Croker is addressing a rather elite audience when he makes these remarks. Indeed, the still current idea that *Frankenstein* was a widely read novel during the Romantic and Victorian periods has been definitively challenged by William St Clair.[26] It is true enough that, having gained a third of the profits of the 500 copies published by Lackington in 1818, Shelley was, during P. B. Shelley's lifetime, a more commercially successful author than her husband.[27] However, St Clair goes on to show how even the 1831 *Bentley's Standard Novels* edition of the text remained at a prohibitively high price for the increasing numbers of lower-class readers of novels, and that a truly mass distribution of the novel did not begin until the 1880s when Routledge published 40,000 copies. The story of *Frankenstein's* fate as a literary text in the nineteenth century is one in which a particular publishing firm, Bentley (no longer associated with Colburn), clinging on to its copyright of the novel, but unable to respond to the increasingly mass trade in cheap novel publication, failed to capitalize on what eventually would become a best seller, a novel which, only at the end of the century, could fulfil its destiny and become 'accessible to the whole reading nation'.[28] It was not, then, as a literary text that *Frankenstein* made its unprecedented mark on Romantic and Victorian culture. As St Clair writes: 'During most of the nineteenth century, it was not the reading of the text of the book, but seeing adaptations of the story on the stage which kept *Frankenstein* alive in culture …'[29] This fact was to have a major impact on the manner in which the wider cultural audience understood Shelley's most famous literary production. Factors such as the publisher's copyright over the text, along with the dominant conservatism and culture of censorship which prevailed in the London and provincial theatres of the nineteenth century, meant that Shelley's politically oriented novel was transformed (we might say 'normalized') in its numerous theatrical versions into a morality play in which 'presumption' is punished and monsters are silenced and side-lined. Being the 'Author of *Frankenstein*' did not mean that Shelley enjoyed a large audience for her subsequent works.[30] It did mean that the general perception of her most famous literary production was wildly divergent from the political radicalism of the novel she had actually written.

We should also note that the reception that the novel did receive in the reviews of her own time was, as the positive example of Scott and the negative example of Croker demonstrate, intensely bound up in the reaction to the work of other writers around her. Frequently reviewers, whilst recognizing the 'power' of the novel, attributed that 'power' to the 'Godwinian school' out of which the text emerges, rather than to any unique capability on the part of its anonymous author. The opening of a review of *Frankenstein* in the *Edinburgh Magazine* is a good example: 'Here is one of the productions of the modern school in its highest style of caricature and exaggeration. It is formed on the Godwinian manner, and has all the faults, but many like-wise of the beauties of that model.'[31] The anonymous reviewer concludes the review by stating that 'We hope yet to have more productions, both from this author and his great model, Mr. Godwin', before adding that these future works would be improved 'if they would rather study the established order of nature as it appears both in the world of matter and of mind, than continue to revolt our feelings by hazardous innovations in either of these departments.'[32] The review, then, is in some respects as much a review of Godwin's novels and their influence as it is a review of *Frankenstein*.

It is important to note this aspect of contemporary responses to the novel, since it can remind us of another major burden associated with the nomination 'Author of *Frankenstein*.' This problem, or burden, takes us back to suggestions that the 'power' of Shelley's first novel stemmed from the inspiration produced 'by her contact with [P. B.] Shelley and Byron during the memorable holiday on the lake of Geneva.'[33] This notion, that *Frankenstein* owed its 'power', if not its actual authorship, to the influence of P. B. Shelley and indeed to Byron, and that as a consequence Shelley could never, after the two poets' early deaths, match her initial success, developed as part of the Victorian domestication of Shelley and persists, at times in quite undiluted forms, today. This is what, beyond anything else, the editors of *The Other Mary Shelley* are alluding to when they figure *Frankenstein*'s canonical assimilation as a burden and a consolidation of marginality.

Masculine adjectives ('power', 'strength', 'force') dominate the early reviews of *Frankenstein*, and that language continued to inform its reception in the nineteenth and twentieth centuries. So did the idea that Shelley could not match her first success due to the death of her 'guide, philosopher, and friend.'[34] The authorial tag, 'Author of *Frankenstein*', becomes subsumed within the Victorian 'biographical wars' which eventuated in a domesticated, politically and ethically cleansed 'Mary Shelley.' A biographically-oriented reception of her work, judging that work in terms of her (passive) relations with the significant male writers in her life, led to a narrative in which *Frankenstein* is a one-off, a uniquely-inspired anomaly, the rest of her literary output (despite *Valperga* being written before P. B. Shelley's death) a decline or, to employ Richard Church's word, a stuttering 'epilogue.' As Bennett has argued, this isolating of *Frankenstein* as a one-off also contributes greatly to the domestication of Shelley as a writer. Bennett demonstrates how challenging to the conventional gender codes of Romantic and Victorian society *Frankenstein* was as a text. Once the gender of that novel's author was widely know, Bennett argues, a general attempt to return Shelley's politically reformist, socially and historically committed novels back to the 'feminine' domain of 'romance fiction' began.[35] Discussing the Victorian rewriting (domesticating, de-politicizing) of Shelley's life and works, Bennett writes that '[s]o efficient was the filter of the era, that even to this day Shelley is often depicted as a victim of conventional expectations for women, the inherent dissonance of her works glossed over as ambiguous subservience or psychological affliction.' (Bennett in F, lxix) In her discussion of *Valperga*, the first of her novels to be fully recognized by reviewers as written by a woman, Bennett writes:

> In ignoring the central theme of the novel, and concentrating instead on the romantic interest, reviewers shifted Mary Shelley from a socio-political Romantic reformer to a writer of romances in the modern sense. During her lifetime, this view became canonical, and was passed on to twentieth-century readers in a skewed patrimony that insisted Mary Shelley was either non-political or interested in politics only when P. B. Shelley was alive. (Bennett, Introduction, F, xli)

The *return to Mary Shelley*, the objective of current reassessments of her life and work, is, in its best forms, an attempt to read beyond and behind this stifling and gender-oriented 'canonical' *romancing* of her work.

III. A NEW MARY SHELLEY?

The amount of scholarly and critical activity dedicated to Shelley has undergone something of a revolution in the past thirty years.[36] Various landmark publications, all utilized in this study, illustrate a growing acceptance of Shelley as a major contributor to Romantic and early Victorian literature.[37] The extensive republishing of Shelley's entire range of work is a conspicuous part of the general scholarly and critical return to women's writing in the Romantic and Victorian periods. Shelley's role within that general return is an important one. Betty T. Bennett and Stuart Curran argue that she 'was virtually unique in the place she held through the shifting mores of her times.'[38] The manner in which critics have responded to the republishing of her oeuvre can also potentially tell us key things about the current state of literary criticism. Has the critical reception of Shelley managed, in the past thirty years, to free itself from the kinds of domesticating and depoliticizing processes we have noted in the nineteenth century? Has it managed to transcend 'the Shelley myth' to which Mary Shelley herself was such an important contributor?[39] Does today's critical work return us to the *other* (for which one might read the 'real') Mary Shelley?

Nora Crook provides a useful map of the various stages the reassessment of Shelley has passed through since the 1970s.[40] Crook refers to a period in the 1970s which she calls '"the Author of *Frankenstein*" phase' when that novel 'rose in eminence as a studied feminist, Gothic and science-fiction text.'[41] Crook cites the publication in 1979 of Levine and Knoepflmacher's edited collection of essays *The Endurance of 'Frankenstein'* as consolidating the emergence of Shelley's novel into the academic literary canon. As Crook adds: 'For the public at large and for most university students this phase has, of course, never passed away; Shelley remains the originating cause of a series of *Frankenstein* films and author of the most widely studied novel in the universities of the USA – and that is that.'[42] Levine and Knoepflmacher's 'take' on *Frankenstein*, however, betrays a certain anxiety regarding the intellectual seriousness of their object of study, an anxiety which indicates a general concern of the period over the emergence into academic study of 'popular' modes of fiction, including the Gothic, science-fiction and, it must be added, women's writing generally. At the beginning of George Levine's own contribution, he writes: 'Of course, *Frankenstein* is a "minor" novel, radically

flawed by its sensationalism, by the inflexibly public and orator-
ical nature of even its most intimate passages.'[43] Against such a
judgement, essays within the collection demonstrate how *Frankenstein* offered up a central test-case for new feminist readings of
Romanticism and the position of women writers within it.[44]

As Crook remarks, however, referring to the 'landmark collection' of Fisch, Mellor and Schor I have already cited, 'the very
success of the canonization of *Frankenstein* itself provoked ... the
"Not *Frankenstein*" or "Other Mary Shelley" phase.'[45] This second phase, pushing beyond the long-established idea of Shelley as
a one novel author, produced an 'explosion' of scholarship and
critical analysis in the 1980s and early 1990s. Crook, in her short
survey, notices the trend, post-1993, to incorporate Mary Shelley's
lesser known works into the canon of critical discussion and thus,
in the terms we have established here, move beyond the Victorian
narrative of strength and decline still evident in some of the critical studies of the 1970s and 1980s. She writes: 'We are now in
a phase of transition towards – let us say – "The Inclusive Mary
Shelley".' Crook describes this phase as 'symptomatic of a read-
iness for progress beyond a simple *Frankenstein*/Not *Frankenstein*
binary opposition and towards a synthesis, where her oeuvre
might be restored to its wholeness.'[46] This phase, as Crook points
out, was fuelled by a number of collections arising from the
various conferences in 1997 which marked the bicentenary of
the death of Wollstonecraft and birth of Shelley.[47] Crook's map
of the different phases of the recent reassessment of Mary Shelley
is a valuable one, so long as we remember that the scholarly
republication and editing of her entire (public and private) oeuvre
is one thing and the critical reception of that work is something else. They are inevitably related, in complex ways, both
requiring the energy created by the other, and yet while the
former can justifiably posit (if not finally achieve) the goal of
synthesis, the latter is inevitably characterized by 'debate and
controversy.'[48]

This book is concerned with the critical reception and interpretation of Shelley as a novelist. It gives equal weight to each of
Shelley's six major novels, plus her novella, *Matilda*. The book
argues that a coherent set of aesthetic and socio-political values
and practices are to be found throughout Shelley's major fictional
works. It argues that for a properly critical *return* to Shelley we
need to activate the reverse direction of her obvious utilization of

biography in her fictional writing. Far from simply fictionalizing, in an unproblematic and 'transparent' manner, the events of her own life and her circle's lives, Shelley's fictional works represent a sustained, life-long intervention into the literary, philosophical, political, aesthetic and ideological concerns of the writers among whom she lived and worked. Shelley's characteristic tendency to fictionalize her own life and the lives of her circle also involves an *intertextual* engagement with the ideological and aesthetic questions of her day.[49] But this study also offers its reading of each novel in the hope that it will provoke debate and counter-readings. It does this by discussing the majority of the interpretations which have collected around each novel and then, instead of attempting an impossible and in fact unhelpful 'synthesis', it presents readings of each novel which attempt to develop and even redirect current debate. The one exception to this method comes in the chapter on *Frankenstein*. It would, of course, require a book-length study even to begin to tackle all the different interpretive trends produced by that novel. Readers can find such synthetic accounts of *Frankenstein* in a number of excellent studies.[50] In the chapter on *Frankenstein*, therefore, I have focused on a reading which returns us to the philosophical and political contexts out of which that novel emerged. This reading is important, since the ideas it establishes provide the foundations for all subsequent chapters. The chapter on *Frankenstein* presumes that readers will also be employing other introductory material on the novel and its critical reception It also, naturally, assumes that readers are in some way familiar with Shelley's most famous novel. The other chapters in the book do not presume any previous knowledge concerning the fictional works in question or their critical reception.

One of the things which makes *Frankenstein* unavoidable as a novel within the history of that literary form is quite how many competing interpretations it has produced. Bennett makes, in this respect, the inevitable move of any engaged form of criticism. She begins by registering, in a positive manner, the multiplicity of interpretations *Frankenstein* has produced ('Gothic, political, biographical, religious, psychological, anti-male feminist, anti-Godwin and anti-Shelley') before suggesting, rightly, that they cannot all be equally valid and that one must, in that case, choose between them (Bennett, Introduction, F, xxvii). Bennett is completely right in her two-fold move here. The vitality of any writer is not found simply in the number of interpretations their work produces; it also stems from the fact that these interpretations produce contradictions which require our selective evaluation. Given the years of scholarly research it required to produce her edition of the letters, Bennett's version of that choice, her own interpretive perspective on Shelley as a writer, comes to us with a special degree of validity.[51] As Mitzi Myers puts it: 'Until Bennett's own biography appears to supplement the letters and journals now available, her own views [as expressed in her various essays and introductions, but above all in her editorial notes to the letters] remain foundational.'[52]

That biography, sadly, will never be completed, since Betty T. Bennett died, with only one volume of the biography completed, in August 2006. The Mary Shelley Bennett's three decades of scholarly work has made available to us is, however, a major corrective to the Victorian myth of Shelley. Bennett's Shelley is an author who remains deeply committed to the liberal cause throughout her life, and constantly asserts her belief in the progressive ideals of a just and ethical society. In 1831 she wrote to Trelawny that 'the Reform Bill swallows up every other thought' (L, II, 146). Bennett's Shelley is a woman who, despite having very different feelings about her own role in the public sphere, shared with her mother a deep concern for the rights of women. She is a correspondent who writes letters against the Imperial ambitions of foreign monarchs, such as Francis II (see L, I, 93, 95), who is appalled by the prospect of a reactionary government and society in England (see L, I, 124), and who could figure her own and her husband's Italian life in terms of a political exile from conservative England (L, I, 137–8). She is a woman and an artist who supported the idea of revolution in Italy throughout her life, as is evident from her first letters and her last book, *Rambles in Germany and Italy* (1840–3). She is someone who knew personally and tried in various ways to assist leaders of the Greek war of Independence against the Turks and, to her cost, various members of the Italian revolutionary movement.[53] She is an author who wrote letters of joy at the news of the Spanish revolution of 1820 (L, I, 140–1) and who, ten years later, wrote a glowing letter of praise to General Lafayette for his part in the July revolution in France (L, II, 117–18). Perhaps above all, Bennett's letters and editorial work have given us, instead of the retiring, morbid 'widow of Shelley', a woman who, after her return to England in 1823, socialized with a host of literary, political and artistic figures (including Prosper Mérimée, Washington Irving, Lady Morgan, the radical feminist Francis Wright), everyone of whom, whatever opinion they eventually formed, treated Shelley as a figure of public interest and undoubted literary achievement.

Bennett's Shelley, a figure emerging from the mists of a Victorian mystifying hang-over, is also an author who possesses an authentic aesthetic and philosophical signature as a writer. She is 'a consistent reformist' who uses biographical approaches, but also mythological intertexts and historical narratives, who develops the radical novel form ('Jacobin fiction') inherited from her father and mother, is deeply concerned with the issue of individual and social education, and shares with her husband a philosophy and politics based on the ideal of 'love' (see Bennett, Introduction, F, xxiv). Such a sustained picture of Shelley's writing career truly begins to liberate her from her previous imprisonment within a Victorian mythology of domestication and de-politicization. It is also, perhaps understandably, a rather too positive (too 'up-beat') picture of Shelley's literary and non-literary work and the world-view that work represents. A certain anxiety can be detected in Bennett's accounts of Shelley over the realist, frequently tragic and apparently pessimistic dimensions of her originally public and originally private writing. The anxiety is simple enough to analyse, since it stems from a concern that attention to Shelley's utilization of negative or pessimistic forms (plots, narrative statements and asides, types of character) will inevitably lead the reception of her work back to the confines of Victorian domestication and de-politicization. Was it not precisely these aspects of her work that were used by her Victorian and post-Victorian commentators in their narrative of her 'back-sliding' after the death of P. B. Shelley?

The Shelley presented in this study is constructed upon the indispensable work that Bennett and others have dedicated to her over the past thirty years. I will argue, however, that Shelley is also a writer who makes a good deal of her philosophical, political, social and aesthetic points through the use of an at times quite astonishing negativity. The emphasis I make on this aspect of Shelley's authorial voice is absolutely necessary if we are to come to a mature interpretive engagement with her oeuvre, and far from leading us back to the Victorian myth it confirms her as a writer with a unique contribution to the forms and ideas of her time.

Shelley's fictional and non-fictional work time and again tests the limits of the idealist philosophy and politics of her immediate familial and intellectual circle, and time and again it corrects idealism in the name of a human-centred mode of philosophical, ethical, political and aesthetic 'realism.'[54]

1

Frankenstein: Or, The Modern Prometheus

I. CRITICISM AND MONSTROSITY

Shelley's *Frankenstein* is something of a monster. Fred Botting discusses at length the manner in which the novel seems to reflect, or mirror back, criticism's hopeless desire to determine a single, closed, interpretatively finalized reading.[55] Chris Baldick argues that it is precisely because *Frankenstein* can be read in so many different ways that it has created what he calls a 'modern myth.'[56] The novel itself is multiple, having been published in 1818, 1823 and 1831 with significant revisions and alterations along the way.[57] Unlike the other chapters in this study, I do not intend to comment on all the different interpretations Shelley's most famous novel has inspired. This analysis of *Frankenstein* focuses on the words 'friend' and 'friendship.'[58] It presents a new reading of *Frankenstein* on the basis of an examination of the various contexts which inform that important concept. What this new reading allows is a contextualization of *Frankenstein* which also establishes some of the fundamental ideas which influenced Shelley's early thought and which she responded to in such a dramatic fictional way. Reading *Frankenstein* in this manner will allow me to establish important features of Shelley's response to her literary, philosophical and political environment which, as the rest of the study will go on to demonstrate, she continued to develop and consolidate throughout the rest of her writing life.

The notion of friendship has distinct political and philosophical connotations in the period we call Romantic. As a term which embodies notions of democracy and even revolution (*fraternity*), it also, in the hands of such Enlightenment thinkers as Godwin, stands for an educational ideal which offers the prospect of individual and social perfectibility. Shelley's response to these notions of friendship in her most famous novel establishes political and philosophical characteristics which, if we follow them, provide us with a foundation for a more general understanding of her thought and work. *Frankenstein*, in its complex engagement with notions of friendship, presents us with Shelley's first attempt to mark a division between her admiration for and support of Enlightenment ideals (democracy, personal and social fidelity, equality between the sexes), and a sustained critique of the unrealizable elements of that same Enlightenment tradition (the idea of perfectibility, the idea that tragedy can be eradicated from human experience). Shelley's response to the Enlightenment ideas she inherited was, in other words, ambivalent; *Frankenstein* as a novel demonstrates that for Shelley human beings are themselves unavoidably ambivalent creatures. It is perhaps a certain kind of ambivalence (speaking for and yet against key Enlightenment ideas and principles) which has led many of its readers to consider the novel as a monstrous text. *Frankenstein*, like all Shelley's novels and major works, reflects back to us a certain monstrosity within the human; it is also written, as I will demonstrate, in the spirit of an authentically human desire for friendship.

II. GODWIN AND THE DISAPPEARANCE OF THE TEACHER

Responding to Walton's confession of his long-term desire for a friend 'who would sympathise with me, and direct me by his counsel', Victor Frankenstein states to his new 'friend': 'I agree with you .... in believing that friendship is not only a desirable, but a possible acquisition. I once had a friend, the most noble of human creatures, and am entitled, therefore, to judge respecting friendship' (F, 19). The fact that Victor is referring to Henry Clerval here, and not Elizabeth, is obviously supportive of all the readings which find within Victor a masculine drive pitted against the feminine and the domestic sphere. It also appears to support an understanding of the word friend in terms of the novel's gendered exploration of the male Romantic discourse of alienation, exile and wandering quest. Both men, Victor and Walton, seem to deny the possibility of friendship with women. Walton's patronizing attitude towards his sister, Margaret Walton Saville, mirrors, in this respect, Victor's lack of confidence with, and sincerity towards, Elizabeth.

In the 1831 edition of *Frankenstein*, Shelley extended the exchange between Walton and Victor on friendship:

> 'I agree with you,' replied the stranger; 'we are unfashioned creatures, but half made up, if one wiser, better, dearer than ourselves – such a friend ought to be – do not lend his aid to perfectionate our weak and faulty natures.' (F, 187)

Nora Crook in her edition of the novel notes that Victor's striking image is an echo of the opening speech of Shakespeare's Richard III: 'Deformed, unfinished, sent before my time/Into this breathing world, scarce half made up' (F, 187). It is significant that in his self-description Richard is presenting himself as an abortion, an 'untimely birth.'

Biographers have always found the subject of the educational and familial situation of the Godwin household at The Polygon and then, with the second Mrs Godwin and her children, at Skinner Street, a source of fascination and debate. One of the documents that stands out in that context is the letter Godwin sent to William Baxter, the day after he had placed his own daughter on board the *Osnaburgh* bound for Dundee. Godwin's sense of the extraordinary intellectual inheritance of his daughter shines out in his comments. The crucial statements, however, concern the apparent inevitably of distance and discipline, and the regrettable authoritarian nature of fathers towards daughters. Godwin writes:

> There never can be a perfect equality between father and child, and if he has other objects and avocations to fill up the greater part of his time, the ordinary resource is for him to proclaim his wishes and commands in a way somewhat sententious and authoritative, and occasionally to utter his censures with seriousness and emphasis.[59]

There are a number of important readings of Shelley which base their interpretation of her life and work on the clearly intense but also fraught relationship between Godwin and his daughter.[60] Documents like these, however, are often read in a rather overly literalistic fashion. The remarks to Baxter are rhetorical and highly ambiguous. Is Godwin stating an inevitable fact here about father-daughter relations? Is he, on the contrary, subtly warning Baxter against too authoritarian a stance, whilst also allowing for the possibility of failure?

The terms of this remarkable letter rehearse various key features of Godwin's philosophical attempts to promote an Enlightenment theory and practice of education. This Enlightenment pedagogy, when presented in its fullest form in the various editions of *Political Justice* (1793, 1796, 1798) and *The Enquirer* (1797), can be said to replace the idea of the teacher (inevitably associated with hierarchy, authority and thus power) with the figure of *the friend*. The idea of the teacher as friend finds its most influential expression in Rousseau's philosophical work on education, *Émile* (1762).[61] The young Émile's preceptor, or teacher, works on what today would be called a child-centred approach, allowing his student the apparent freedom to discover and learn by his own actions.[62] Godwin, in *The Enquirer*, however, accuses Rousseau of betraying the very Enlightenment ideal of teaching which he purportedly defends and promotes. Fifteen years before his letter to Baxter, yet in a strikingly similar fashion, Godwin writes: 'There is no problem in the subject of education more difficult and delicate of solution, than that which relates to the gaining the confidence, and exciting the frankness of youth .... There is an essential disparity between youth and age' (Godwin, *Political*, V, 131). Godwin goes on to criticize Rousseau because he wants, despite what he suggests here, to argue that true friendship (understood as sympathy, sincerity or confidence, and thus equality) is possible in the teaching scenario. In *Political Justice*, he writes: 'Rousseau, notwithstanding his great genius, was full of weakness and prejudice. His *Émile* is upon the whole to be regarded as the principal reservoir of philosophical truth as yet existing in the world, but with a perpetual mixture of absurdity and mistake' (Godwin, *Political*, III, 273). In *The Enquirer* he calls Rousseau's system 'a series of tricks, a puppet-show exhibition, of which the master holds the wires, and the scholar is never to suspect in what manner they are moved' (Godwin, *Political*, V, 126). Whilst Rousseau's preceptor pretends to be the friend, allowing the child to learn what it wants at its own pace, he in fact constantly rigs the scene, preparing obstacles and openings for the child to then experience.[63] Against such a duplicitous pedagogy, Godwin writes: 'children are not inclined to consider him entirely as their friend, whom they detect in an attempt to impose upon them' (Godwin, *Political*, IV, 25).

Political Justice, Godwin's politico-philosophical masterpiece of the revolutionary decade of the 1790s, presents a vision of humanity as perfectible, capable of establishing through the exercise of its rational faculties a truly just and equal society. In the original, 1793 version, Godwin describes political justice as 'that all comprehensive scheme, that immediately applies to the removal of counteraction and contagion, that embraces millions in its grasp, and that educates in one school the preceptor and the pupil' (Godwin, *Political*, III, 18). That post-Rousseauean image of preceptor and pupil, equals in the 'one school', is a central principle of Godwin's perfectibilist philosophy and is reinforced in *The Enquirer* in the rhetorical reversal of the traditional understanding of teacher-pupil relations. There Godwin imagines the pupil leading the teacher in the voyage of knowledge (Godwin, *Political*, V, 115). In Book 8, Volume VI of *Political Justice*, Godwin portrays a society in which this kind of education would be possible (Godwin, *Political*, III, 455). Godwin's readers are given there an image of a rational society which has transcended the irrational forces of property, of domestic hierarchies between parents and children, along with the institutionalized hierarchies evident in public schools and universities. It is a society of friends, willing to assist the rational enquiries of the young as they make their own way along the path of enlightenment. Here, the claims of parental power over children have been transcended so completely that Godwin can state: 'It is of no consequence that I am the parent of a child, when it has once been ascertained that the child will receive greater benefit by living under the superintendence of a stranger' (Godwin, *Political*, III, 92).

Godwin's imagined society is one which precisely does not malform and contort its young by the exercise of modes of pedagogical power and coercion.[64] For Godwin, as for all philosophers of the subject, education reflects the wider social system, so that a Jacobin juxtaposition between 'things as they should be' and 'things as they are' structures his various discussions of the subject.[65] Against Godwin's imagined, future-state of society and education, in which teachers disappear in favour of a community of friends, we can place a central passage from *The Enquirer*: 'All education is despotism. It is perhaps impossible for the young to be conducted without introducing in many cases the tyranny of implicit obedience. Go there; do that; read; write; rise; lie down; will perhaps for ever be the language addressed to youth by age' (Godwin, *Political*, V, 107).[66] The word 'impossible' and the phrase 'perhaps for ever' are extremely important here, since it is for Godwin, above anything else, education which will allow us to move from 'things as they are' to 'things as they should be'. The bar these words place between *now* and *then* can appear confusing as well as daunting when reading Godwin's perfectibilist, proto-anarchist and in many senses utopian political and philosophical works. Readers indeed might be reminded of Shelley's less than neutral comment on her husband in her note on *Prometheus Unbound*: 'Shelley believed that mankind had only to will that there should be no evil, and there would be none' (Shelley, *Novels*, II, 277). For Godwin, education, conducted on the rational basis of confidence and sincerity (friendship rather than power) is the key solution to the problem of how humanity moves from its current corrupt state to an enlightened one. And yet, as he also acknowledges, it is difficult to see how parents and teachers can sufficiently free themselves from the current political environment to begin the exercise of rational, enlightened pedagogy (Godwin, *Political*, IV, 26).

Godwin's answer to such seemingly intractable problems is, throughout *Political Justice*, to evoke the transformative power of reason. Godwin's work on education constantly comes up, however, against the problem of pedagogy in the strictest sense: the education of young children and infants. John Locke's resolution of this problem was still perhaps the dominant model in the 1790s. In his *Some Thoughts Concerning Education* (1693) Locke compares the teaching of young children to the political system of benign monarchy; only after the child has been moulded into an adult with independent reason can friendship, equality and thus a relationship figurable as democratic exist between father and son.[67] Such a resolution, in its rhetorical confirmation of the necessity for monarchical rule, was not one that Godwin could ever countenance. How enlightened parents and teachers are to deal with the period in which reason has yet to assert its independence in young children remains an especially thorny issue for Godwin's pedagogical theory and practice. He writes in *The Enquirer*: 'When a child is born, one of the earliest purposes of his institutor ought to be, to awaken his mind, to breathe a soul into the, as yet, unformed mass' (Godwin, *Political*, V, 84). Later on in *The Enquirer*, Godwin follows up this image of animating 'unformed' material in language which cannot but remind us of the subtitle of his daughter's first novel, along with the Miltonic intertext which runs throughout it: 'The pupil', states Godwin, 'is the clay in the hands of the artificer'(Godwin, *Political*, V, 113). In the important chapter 'The Characters of Men Originate in Their External Circumstances' added to the 1796 and 1798 revised *Political Justice*, Godwin extends this Promethean-Miltonic imagery: 'Children are a sort of raw material put into our hands, a ductile and yielding substance, which if we do not ultimately mould in conformity to our wishes, it is because we throw away the power committed to us, by the folly with which we are accustomed to exert it' (Godwin, *Political*, IV, 25).

The clear tensions within Godwin's enlightenment accounts of education, between the promotion of confidence, sincerity and equality and the, apparently unavoidable, god-like shaping and moulding powers of the parent over the young child, are never successfully resolved. Such tensions are, perhaps, beyond any possible resolution. Yet without some resolution of this tension, between the ideal of equality and friendship and the reality of an initial monarchical despotism, it is difficult to conceive of any way out of 'things as they are.' Shelley's *Frankenstein* can be read as a rigorous fictionalization of this pedagogical and political impasse.

III. 'O MY FRIENDS, THERE IS NO FRIEND'[68]

All three of the novel's central male protagonists seem to have been malformed by a faulty education. This fact, on its own, would seem to support the view that *Frankenstein* presents a negative critique of the Enlightenment idea of the disappearance of the teacher. Walton bemoans his lack of formal education, as we have already seen. In his second letter to his sister he writes of his lack of a friend: 'I desire the company of a man who could sympathize with me; whose eyes would reply to mine' (F, 13). He quickly relates this desire for a friend to his lack of formal education and goes on to refer to his discovery of 'the celebrated poets of our own country' and to the fact that only when it was too late did he realize 'the necessity of becoming acquainted with more languages than that of my native country' (F, 13). This feature of Walton's early years is clearly meant to be related by the reader to Victor Frankenstein's own educational experiences. It is common in criticism of the novel to highlight the lack of guidance Victor's father provides for his son. Discussing his discovery of the works of Cornelius Agrippa at thirteen, on the family holiday at Thonon, Victor states:

> I cannot help remarking here the many opportunities instructors possess of directing the attention of their pupils to useful knowledge, which they utterly neglect. My father looked carelessly at the title-page of my book, and said, 'Ah! Cornelius Agrippa! My dear Victor, do not waste your time upon this; it is sad trash.' (F, 25)

In the 1831 version Shelley adds to our sense of the father's neglect of Victor's study: 'My father was not scientific, and I was left to struggle with a child's blindness, added to a student's thirst for knowledge' (F, 195–6). In 1818 the 'unscientific' nature of the father's knowledge is somewhat contradicted by his explanation of electricity to his son after the storm.[69] In 1831 Shelley changes this to the explanations of a visitor, 'a man of great research in natural philosophy' (F, 197), thus emphasizing the father's lack of scientific knowledge and his inability to guide his knowledge-thirsty son. The fact that the creature himself is left without educational guidance seems unnecessary to state. The creature has to fend for itself and, as various commentators have remarked, its acquisition of an education by stealth appears to align it with a feminine tradition in which young women gain access to an almost exclusively male education by accident, or some other exceptional circumstance.

This reading appears to provide us with a novel that fictionally stages a critique of the Enlightenment idea of the disappearance of the teacher, so associated with the work of Godwin. In such a reading, all three male protagonists of the novel appear to be mal-formed by a lack of direct pedagogical guidance. The reading could be seen to be confirmed by the fact that Victor repeats the sins of his father by abandoning his creature. We should remember here Rousseau's notorious abandonment of his five children in the Parisian Foundling Hospital (see LL, III, pp.320–66). Not only does Victor abandon his 'child', he also cannot be the friend Walton wishes him to be. Such a reading would pit Walton's confused motives and understanding at the end of the novel against an assumed moral, clearly received by the reader, in which the devastating consequences of the abnegation of pedagogical responsibility are exposed and understood.

Such a moralizing reading is achieved, of course, at the expense of a gross reductionism. Readers possessing a knowledge of Godwin's own novels are aware, for example, of the fact that the theme of untutored education has a major intertext in *Caleb Williams*, in which Caleb's early love of romances and Falkland's obsession with the outmoded ideals of chivalry strikingly map on to the histories of Walton (substituting romance novels for accounts of 'voyages') and Victor (substituting chivalry for alchemical texts). The resistance of Henry Clerval's bourgeois father to his educational plans would also complicate such a morally transparent reading: in the 1831 revisions the father is made far more aggressive in his resistance, and Clerval consequently more of a rebel. However, the father's reluctance to provide a university education for his son cannot be read as part of any critique of Enlightenment pedagogical theory: in fact Henry's father's motives stem from commercial, conservative concerns.

It could also be objected that the two main family units described in the novel support and even celebrate the kinds of Enlightenment values we have been discussing. Anne K. Mellor argues that both the De Lacey family and the Frankenstein family are versions of a bourgeois familial ideal which Shelley desired and yet ultimately found wanting. It is perhaps more accurate to state that these central family units are examples of a Republicanism untainted by the corruption of the revolutionary ideal in the 1790s. Felix's heroism in his attempts to save Safie's Muslim father from an unjust Parisian authority out of step with its own populace (F, 91), and his use of Volney's *The Ruins: or A Survey of the Revolutions of Empires* (1791) to instruct Safie into the French language, are indicators of his and his family's Enlightenment, radical credentials.[70] Their domestic relations mirror this Enlightenment position, a statement which, with certain reservations, could also be applied to the Frankenstein family in their home in Geneva, historical site of Rousseau and the revolutionary, Promethean ideal.[71] What is crucial about the Frankenstein family, however, and in this it seems to mirror the De Lacey household, is that it is characterized by a reciprocal structure in which sympathy and equality have replaced hierarchy and parental despotism. In an important early paragraph in Chapter 1, the same chapter in which Victor looks back at his father's lack of guidance over Cornelius Agrippa, Victor describes his family thus: 'My parents were indulgent, and my companions amiable. Our studies were never forced; and by some means we always had an end placed in view, which excited us to ardour in the prosecution of them. It was by this method, and not by emulation, that we were urged to application' (F, 24). In case we are unsure whether such an upbringing is a wholly good thing, Victor goes on to emphasize the Enlightenment nature of the education of the Frankenstein children (F, 24). An addition in the *Thomas* version adds an even greater emphasis to the Enlightenment context of the Frankenstein children's upbringing: 'My parents were possessed by the very spirit of kindness and indulgence. We felt that they were not the tyrants to rule our lot according to their caprice, but the agents and creators of all the many delights which we enjoyed' (F, 194).

The Frankenstein household, then, is an ideal one in which friendship rather than pedagogical coercion reigns. The 1818 version ends Chapter 1 with precisely this point:

> Such was our domestic circle, from which care and pain seemed for ever banished. My father directed our studies, and my mother partook of our enjoyments. Neither of us possessed the slightest pre-eminence over the other; the voice of command was never heard amongst us; but mutual affection engaged us all to comply with and obey the slightest desire of each other. (F, 28)

There seems to be no clear reason why the Frankenstein family's exemplary economy of reciprocity and equality should have produced, in Victor, the disastrous consequences it did. The novel appears to celebrate modes of rational education and enlightened domestic relations at the same time that it demonstrates their inability to guarantee against irrationality, violence and tragedy. A closer look at the educational scenes concerning the creature itself can help us to better understand these apparent paradoxes.

IV. READING MONSTERS

In a stimulating account of the creature's education in the 'hovel' by the De Lacey's cottage, Anne McWhir suggests that the books the creature reads offer him 'a confused curriculum': 'Either he reads the wrong books or, more probably, Shelley (as author and teacher) denies him the ability to read them critically.'[72] Whilst this reading is insightful and challenging, it misses the consistency and coherence of the lessons the creature learns from the texts he reads (and these texts include the 'history' of the De Laceys and

Safie themselves). We should remember that, for the creature, language itself appears like a 'godlike science' (F, 83). When Felix reads Volney to Safie, this 'godlike' quality of human beings appears to be reinforced and yet discredited by the same text: 'These wonderful narrations inspired me with strange feelings. Was man, indeed, at once so powerful, so virtuous, and magnificent, yet so vicious and base? He appeared at one time a mere scion of the evil principle, and at another as all that can be conceived of noble and godlike' (F, 89). The sense of strangeness, or the uncanny, derived from the creature's reading of these narratives, has to do, then, with what appears to be the radical ambivalence of humanity. The conversations between the cottagers are, the creature tells us, another important text for him to read, and what he learns from them appears to support the lesson taken from Volney: 'While I listened to the instructions which Felix bestowed upon the Arabian, the strange system of human society was explained to me. I heard of the division of property, of immense wealth and squalid poverty; of rank, descent, and noble blood' (F, 89).

As his understanding of human society increases, of course, the creature begins to attempt to apply what he has learnt to himself and his own situation. This move produces the classic Romantic anti-self-consciousness topos of knowledge as a version of the Fall.[73] Knowledge communicated through language does not lead to 'godlike' status; rather, it confirms, each time, the radical ambivalence (between good and evil, divinity and monstrosity) within the human frame and human society. The 'history' of his 'friends', their exile and their joyous reunion with Safie, only goes to demonstrate the inability of human virtue to exist outside of human depravity: 'Such was the history of my beloved cottagers. It impressed me deeply. I learned, from the views of social life which it developed, to admire their virtues, and to deprecate the vices of mankind' (F, 95). The De Laceys and Safie, despite their virtues, are examples of and are part of 'mankind.' They cannot be extricated from the ambivalence which seems to sit at the very centre of human affairs and which is profoundly deepened in resonance and reach by the books the creature now discovers in the 'leathern portmanteau', books which fill him with responses 'that sometimes raised me to ecstasy, but more frequently sunk me into the lowest dejection' (F, 95).

Part of that ambivalent reaction on the part of the creature has to do with what these new texts tell him about his relation to human society. Like the De Laceys in relation to the wider human society, the creature, reading Goethe's *Werter*, finds himself 'similar, yet at the same time strangely unlike the beings concerning whom I read, and to whose conversations I was a listener' (F, 96). If human beings are essentially ambivalent, a mixture of good and evil, rational and yet irrational, virtuous and yet corrupt, then this sense of being 'similar' and yet 'unlike' is in fact an accurate impression. You cannot simply be *like* creatures who are so radically divided within themselves, since there is not a singular essence or characteristic to uncomplicatedly resemble or from which to differ. Plutarch's *Lives* appears, initially, to offer the creature something wholly positive: 'he elevated me above the wretched sphere of my own reflections, to admire and love the heroes of past ages' (F, 96). However, Plutarch's text cannot hide the divided, conflictual nature of human beings: 'I felt', the creature states, 'the greatest ardour for virtue rise within me, and abhorrence for vice, as far as I understood the signification of those terms, relative as they were, as I applied them, to pleasure and pain alone' (F, 96). The creature's qualifying of the purely sensational nature of its response to human ambivalence prepares the reader for the last in the series of classic texts fortuitously (or not) found by the creature, Milton's *Paradise Lost*. This text, written to 'explain the ways of God to men', will surely allow the creature to transcend its sense of the ambivalence of humanity by providing a religious super-structure on which to understand the presence of good and evil in the universe? The creature's famous, literalistic response to the text is something of a disappointment in that regard: 'It moved every feeling of wonder and awe, that the picture of an omnipotent God warring with his creatures was capable of exciting' (F, 97). Even the God of human beings manifests an ambivalent nature, at once 'omnipotent' and yet in conflict with 'his creatures.' The creature's much discussed attempts to compare himself to Adam and to Milton's Satan suggest the difficulties of singular relation and identification we have already noted. He is, in deed, like and 'unlike' both of these characters, a fact which is accentuated when, employing the religious terms he has gained from Milton, he turns to his own origins in Victor's journal of creation.

The creature's response to learning the details of his origins is dominated by a sense of contamination and filth, clearly reflecting Victor's own response to his act of animation: 'the minutest description of my odious and loathsome person is given, in language which painted your own horrors, and rendered mine ineffaceable' (F, 97). Despite emphasizing his apparent difference from his creator, the creature's reaction to Victor's journal cannot suppress the fact that it is his 'resemblance' which is most troubling to both creature and creator: 'God in pity made man beautiful and alluring, after his own image; but my form is a filthy type of your's (sic), more horrid from its very resemblance. Satan had his companions, fellow-devils, to admire and encourage him; but I am solitary and detested' (F, 97). In the 1831 edition of the text the last word 'detested' is changed to 'abhorred.' That word, and its, at least partly, homophonous relationship to the word 'abortion', can take us further in our understanding of the radical ambivalence which connects the creature and his creator and the species to which they both, in different ways, belong.

V.   ABORTIVE MEN

Even before he had experienced the tragic events of the birth of his daughter, Godwin had come to the opinion that the standard Lockean understanding of human beings as *tabula rasa* was an insufficient explanation for the differences clearly evident between children. These differences are a continuing problem for Godwin in his attempt to erect a philosophy which would prove the perfectibility of human society on the basis of a universal rational faculty. In his revised *Political Justice*, Godwin goes out of his way to reject Lockean arguments: 'at the moment of birth', he writes, 'man has really a certain character, and each man a character different from his fellows.' However, Godwin is as quick to argue that reason, when politically and socially enshrined, will make as nothing these original differences: 'Speak the language of truth and reason to your child, and be under no apprehension for the result.' He also argues that the differences perceivable between infants are not metaphysical, but are in fact the results of material experiences prior to birth. These pre-natal differences ('the confused and unpronounced impressions of the womb') are not important, he argues, and can easily be 'obliterated' by education (Godwin, *Political*, IV, 23).[74] Philosophically speaking, Godwin's desire to obliterate the traces of the womb is perfectly understandable, since these are experiences which even his towering faith in the transformative powers of reason will never be able to reach. The issue is serious for Godwin, and indeed for any rationalist political philosophy, since anything which supports the idea of a limit to reason's transformative powers threatens, using words carefully here, to give more life to a figure (perhaps best described as a spectre) which necessarily haunts such philosophies. This spectre can be spotted throughout Godwin's philosophical and fictional work. This figure, or spectre, concerns the possibility of a human being who is not subject to the claims of reason, a figure for whom reason (successfully communicated) is not a sufficient foundation for identity and action. In his revised Chapter 5, Volume I, 'The Voluntary Actions of Men Originate in Their Opinions', Godwin introduces this figure thus:

> Man is a rational being. If there be any man, who is incapable of making inferences for himself, or of understanding, when stated in the most explicit terms, the inferences of another, him we consider as an abortive production, and not in strictness belonging to the human species. (Godwin, *Political*, IV, 42)

Godwin's *Mandeville*, published one month before the publication of *Frankenstein*, is a novel which presents the narrative history of an 'abortive character.' Malformed by his childhood experiences in seventeenth-century Ireland and then England, and having developed an insane hatred for his nemesis, the virtuous Clifford, Mandeville's attempts late in the novel to thwart the marriage of Clifford and his sister, Henrietta, are proof positive of his abortive reason and character. Henrietta, in a fit of despair, asks: 'Of what use is his life? He is an abortion merely, and appertains in no way to the scene of the living world. He never will be anything but miserable; and his existence answers to no purpose but that of intercepting the happiness of others' (Godwin, *Novels*, VI, 294–5). The novel itself, of course, contains, as a narrative, its own transcendence of such irrationality, in that Mandeville truthfully (and thus rationally) narrates the history of his own irrationality and abortiveness. He says of himself: 'I was necessarily an abortion', someone 'who could never become useful to society, and whose existence would be a burden to his fellow-creatures' (Godwin, *Novels*, VI, 298). *Mandeville* performs in itself the primary function of the figure of the abortion in Godwin's philosophical work: in raising the possibility of the narrative of an abortive man, *Mandeville* transcends that possibility, returning the reader to the securities and guarantees of reason, in the very fact that Mandeville, the abortive man, narrates the history of his life and malformation. Throughout Godwin's political, philosophical and pedagogical work the abortive man serves this purpose, of raising the possibility of a limit to reason only for that limit to be transcended. Abortive men are necessary for Godwin, in that they are the exception that proves the rule of the inevitable triumph of reason if men would only learn to trust and exercise it.

P. B. Shelley's additions to the Draft version of *Frankenstein* have caused a good deal of debate in recent years.[75] One of the most conspicuous changes he made occurs near the very end of the novel and creates a link to the review he wrote, but which was not published until November 1831 (see FN, I, xciii). Addressing Walton by the dead body of Victor, the creature delivers his own version of the tragic events that have unfolded. Reminding Walton of the rejection he has suffered from everyone, the creature's question is simple: can Walton really state that only he, the creature, has been to blame, that only he is a monster? He goes on: 'Nay, these are virtuous and immaculate beings! I, the miserable and the abandoned, am an abortion, to be spurned at, and kicked, and trampled on. Even now my blood boils at the recollection of this injustice!' (F, 169). In the Draft Notebook Mary Shelley's 'the devil' has been cancelled by P. B. Shelley and 'an abortion' substituted (FN, II, 639). In his review of the novel, P. B. Shelley describes the creature (making sure to avoid the word 'monster') as 'an abortion and an anomaly' (*Shelley's Prose*, 308). The description is perhaps a self-conscious pleonasm, since, in Godwinian terms, an abortion *is* an anomalous man, a man who cannot hear and cannot respond to the call of reason. Since all men possess the faculty of reason, those men who apparently lack that faculty or have it in a faulty or malformed manner, are not entirely, properly men.

P. B. Shelley's addition to the novel here simply reinforces the logic Mary Shelley had already consistently expressed in her text. It is precisely the creature's anomalous status that makes him so terrifying to the human others who encounter him. But that terror is founded on the possibility that the creature's anomalous nature might reflect the human rather than simply differing from it. As David Marshall has suggested, what is perhaps 'most horrible about Frankenstein's experiment' to create a being like himself, 'is that it is too successful.'[76] The creature is such a threat to human society because he is a visible sign and reminder of the abortive nature of humanity itself. As Marshall puts it: what the creature fails to recognize is 'that it is his sameness that is most threatening.'[77]

Marshall has discussed this issue in terms of a reading of *Frankenstein* which returns it to a major intertext in Rousseau's philosophy of sympathy. Victor, and all others who encounter him, fail in sympathy towards the creature because in his physical appearance he is a literalized metaphor for the repressed truth of humanity itself. The creature understands this and so, as he attempts to persuade Victor of his right to society and companionship, he places his hands in front of his creator's eyes: 'thus I take from thee a sight which you abhor', he says, 'Still thou canst listen to me, and grant me thy compassion' (F, 75). As various commentators have noted, the word *monster* comes from the Latin *monstrum*, 'a divine portent or warning', 'a prodigy or marvel', 'a malformed animal or plant; a misshapen birth, an abortion.' Medieval meanings include imaginary animals, part brute, part human, or a mixture of 'two or more animal forms.' The Latin *monstrare* meaning 'to show', hence giving the medieval meaning to the word *monstrance* ('Demonstration, proof'), provides another, related association for the modern word monster. The creature demonstrates something about those who encounter him, and so he is *abhorrent*. The various modulations of the verb *to abhor* resound throughout the novel, but nowhere more so than when the creature comes face to face with Victor on the Mer de Glace and with Walton at the end of the novel. It does not seem improbable, in fact, to suggest a deep connection between the idea .of abortive men and the psychological and phenomenological *abhorrence* unfailingly generated by the creature. From the Latin *abhorrēre*, meaning 'to stand aghast', to *abhor* can mean to shrink from something in horror, but also to cause horror or disgust in another (OED). As Marshall puts it: 'What is so hideous about the monster is his embodiment of *phantasma*: the monstrous image of that which is made visible, shown, presented to the eye, brought to light. This is the monstrous figure that will not disappear when one shuts one's eyes, or one's book.'[78]

The creature is 'unfashioned', 'half made up', in the sense that he has not been provided with the education and socio-familial environment which would have, to employ Godwin's terms, *formed* and *moulded* him correctly. Yet the same can be said, as we have seen, for all significant male characters in the novel. Victor, Walton, Henry, M. Frankenstein are all in this sense abortive men. When the creature finally speaks to De Lacey he makes it quite clear that his 'friends' (in other words, De Lacey and his family) are themselves, even though they have never met him, already prejudiced against him. The figure he employs to express this is importantly one of the novel's numerous references to watery, yellowy, cloudy or filmy eyes. Speaking to the blind De Lacey, the creature refers to a blindness which affects all of humanity: 'a fatal prejudice clouds their eyes, and where they ought to see a feeling and kind friend, they behold only a destestable monster' (F, 100). The strange temporality of the creature's grammar (they do not know me, have never seen me, but are prejudiced against me) can alert us to another dimension of abortiveness which brings us back to the issue of education.

An abortion is an 'untimely birth', and at least figuratively appears to suffer from coming too late as much as from arriving too early. The creature waits and waits before he presents himself to De Lacey. It is not possible, however, to determine whether his choice of moment is too early or doomed, given their pre-existent prejudice, always to be too late. Entering the region of Geneva he meets Victor's brother, William, and, imagining him to be too young to have 'imbibed a horror of deformity', considers whether he could not 'educate him as my companion and friend '(F, 106). The creature is, however, wrong about William's lack of prejudice and this idea of the creature educating him collapses into the scene of his first murder. The idea of the creature (the 'monster') as teacher is a compelling one, however. The creature arrives too late to teach William what he could, potentially, learn. But then, throughout the novel, teachers appear to arrive too late. At Ingolstadt Victor announces that in Waldman he has finally found the teacher-'friend' we have already observed his father to be and yet not to be: 'In M. Waldman I found a true friend. His gentleness was never tinged by dogmatism; and his instructions were given with an air of frankness and good nature, that banished every idea of pedantry' (F, 34). Yet Waldman's Enlightenment pedagogy comes far too late to save Victor from his 'fate' and in fact his teaching seems to hasten his student's ruin. Another alteration to the Draft version by P. B. Shelley is of moment here. It was in fact P. B. Shelley who added the following, quintessentially Godwinian statement to Waldman's unprejudiced and yet corrective opinions about Agrippa and Paracelsus: 'The labours of men of genius however erroneously directed scarcely ever failed in ultimately turning to the solid advantage of mankind'

(FN, I, 62–5; see F, 33). The addition, once again, adds a more direct connection to the Godwinian ideas being critiqued in the novel; it is a reinforcement, rather than an interruption. The 'labours of men of genius' can, in fact, as Victor is about to demonstrate, produce something not especially advantageous to 'mankind', as can the teaching of a man so enlightened and lacking pedantry as Waldman.

As we know, by the time Victor arrives on board Walton's ship it is far too late for him to be 'the friend' for whom Walton has been searching. Victor, in fact, as we learn, was never in the position to be such a 'friend.' Untimeliness is a problem which, like the abortive man, haunts Godwin's Enlightenment accounts of teaching, since, despite his meliorist rather than revolutionary approach to social reform, it is not clear how, if all men live within the corrupt state of 'things as they are', someone with the credentials to act as the 'friend', the Enlightened preceptor, can ever emerge from our malforming social environments (see Godwin, *Political*, V, 94). Victor's dream at the beginning of his scientific labours appears a particularly intense version of blindness on this score, since in animating a human being he ends up not a 'friend' (someone who can intellectually and spiritually animate) but a monarch and a god, before, that is, he falls, like Lucifer, into his own version of monstrosity and abhorrence. 'No father', he exclaims, 'could claim the gratitude of his child so completely as I should deserve theirs' (F, 37). Victor, however, is in no position to animate a new being into intellectual light. His labours produce only an abortive man, an 'unfashioned creature, but half made up', a creature, that is, who resembles him. Against Victor's visions of animating new human beings, the creature's desire for an animated creature sounds wholly rational and reasonable: 'It is true', he states:

> we shall be monsters, cut off from all the world; but on that account we shall be more attached to one another. Our lives will not be happy, but they will be harmless, and free from the misery I now feel. Oh! my creator, make me happy; let me feel gratitude towards you for one benefit! Let me see that I excite the sympathy of some existing thing; do not deny me my request! (F, 109)

The creature here may seem to contradict itself on the question of happiness, but, as we have seen, the creature has had an education that has taught him truths still not fully understood by Victor, despite his quoting of P. B. Shelley's 'Mutability' as he ascends Montanvert (F, 73). The happiness the creature refers to concerns Victor's possible consent. It will make the creature happy if his creator for one time shows sympathy for him and agrees to his demands. The result of that consent, however, life with his female companion, will not in itself be a life that could be described as 'happy.' The creature knows the nature of humans (naturally born or animated by scientists) well enough to understand that the idea of a singular state such as happiness is not a possibility. His life with the female creature will be ambivalent, just as all human life is ambivalent; it will be abortive, in the sense of being 'untimely', not in the right place and not at the right time. He could have with equal truth have asserted: we will not be *unhappy*. Not singularly, and not permanently. The female creature remains literally an 'unfashioned creature, but half made up' because Victor, as his vacillating statements on the ship at the end of his life demonstrate, cannot see this essential feature of himself and of human life. Even at the very end of his life, Victor is still holding out for that most singular of notions, *heroism*. Immediately after his advice to seek 'happiness in tranquillity', Victor reverses his counsel to Walton: 'Yet why do I say this? I have myself been blasted in these hopes, yet another may succeed' (F, 166). To the crewmen and their desire to return home, he says: 'Oh! be men, or be more than men. Be steady to your purposes, and firm as a rock. This ice is not made of such stuff as your hearts might be; it is mutable, cannot withstand you, if you say that it shall not' (F, 164). Victor has forgotten the P. B. Shelley of 'Mutability' here, and returned to the idealism of *Prometheus Unbound*. He has returned to the dream of a singular and superior humanity who will be 'men, or ... more than men.'

Although he created some of the most compelling novels of the Romantic period out of their histories – Falkland, St Leon, Fleetwood, Mandeville, Deloraine – Godwin's philosophy tended to *other* abortive men, viewing them as alien to what was truly and properly human. P. B. Shelley's poetry and prose displays a similar vacillation between a recognition of the ambivalence of human beings and a desire to transcend such mixed and conflictual qualities through an idealism of pure reason and, more frequently, pure love. Shelley created her most famous novel by staging and subtly exploring that process of othering human ambivalence, but it was her belief that true monstrosity was born from a refusal to countenance the monstrous and the abortive in that antithetically mixed species we call human. This process, she also believed, was characteristic of men.

VI. SAFIE'S LETTERS AND WOLLSTONECRAFT'S WAGER

It is a commonplace move to associate the name of the Christian-Arab Safie with the female character Sophie in Rousseau's *Émile*.[79] This move on its own already draws our attention to the work of Mary Wollstonecraft, since it is Rousseau's arguments about the lack of need to provide Sophie (and thus, by extension, all women) with a rational education which forms one of her most obvious targets in *A Vindication of the Rights of Woman*. Paraphrasing Rousseau's arguments in *Émile*, Wollstonecraft writes: 'Rousseau, and most of the male writers who have followed his steps, have warmly inculcated that the whole tendency of female education ought to be directed to one point: – to render them pleasing' (Wollstonecraft, *Works*, V, 96). What Shelley was to call in *Lodore* a 'sexual education' is one of the principal targets of Wollstonecraft's critique in her most famous and influential text. The masculine notion that there is a 'sexual difference' in intellect and in ethics is, as Wollstonecraft demonstrates, a disastrous one in that it generates the very inequalities it then points towards as 'natural' proofs. The tautologous nature of such arguments are compared by Wollstonecraft to the traditional arguments defending the rights of monarchs over the people: 'The many have always been enthralled by the few; and monsters, who scarcely have shewn any discernment of human excellence, have tyrannized over thousands of their fellow-creatures' (Wollstonecraft, *Works*, V, 105). Wollstonecraft constantly returns to the issue of friendship as part of her critique of this ideology of 'sexual difference.' The whole of *A Vindication of the Rights of Woman*, in fact, can be described as a call to friendship between men and women, or in other words a call to allow women into the until now exclusively male realm of primary friendship. In citing writers like La Rochefoucauld ('rare as true love is, true friendship is still rarer'), Wollstonecraft subtly parodies the androcentric tradition of male friendship which relegates women to a position which is less than fully human (Wollstonecraft, *Works*, V, 98–9). Education plays a crucial role in this recovery of women to the realm of the human. 'But I still insist', she writes:

> that not only the virtue, but the *knowledge* of the two sexes should be the same in nature, if not in degree, and that women, considered not only as moral, but rational creatures, ought to endeavour to acquire human virtues (or perfections) by the *same* means as men, instead of being educated like a fanciful kind of *half* being – one of Rousseau's chimeras. (Wollstonecraft, *Works*, V, 108)

It is not difficult to see that Wollstonecraft's critique of patriarchy concerns that system's tendency to figure women as abortive men (*half* beings). She writes elsewhere in her text: 'instead of a part man, the inquiry is whether she have reason or not' (Wollstonecraft, *Works*, V, 122). Joyce Zonana's insightful reading of the role of Safie's letters in *Frankenstein* helps us to understand how her mother's arguments against this cultural and historical figuring of women is inscribed at the very heart of Shelley's *Frankenstein*.

There are two occasions, as Zonana reminds us, in which the creature's copies of the letters sent from Safie to Felix are mentioned. The first, when the creature confronting Victor on the Mer de Glace states that at the end of their dialogue he will give them to his creator and that 'they will prove the truth of my tale' (F, 92). On the second occasion these letters are mentioned, they have been seen by Walton. His recorded reaction to them reinforces their role as material evidence: 'His [Victor's] tale is connected, and told with an appearance of the simplest truth', Walton writes to his sister, 'yet I own to you that the letters of Felix and Safie, which he shewed me, and the apparition of the monster, seen from our ship, brought to me a greater conviction of the truth of his narrative than his asseverations, however earnest and connected' (F, 159–60). Thus, as Zonana points out, the role the letters play as evidential proof is passed on from the creature to Victor, from Victor to Walton, and from Walton ultimately to his sister and the novel's readers: 'Safie's letters', she writes, 'are the only tangible, independent evidence of the truth of Walton's tale.'[80] Safie's mother had been 'a Christian Arab, seized and made a slave by the Turks', and before her death she had 'instructed her daughter in the tenets of her religion, and taught her to aspire to higher powers of intellect, and an independence of spirit, forbidden to the female followers of Mahomet.' As a consequence of her mother's teaching, Safie struggles against her manipulative father and sickens 'at the prospect of again returning to Asia, and the being immured within the walls of a haram, allowed only to occupy herself with puerile amusements, ill suited to the temper of her soul, now accustomed to grand ideas and a noble emulation for virtue' (F, 92). As Zonana reminds her readers, Wollstonecraft used the imagery of the 'harem' to describe the position of Western women trapped within the patriarchal confines of European society. As she puts it, referring to *A Vindication of the Rights of Woman*: '"Mahometanism", for Mary Wollstonecraft, is a figure for an error she finds central to Western culture: the refusal to grant women full membership as rational beings in the human race.'[81] This 'error', in fact, as Zonana also rightly states, modulates between denying women reason and denying them a soul. Thus, Walton's statements about Safie's letters and the appearance of the creature are highly significant, since what the creature shares with Safie is the desire to be treated as an animate being, a being possessing reason and a soul. What we might add to Zonana's reading is a point about the manner in which Wollstonecraft argues this point on behalf of women. Attacking the common association of women and sensibility, Wollstonecraft writes:

> I come round to my old argument: if woman be allowed to have an immortal soul, she must have, as the employment of life, an understanding to improve. And when, to render the present state more complete, through every thing proves it to be but a fraction of a mighty sum, she is incited by present gratification to forget her grand destination, nature is counteracted, or she was born only to procreate and rot. Or, granting brutes, of every description, a soul, though not a reasonable one, the exercise of instinct and sensibility may be the step, which they are to take, in this life, towards the attainment of reason in the next; so that through all eternity they will lag behind man, who, why we cannot tell, had the power given him of attaining reason in his first mode of existence. (Wollstonecraft, *Works*, V, 132)

The paragraph is an often cited one, and yet very frequently commentators do not recognize the mixture of satirical humour and anger with which Wollstonecraft argues the case. Confronting the sexual differences of canonical male writers such as Milton, Rousseau and, here, Dr. Johnson, Wollstonecraft exposes the logical and ethical absurdities in their depictions of women. More than that, however, she offers up a response which can best be characterized as an ethical gamble or wager. I will take another famous passage to demonstrate the frequency of this rhetorical wager in Wollstonecraft's text:

> It is time to effect a revolution in female manners – time to restore to them their lost dignity – and make them, as part of the human species, labour by reforming themselves to reform the world .... If men be demi-gods – why let us serve them! And if the dignity of the female soul be as disputable as that of animals – if their reason does not afford sufficient light to direct their conduct whilst unerring instinct is denied – they are surely of all creatures the most miserable! And, bent beneath the iron hand of destiny, must submit to be a *fair defect* in creation. (Wollstonecraft, *Works*, V, 114)

Either women are human brutes (lacking a soul and reason) or they are the intellectual and spiritual equals of men. Either women are, for some reason religious discourse seems unable to explain, abortive men, or they are not. Writing in the context of the question of what we can expect from education, Wollstonecraft writes: 'whatever effect circumstances have on the abilities, every being may become virtuous by the exercise of its own reason; for if but one being was created with vicious inclinations, that is positively bad, what can save us from atheism? or if we worship a God, is not that God a devil?' (Wollstonecraft, *Works*, V, 90). The relevance of the passage to her daughter's novel, *Frankenstein*, is obvious. If we are to retain our notions of religion and of Enlightenment, the notion of abortive men (whether they be women or other races or essentially 'bad' or irrational men) does not make sense. Do we want a society in which half the human race are figured as lesser beings? Do we want a just and equal society in which all human beings are treated with respect? If we want the latter, then we must wager on that idea. Equality, Wollstonecraft states again and again, will only come if we make the experiment. As Wollstonecraft puts the issue: 'when morality shall be settled on a more solid basis, then, without being gifted with a prophetic spirit, I will venture to predict that women will be either the friend or slave of man' (Wollstonecraft, *Works*, V, 104). Equality and justice might arrive if we treat women like beings deserving equality and justice. If we allow human beings to be equal *then* there might, possibly, be equality. The rights of man and of woman, in Wollstonecraft's famous text, are, without 'a prophetic spirit', a wager. But a wager well worth risking, given the appalling alternative prospects.

In *Frankenstein* Victor is faced with a wager which is comparable to the one Wollstonecraft stages frequently in the *Vindication*:

'I was now about to form another being, of whose dispositions I was alike ignorant .... She also might turn with disgust from him to the superior beauty of man; she might quit him, and he be again alone, exasperated by the fresh provocation of being deserted by one of his own species' (F, 128). Who knows the answers to the series of questions and hypotheses he poses to himself, on the brink of that new act of creation? Certainly not Victor, nor his creature, nor the reader. The female creature is a wager and Victor refuses to take the bet. He does so because he cannot confront the fact that chance is involved and there is no guarantee concerning the results. He requires certainty before the act, and that simply is not available. His great anxiety is that he might bring greater horror and injustice into the world, and on that basis the reader has some sympathy for his predicament. However, he does not understand that justice, like friendship, is always based on a wager, is never certain but always worth speculating upon. Knowledge of this fact is something Shelley possessed and which she shared with her mother. It is this knowledge, amongst many other things, which *Frankenstein* offers to its readers, in the hope of a friendship which still might one day be possible.

2

Matilda

I. *MATILDA* AND PSYCHO-BIOGRAPHY

Shelley's *Matilda* has become one of the most widely read and studied of her fictional works. Although written in 1819, *Matilda* was not published until Elizabeth Nitchie's edition in 1959.[82] The story behind that one hundred and forty year hiatus is an inevitable part of any reader's engagement with *Matilda*. The text concerns the incestuous desire of a father for his daughter, his suicide after confessing that desire and then the daughter's melancholic movement towards a wished-for death. Shelley sent *Matilda*, in the care of her friend Maria Gisborne, to her father in 1820. Godwin pronounced the story 'disgusting and detestable', lamented the lack of 'a preface to prepare the minds of the readers, and to prevent them from being tormented by the apprehension from moment to moment of the fall of the heroine', and seems to have refused to return the manuscript to his daughter after deciding not to send it to the publishers.[83] These facts, alone, are enough to start most readers wondering about Shelley's motivation in writing the text and in addressing it, as it were, to Godwin. *Matilda* is such a popular text today because it appears to confirm the rebellious, gender-conscious critique of male Romanticism many readers have argued exists more implicitly within *Frankenstein*.[84] It has also become something of a test-case against which contemporary critics have debated the positive and negative dimensions of psycho-biographical forms of critical reading.[85]

Confronted with the text of *Matilda* and with the biographical contexts in which it was written, it can seem perverse of critics to pursue anything but a psycho-biographical reading. When we remember the situation in which Mary Shelley wrote *Matilda* it appears simply incontrovertible that the text is a fictional expression of her deep sense of loss at the deaths of her children and her melancholia over her emotional estrangement from the two most important men in her life, her husband and her father. The death of William Shelley (aged 3) in Rome on 7 June 1819, coming as it did less than a year after the death of her daughter Clara (aged 1) on 24 September 1818, sent Shelley into a depression which clearly affected her relationship with P. B. Shelley. The most intense period of Shelley's depression before 1822 covers the period in which she composed her novella, first as a text entitled *The Fields of Fancy* and then as *Matilda*.[86] P. B. Shelley wrote a number of minor and fragmentary lyrics during this period expressing his sense of Mary's emotional withdrawal into melancholia, including one that begins 'My dearest Mary, wherefore hast thou gone/And left me in this dreary world alone?' (Shelley, *Poems*, II, 709).

Shelley's troubles in 1819 were increased by a rapidly deteriorating relationship with her father. In troubled financial circumstances, Godwin, never having forgiven P. B. Shelley for eloping with Mary, was increasingly feeling that the poet had broken his promises about helping him with his money problems. As P. B. Shelley was to remind Godwin in 1820, however: 'I have given you within a few years the amount of a considerable fortune' (*Letters of Percy Bysshe Shelley*, II, 225). Despite such reminders, Godwin's need for money and his sense of betrayal with regard to P. B. Shelley was increasingly mixed, from 1818 onwards, with his rather harsh, puritanical manner of consoling his daughter for her losses. In a letter to Leigh Hunt dated 15 August 1819, P. B. Shelley describes the situation: 'We cannot yet come home. Poor Mary's spirits continue dreadfully depressed. And I cannot expose her to Godwin in this state' (*Letters of Percy Bysshe Shelley*, II, 109).

Since 1959 and Nitchie's edition, many readers have taken such contexts and read them into *Matilda*.[87] Such a psycho-biographical approach has various consequences, not least that it tends to present us with a text which reads as a confession of melancholia alongside aggressive feelings towards Godwin and P. B. Shelley. Nitchie writes, for example, that 'Mary poured the suffering and the loneliness, the bitterness and the self-recrimination of the past twelve months' into *Matilda*.[88] She goes on to state: 'Certainly Mary is Mathilda.'[89] Psycho-biographical readings like these appear to have much in their favour, and certainly the frequently cited letter Godwin sent to Mary after the death of William appears to confirm arguments that would read *Matilda* as a bitterly angry response.[90] This letter, sent on 9 September 1819, is written with 'the privilege of a father and a philosopher' and expostulates with Mary on her depression. Godwin writes: 'You have all the goods of fortune, all the means of being useful to others, and shining in your proper sphere. But you have lost a child: and all the rest of the world, all that is beautiful, and all that has a claim upon your kindness, is nothing, because a child of two years old is dead.' He then goes on to argue that '[t]he human species may be divided into two great classes: those who lean on others for support, and those who are qualified to support.' It is unsurprising what class of people Godwin favours. He has some rather specific things to say about melancholia and the nature of family relations: 'Above all things, I entreat you, do not put the miserable delusion on yourself, to think there is something fine, and beautiful, and delicate, in giving yourself up, and agreeing to be nothing.' Having made his points, Godwin reinforces the method by which he has made them by invoking his own philosophy of sincerity: 'Depend upon it, there is no maxim more true or more important than this; Frankness of communication takes off bitterness. True philosophy invites all communication, and with-holds none.'[91]

Matilda can be read as a text which not only defiantly reiterates the melancholia Godwin so deplores here, but also demonstrates the damaging, in this case disastrous, results of this very philosophy of sincerity and confidence. At the very moment that Mathilda is urging her father to confess his secret and the cause of his sudden change towards her, she retrospectively comments on her 'pertinacious folly' in urging him to include her in his confidence: 'I was led by passion and drew him with frantic heedlessness into the abyss that he so fearfully avoided' (M, 27). When the father writes what turns out to be his suicide-note to Mathilda, he accuses himself in this manner: 'I have betrayed your confidence; I have endeavoured to pollute your mind, and have made your innocent heart acquainted with the looks and language of unlawful and monstrous passion' (M, 32). The father betrays Mathilda's confidence by succumbing to her entreaties to let her into his confidence. As Pamela Clemit has put it: 'Mathilda's trenchant advocacy of frankness and sincerity leads to disaster.'[92] Clemit's comment is part of a sustained reading of *Matilda* as 'a carefully crafted work employing many of the conventions associated with the fictional model which Godwin originated in *Caleb Williams*' and as a text which experiments with and re-evaluates 'a range of literary themes and techniques shared with Godwin and Shelley.'[93] In a text which clearly critiques Godwin's faith in a philosophy of unflinching sincerity and truth-telling, Shelley created a narrative which has profoundly challenged her readers' sense of the relationship between fiction and fact, life and work. To read *Matilda* as a purely confessional work, as a literal act of confidence or sincerity, unproblematized by literary and mythic codes and conventions, is to miss the very essence of Shelley's text, since, as I will demonstrate, far from being a simple outpouring of grief and melancholia, *Matilda* is *about* grief and melancholia. As Clemit writes: 'To read *Matilda* merely as an expression of psychic crisis is to underestimate Mary Shelley's achievement as a self-conscious artist.'[94] It has also frequently involved the perpetuation of a series of factual errors with regard to what Harpold calls the 'circulation' of Shelley's text.

There are two main misconceptions, or at least unprovable hypotheses, which continue to dog the critical reception of *Matilda*. They stem from the same root cause. It has been assumed that Godwin's apparent refusal to return the manuscript to his daughter caused the text to remain unpublished. It has also been assumed, on no evidence, that as she would do with her next major novel, *Valperga*, Shelley sent *Matilda* to her father as a gift, so that he could profit from its publication.[95] In fact, as we know from her journal, Shelley retained some kind of copy of *Matilda* which she read to Edward and Jane Williams on 4 September 1821 (see J, 379).[96] Whatever we think of Godwin's response to the text, as recorded by Maria Gisborne, the idea that he suppressed it against Shelley's own wishes is not tenable. The point is crucial in coming to a reading of *Matilda*, since it alerts us to the dangers of a too hasty interpretive narrative of oppressive fathers and victimized daughters which seems so perfectly to match the subject of the text itself. As Bennett suggests, there were very particular reasons why both Godwin and Shelley may have come to the mutual recognition that publication of *Matilda* might be a mistake. The most compelling of these is a fear of provoking into renewed life the spectre of public scandal which had been generated by Mary and Claire's association with P. B. Shelley and Byron and which hovered over Mary and Claire for the rest of their lives.[97]

Despite many claims to the contrary, it appears likely that Mary Shelley came to share her father's sense that *Matilda* was an unwise publication. When one remembers the circumstances in which she finally returned to England in 1823, including her need to palliate Sir Timothy Shelley, Godwin's response comes to seem prophetically wise rather than oppressive. The question still remains, however: what kind of text is *Matilda* and its former version, *The Fields of Fancy*? Muriel Spark argues that 'on reflection' Shelley came to see that in *Matilda* 'she had been merely relieving her feelings by over-dramatising her situation.'[98] Jane Blumberg shares this assessment, stating: '*Mathilda* is an uncontrolled, certainly therapeutic purge of psychological tensions and anxieties surrounding Shelley's relationship with her father. Shelley herself came to see how inappropriate it was for public consumption, unworthy to follow the distinguished *Frankenstein*.' She goes on to describe it as presenting 'the raw feelings and unbridled emotional expression that one would expect to find in an author's private writings.'[99] We can turn this argument around, however, and state that since it appears that during composition and in the immediate period afterwards Shelley did in fact believe that she was writing her text for publication, it makes little sense to conclude that what she did write was *merely* personal, *merely* confessional as opposed to literary. The primary question here, as various critics have recognized, is one of readership. Who is the imagined reader of *Matilda*? At the very beginning of the text, prefacing her story and addressing Woodville, her apostrophized reader, Mathilda writes the following: 'I do not address them [my pages] to you alone because it will give me pleasure to dwell upon our friendship in a way that would be needless if you alone read what I shall write. I shall relate my tale therefore as if I wrote for strangers' (M, 5–6). If this passage is intended as a metanarrative comment on the status of the text as a whole, and Shelley is, like her father, a frequent user of such moments within her fiction, how are we to read it? Should we understand this passage as suggesting that the text is directed at a personal readership (Godwin, P. B. Shelley, her immediate circle) but written as if it were a public narrative? should we interpret it as a moment in which personal and public are disrupted as oppositional terms? Does the text utilize the social conventions of literary narrative in order to encrypt a personal message to Godwin and/or to P. B. Shelley? does it seek to deconstruct the very categories of private and public writing in the hope of challenging readers familiar with the literary debate about these categories in the period? A further option must at least be mentioned here: was Shelley simply too engrossed in her melancholy, as Spark and Blumberg suggest, to produce a text which could negotiate between the realms of public and private discourse?

In one of the most profound essays yet written on *Matilda*, Tilottama Rajan presents a reading which would support the idea that the text produces a deliberate confusing of public and private registers. Balancing a focus on psycho-biography *and* the literary (formal, intertextual) dimensions of the text, Rajan argues that *Matilda* is an unclassifiable text, a novella which in many ways is closer to lyric than the novel. Employing Julia Kristeva's theory of abjection, Rajan suggests that *Matilda* refuses to fit into the recognized forms of narrative fiction and so, as an abject text, does not address itself directly to any reader.[100] As she writes: 'the abject has no clear sense of how it wants to influence a reader, indeed whether it wants a reader at all.' For Rajan, *Matilda* presents to its readers, whoever they may be, a piece of 'unusable negativity' which cannot be absorbed back into standard interpretive frames, or what Rajan herself calls *the supplement of reading*.[101] In this sense, although one submits the text to lengthy discussion and the other omits it from the canon of *Mary Shelley's Early Novels*, Rajan and Blumberg agree on the fact that *Matilda* is a singular text, one that resists being read in terms of the standard conventions of literary fiction. For Rajan, *Matilda* aims at *affect* rather than *effect*, which is to say that instead of calling (like conventional narrative works) for an interpretive response in the reader, it seeks to convey the 'unusable negativity' of trauma. Such a reading might find confirmation, in fact, in Mathilda's description of herself at the end of Chapter 11 as a figure of pollution, a female version of Cain, and a 'monster'. She asks:

> Why when fate drove me to become this outcast from human feeling; this monster with whom none might mingle in converse and love; why had she not from that fatal and most accursed moment, shrouded me in thick mists and placed real darkness between me and my fellows so that I might never more be seen?, and as I passed, like a murky cloud loaded with blight, they might only perceive me by the cold chill I should cast upon them; telling them, how truly, that something unholy was near? (M, 61)

Matilda, as a text, is that 'cold chill' sent by a creature 'set apart by nature', a monster outside of the network of human social relations. It is a text which appears intended to convey not meaning but a pollution or contamination, a disturbing and disruptive communication of negative feeling. The difficulty *Matilda* presents to the reader (whether that reader be Godwin, P. B. Shelley, or the contemporary reader) is centred in the relation between its affective singularity and the thematics of trauma. How can one have a thematics of trauma? If we thematize trauma we transform a singular event and feeling into the structure of a generalized discourse. In so doing we lose the singularity, the individuality, and ultimately the subjectivity of these experiences and subjective states. Trauma, in its singularity, stands outside of the socially signifying structures of narrative, whether they be psychological, political, philosophical or literary. It refuses the meaning such socially signifying discourses would ascribe to it since in that ascription of meaning singularity is eradicated, transformed into generalized meanings and categories. That is what Rajan is referring to through her use of the word abjection. The abject is that which refuses to be assimilated into general, socially signifying structures. To suggest that trauma and melancholia are private, whilst the signifying languages of narrative fiction, psychology or philosophy are public, however, is in itself to fail to recognize the disturbing and disruptive existence of such phenomena in human life. Another word for the phenomenon we are examining here is *tragedy*. Tragedy, as a concept, is divided between a codifiable, formal tradition and a singular, unrepeatable event, *the tragic*. Every literary example of tragedy confronts the problem that in presenting events and subjective states in the classical form of tragedy the singularity of those very events and states might be lost. *Matilda* is a text which confronts this problem and does so by finding a form in which the subjective experience of the tragic is both conveyed in its singularity and introduced into a philosophical, political and aesthetic debate about tragedy. It does so by intervening, as a text, into the Romantic discourse on incest.

II.   'A VERY POETICAL CIRCUMSTANCE'

Matilda's theme of incest may shock modern readers coming unprepared to the text; the theme, however, was a very common one within Romantic and particularly second-generation Romantic writing.[102] Byron's poetry, including *Manfred* (1816), along with his life, present an obvious example of the currency of the theme in Regency England. From Horace Walpole's *The Castle of Otranto* (1764), through Matthew Lewis's *The Monk* (1796), onto Godwin's *Mandeville* (1817), the theme had been a stock feature of the Gothic novel tradition.[103] P. B. Shelley, like Byron, found the subject peculiarly suited to his poetry, and in a letter to Maria Gisborne, discussing Calderon's treatment of the Biblical incest story of Amon and Tamar, he wrote: 'Incest is like many other *incorrect* things a very poetical circumstance' (*Letters of Percy Bysshe Shelley*, II, 154). Incest, as a theme, is poetical for P. B. Shelley partly because it can be made to represent the worst forms of human behaviour and to represent the 'highest heroism.' For P. B. Shelley this distinction divides up into generational (father-daughter) incest and sibling incest respectively. The former is an obvious symbol for tyranny and oppression and finds its great expression in the play, *The Cenci* (1819), which P. B. Shelley wrote just before the period in which Mary Shelley composed *The Fields of Fancy* and *Matilda*.[104] The latter is more difficult for modern readers to immediately comprehend, but for P. B. Shelley, as in a more ambivalent manner for Byron, it involves a form of idealized love so original, and thus so primary, that it stands outside of the unjust, unequal and distorting codes of social love, family structures and marriage. The symbol of that kind of pure, originary love is the desire between sister and brother, and is given its greatest expression in P. B. Shelley's *Laon and Cythna* (1817), a poem which because of its celebration of sibling desire had to be reissued, in modified form, as *The Revolt of Islam* (1818).[105]

It is the relation between *Matilda* and *The Cenci* that is of primary importance for Mary Shelley's readers. In her 'Note' on *The Cenci* for the 1839 *Poetical Works of Percy Bysshe Shelley*, she discusses the manner in which the Shelleys passed between them the idea of writing a tragic drama (Shelley, *Novels*, II, pp.282–3). After viewing what they believed to be a portrait of Beatrice Cenci by Guido Reni, and having been given (by John Gisborne) the account of 'the story of the Cenci', P. B. Shelley urged his wife to attempt a tragedy on the subject, only for her to convince him to make the attempt. 'This tragedy', Mary states, 'is the only one of his works that he communicated to me during its progress', and her translation of the Cenci narrative was crucial in P. B. Shelley's research for his drama.[106] Mary had also been translating Alfieri's *Mirra* (1784), a play based on Ovid's account of Myrrha's incestuous desires for her father Cinyras in *Meta-*

morphosis Book X.[107] These intertexts are crucial because they establish another parallel structure to add to the generational/ sibling one we have discussed. In Ovid, Alfieri and the Cenci history we have parental, father-daughter incest; however, in the first two texts desire goes from daughter to father, whilst in the story P. B. Shelley dramatized desire runs from father to daughter. *Matilda* appears to replicate *The Cenci* in presenting us with a desiring father. As many have noted, this desire is considerably complicated by Mary Shelley. The father's desire, in *Matilda*, is in some uncomfortable way, made the object of sympathy, if not identification, and the daughter appears at one moment to view that desire as alien and catastrophic, and yet at others to take responsibility for it: 'I believed myself to be polluted by the unnatural love I had inspired ....' (M, 60)

A comparison between P. B. Shelley's Beatrice Cenci and Mary Shelley's Mathilda is, to say the least, instructive. Beatrice Cenci is a daughter-victim who, in the course of the play, moves from a position of abjection and loss of identity to that of sublime, even terrifying, agency. In Act 3, scene i, after Orsino Cenci has raped his daughter as an act of arbitrary vengeance against his family, Beatrice appears, Ophelia-like, to have been driven to the point of insanity. She comments on herself as if she were an alien, a character in an implausible play (Shelley, *Poems*, II, 779–80). The deed itself remains unspeakable (P. B. Shelley marks it with a hyphen): it is so unnatural and unprecedented that it cannot figure within the social system of society and law. In her marginal notes to her translation of the 'Relation', at the moment when she comes to Cenci's violation of his daughter, Mary writes: 'The details here are horrible, and unfit for publication' (LL, IV, 297). The fate of Beatrice Cenci at the hands of her father is a primal crime, something beyond the levels of violence and bloodshed associated with human society and human history.[108] It is unspeakable, it cannot be incorporated into human discourse, and as such it turns Beatrice, at least at this point of Act 3, into a mythical figure, a figure from a 'woeful story' created by an imagination with unprecedented negative capabilities. The degree of Beatrice's violation, a systematic assault on her very identity, is measured by her confusion over her own role in the unnameable act. 'Oh, what am I?' she asks (Shelley, *Poems*, II, 781). Beatrice at this point has lost her sense of self, even her sense of being. The unique, unprecedented, singular act of parental violation takes her out of the symbolic order, which relies on repeatability, codes and conventions, the categorization of names and naming. In this state of subjective oblivion, she reaches the point where she contemplates suicide, only to reject it as a way out of her monstrous position: 'Self-murder? no, that might be no escape' (Shelley, *Poems*, II, 783).

The logic of P. B. Shelley's play is established in these speeches and Beatrice soon realizes that the only power which exists in the world to 'adjudge and execute the doom' of the crimes committed by her father lies in her own hands and those of her fellow victims. Beatrice Cenci becomes an agent of 'vindication' and the 'law', describing herself (and those who perform her desire for parricide) as 'a weapon in the hand of God', 'A sword in the right hand of justest God' (Shelley, *Poems*, II, 820, 828). It is in this adoption of divine justice that the political allegory of Beatrice's tragedy emerges for P. B. Shelley. Her hugely compelling embodiment of the spirit of just revenge is, according to P. B. Shelley, a mistake and a crime. He famously writes, in the preface to his poem, that 'no person can be truly dishonoured by the act of another; and the fit return to make to the most enormous injuries is kindness and forbearance' (Shelley, *Poems*, II, 730). These are not simply ethical and political opinions, however. P. B. Shelley makes his famously critical assessment of his heroine's actions in the context of a discussion of tragedy: he states that she should have acted differently, but then adds: 'but she would never have been a tragic character' (Shelley, *Poems*, II, 731). Beatrice could have acted differently and resisted the urge to 'revenge, retaliation' and 'atonement', but such an ideal character would have been just that, ideal rather than tragic. Tragedy, in these seminal remarks, appears less to do with the violence which Beatrice suffers than in an aesthetic distinction between realism and idealism. Tragedy, it would appear, is transcendable and transformable through ideal human action, by a 'fit return' to injury and insult.

Shelley's Mathilda does not suffer physical injury from her father. Incest in *Matilda* is an idea, associated with a dreadful sentence spoken by the father. The sentence in question is the one Mathilda finally drags from her resistant father's mouth: 'My daughter, I love you!' (M, 28), a sentence the young Mathilda, growing up in the absence of the wandering father, had often imagined in a wish-fulfilment fantasy (M, 14). The father's confession of incestuous desire, however, shatters the daughter's subjectivity just as completely as does physical violation in *The Cenci*. In

Matilda, Shelley takes the network of incest narratives from Ovid through to her husband's dramatic text and stripping the scenario of the actual violence of physical abuse, or the taboo of socially forbidden sexual relations, concentrates on the singularity of tragedy and the experience of what we might call the (de)figured female subject.

III. WANDERING FIGURES

It is useful to consider another network of intertextual allusions which are employed throughout the text. This network of allusions involves frequent references to the myth of Proserpine, along with the figures from Dante.[109] The image of wandering by a riverside gathering flowers connects Proserpine to Dante's Matelda, who helps the poet cross the two-fold river of Eunoe and Lethe (the rivers of remembering and forgetting) and so assists the poet in reaching the outer regions of Paradise. In the central scene of confession between the father and Mathilda, images of crossing an abyss play a vital role. The father warns Mathilda, as she attempts to get him to answer her question ('Am I the cause of your grief?): 'There is a fearful chasm; but I adjure you to beware!' In reply, Mathilda positions herself as Dante's Matelda, helping the father over that divide: '"Ah, dearest friend!" I cried, "do not fear! Speak that word; it will bring peace, not death. If there is a chasm our mutual love will give us wings to pass it, and we shall find flowers, and verdure, and delight on the other side"' (M, 27). Having made his terrible confession the father returns to the Dantean imagery associated with Matelda, along with the Proserpine myth of the natural world and the underworld: 'We have lept the chasm I told you of, and now, mark me, Mathilda, we are to find flowers, and verdure and delight, or is it hell, and fire, and tortures?'(M, 28).

The most important dimension these intertexts help to establish, however, is figured through the trope of wandering. After Diana, the mother of Mathilda, dies, the father leaves his infant daughter in the care of his sister and becomes a wanderer around Europe until, when she has attained the age of sixteen, he returns to his daughter. Mathilda, in her adolescence, during the father's wandering absence, imagines herself pursuing her father and thus, through her own agency, realizing her fantasy of a 'scene of

recognition.' The fantasy of becoming a wanderer herself necess-
itates, however, cross-dressing: 'My favourite vision', she writes,
'was that when I grew up I would leave my aunt, whose coldness
lulled my conscience, and disguised like a boy I would seek my
father through the world' (M, 14). Katherine Hill-Miller's description of Mathilda's fantasy in terms of 'a Telemachus figure who
wanders the world in search of his lost father' is highly suggestive
here.[110] Fénelon's *Telemachus*, one of Godwin's favourite philosophical and political texts, presents us with the son of Ulysses
questing for his father at the same time as Ulysses himself is
engaged in his Homeric quest to find a way home to Ithaca after
the Trojan Wars.[111] In such male narratives, wandering is associated with heroic questing, as it is indeed in P. B. Shelley's *Alastor*,
a text which itself echoes throughout *Matilda*.

The gender politics of *Matilda* can be pursued in terms of the
figure of wandering. When the father writes his long letter to
Mathilda, he describes his period of absence during her childhood in a language which is remarkably close to that presented
in P. B. Shelley's *Alastor*. Just as the poet-figure of that poem
wanders the earth in search of his epipsyche, the vision of his ideal
other (his 'soul out of my soul') that he has on one occasion
been granted, so does the father. He says to his daughter: 'You
appeared as the deity of a lovely region, the ministering Angel of
a Paradise to which of all human kind you admitted only me'
(M, 33). That statement contains within it the difference Shelley
would mark between male and female wandering. P. B. Shelley's
poet-figure wanders the earth hoping for a material female realization of his vision of the epipsyche, but the quest, as P. B. Shelley
makes clear, is, however noble and even heroic it may appear, a
doomed one. The female epipsyche is a metaphor, a figure for
the ideal, which in P. B. Shelley's dialogic rendition we must pursue and yet which cannot be realized in the material world. Both
the father and Woodville, the young poet who befriends Mathilda
after her father's death, are wanderers in this sense. Shelley even
makes Woodville a poet who gains the admiration of 'the whole
nation' by publishing his first poem when 'he was three and twenty
years,' the same age at which P. B. Shelley published *Alastor*.

For the text's two male characters, wandering is associated with a
male Romantic discourse of quest and idealism; for Mathilda, however, it involves a loss of identity. As the father's words suggest, his
return, after sixteen years of wandering from his daughter, imme-

diately figures her 'as the deity of a lovely region, the ministering Angel of a Paradise.' The scene in which the father finally returns to his daughter is narrated by Mathilda, and is worth remembering here. Mathilda begins by describing a situation in which, like Proserpine and indeed Dante before her, her wandering leads to a loss of direction:

> My father was expected at noon but when I wished to return to me[e]t him I found that I had lost my way: It seemed that in every attempt to find it I only became more involved in the intricacies of the woods, and the trees hid all trace by which I might be guided. I grew impatient, I wept, and wrung my hands but still I could not discover my path.

Mathilda does finally find her way to the lake and sees her aunt and her father walking on the opposite side, and she describes herself 'dressed in white, covered only by my tartan *rachan*, my hair streaming on my shoulders, and shooting across with greater speed than it could be supposed I could give to my boat, my father has often told me that I looked more like a spirit than a human maid' (M, 15). Those words are, of course, uncannily prophetic, in that for the father Mathilda will eventually become a 'spirit.' As he explains in his letter: 'in my madness I dared say to myself – Diana died to give her birth; her mother's spirit was transferred into her frame, and she ought to be as Diana to me' (M, 35). The father's return to Mathilda is, from the very beginning, a wandering from her, in that he sees not her but a 'spirit' and we might add a 'spectre' of the mother. Mathilda equally complains of Woodville that his perception of her is in fact a wandering, a figuring of her as something other. In the following example she complains that for Woodville she is Proserpine: 'You never regarded me as one of this world, but rather as a being, who for some penance was sent from the Kingdom of Shadows; and she passed a few days weeping on the earth and longing to return to her native soil' (M, 66). In two conspicuous scenes of reading, which confirm the importance of the intertextual networks we are tracing, the reader is shown further instances of the father's figuration of his daughter. The first concerns the father's, at that moment, inexplicable reaction to Mathilda's venturing of the opinion that 'Myrrha [was] the best of Alfieri's tragedies' (M, 20), the second displays the father's struggle with his desire for the daughter to be the mother when he asks Mathilda to read Dante from where her mother had 'left off' and then abruptly changes his mind (M, 23). At the beginning of the last chapter, after Woodville has taken his leave of Mathilda in order to go to his sick mother, she imagines a reunion with her father in 'some sweet Paradise' like that in which 'Dante describes Mathilda gathering flowers' (M, 62). Wandering on in this reverie of reunion in the afterlife, Mathilda appears to become the intertext that she imagines:

> I was so entirely wrapt in this reverie that I wondered on, taking no heed of my steps until I actually stooped down to gather a flower for my wreath on that bleak plain where no flower grew, when I awoke from my day dream and found myself I knew not where .... I had lost myself. (M, 63)

Shelley's *Matilda* takes up the incest narratives which are so important to both Shelleys in 1819, along with poems such as *Alastor*, and transforms them into an account of female figuration, a description of the manner in which for a woman like Mathilda, the result of masculine desire appears to be loss of subjectivity, a wandering identity best expressed through the processes of figuration itself. What Mathilda shares with Beatrice Cenci is not physical violation by the father, but the loss of identity (a fall into figuration) due to the singularity (the socially unnameable trauma) of a tragedy caused by the father. Unlike Beatrice Cenci, however, Mathilda cannot escape from her wandering identity; she makes no return to agency through tragic, if understandable error. In a much quoted statement, addressed to the poet Woodville, she complains: 'I am, I thought, a tragedy; a character that he comes to see act: now and then he gives me my cue that I may make a speech more to his purpose' (M, 56). Mathilda here is describing how 'unreasonable' she could be towards the noble and virtuous Woodville. In attempting to counter-act the over-dominance of psycho-biographical readings, some recent critics have taken up the theatrical imagery employed by Mathilda here and elsewhere, and have argued that she is in fact either a self-conscious manipulator of her narrative, theatrically exaggerating the events of her own history, or an example of the disastrous consequences resulting from taking theatrical metaphors for literal realities.[112] Interesting as such readings are, it is far more convincing to take her at her word. Mathilda *is a tragedy*, a female character who loses her relation both to self and to the world around her because of a singular experience which positions her outside of the symbolic order.

In the famous last paragraph of her 'Note on *The Cenci*', Shelley praises her husband's poem in the most unreserved terms. The fifth act, she writes, 'is the finest thing he ever wrote .... often after was he earnestly entreated to write again in a style that commanded popular favour, while it was not less instinct with truth and genius.' The 'bent' of P. B. Shelley's mind, however, she continues, 'went the other way', taking him away from 'the delineations of human passion .... [towards] fantastic creations of his fancy, or the expression of those opinions and sentiments with regard to human nature and its destiny; a desire to diffuse which, was the master passion of his soul' (Shelley, *Novels*, II, 286). For P. B. Shelley in *The Cenci*, tragedy, including Beatrice's tragic adoption of an ethical 'vindication' ending in parricide, is distinct from a philosophical understanding and enactment of Justice and Love. Tragedy and philosophy (or wisdom), in this sense, are not equatable, since the latter must always transcend and thus transform the former.[113] To understand how *Matilda* critically responds to such a position, we need to look more closely at the issue of narrative form and how it alters in the move from the rough draft *Fields of Fancy* to the fair copy *Matilda*.

IV.   FRAMES AND DIGRESSIONS

At some point after 12 September 1819, Shelley changed her mind about how to present her text and, dropping the long frame-narrative structure of *The Fields of Fancy*, moved to the first-person narrative structure that is *Matilda*.[114] In *The Fields of Fancy*, which is partly modelled on Wollstonecraft's unfinished *The Cave of Fancy*, a female mourner is visited by Fantasia. This mythological figure, which readers inevitably associate with the imagination and thus with writing, tries to persuade the unnamed female mourner to accompany her to the Elysian Fields. Most commentators agree that this framing technique creates a distancing effect between Mathilda's narrative and Shelley herself, partly because the unnamed female mourner who narrates the frame seems equally suitable as a fictional figuration of the author.[115] The mourner opens her narrative by stating: 'It was in Rome – the Queen of the World that I suffered a misfortune that reduced me to misery & despair' (Shelley, *Novels*, II, 351). The mourner's reluctance to accompany Fantasia establishes a tension between mourning and philosophy. The mourner's reluctance stems from a desire to remain on earth linked to the memory of those whom she has lost (Shelley, *Novels*, II, 352–3). When Fantasia, in a revision of the Proserpine myth, abducts the mourner during sleep and carries her to the Elysian Fields, she explains the 'chief care' of those who inhabit this particular part of this spiritual domain. 'This part of the Elysian Gardens', Fantasia states:

> is devoted to those who as before in your world wished to become wise & virtuous by study & action here endeavour after the same ends by contemplation .... Nor do they only study the forms of this universe but search deeply in their own minds and love to meet & converse on all those high subjects of which the philosophers of Athens loved to treat. (Shelley, *Novels*, II, 353)

The last part of that speech indicates the connection between *The Fields of Fancy* and P. B. Shelley's translation of Plato's *The Symposium*.[116] Diotima, Socrates's instructress on love in Plato's text, is given centre stage in the frame narrative of *The Fields of Fancy* once the female mourner has arrived in the Elysian Fields. Diotima does not directly address her philosophical meditations to the mourner, however, but presents them chiefly to a young woman 'of about 23 years of age in the full enjoyment of the most exquisite beauty' and a 'youth beside her', who has 'a far different aspect.' The young woman is Mathilda, and her 'aspect' is melancholic. The young man beside her has his biographical and intertextual referent in P. B. Shelley: 'his form was emaciated nearly to a shadow – his features were handsome but thin & worn.' The young man's difference from that of the Mathilda figure appears to embody the distinction between philosophical contemplation and mourning I have already noted (Shelley, *Novels*, II, 355).

As the narrative moves on to Diotima's instruction, Shelley fuses the Platonic ideal of love as the philosophical desire for the Beautiful and the Good, with P. B. Shelley's most idealistic works of poetry and prose of this period. In particular, *The Fields of Fancy* at this point becomes a revisionary encounter with Acts 1 to 3 of *Prometheus Unbound*.[117] Diotima presents an account of her own philosophical development, a narrative which has for its fundamental impetus a desire to explain the apparent intermixture of good and evil in the natural world. Her speeches can profitably be read alongside the appalling history lesson presented by the Furies to the still bound Prometheus in Act 1 and Asia's parallel account of natural and human history in Act 2. Diotima states: 'It requires a just hand .... to weigh & divide the good from evil – On earth they are inextricably entangled and if you would cast away what there appears an evil a multitude of benef[ic]al causes or effects cling to it & mock your labour' (Shelley, *Novels*, II, 355). The natural world, as she continues, is incredibly beautiful, and yet it itself is full of horror and evil; the human world seems no different, mingling 'love & virtue' with 'selfishness & vice' (Shelley, *Novels*, II, 356).

To the many critics who have argued that *Matilda* is a simple, pre-literary outpouring of personal grief, it is salutary to note that in this first version of her text (thus closer to the tragic event of the death of William in Rome) Shelley produced perhaps her most sustained engagement with the visionary epic poetry her husband had been developing in 1818 and 1819. Diotima's vision of natural and human history is clearly a response to the climactic words of torture spoken by the Furies to Prometheus:

> The good want power, but to weep barren tears.
> The powerful goodness want: worse need for them.
> The wise want love, and those who love want wisdom;
> And all best things are thus confused to ill. (Shelley, *Poems*, II, 514)

Diotima's vision of the entanglement of good and evil in the natural and human spheres may be realistic, but, as she says, it is 'one side of the picture', and she separates such a vision from 'wisdom' and thus 'philosophy.' Diotima describes how, in failing to disentangle good and evil, she was tempted to imagine the earth 'as an imperfect formation where having bad materials to work on the Creator could only palliate the evil effects of his combinations' (Shelley, *Novels*, II, 356). This vision looks forward to the Paterin heresy adopted by Beatrice in Shelley's next major novel, *Valperga*. Only when Diotima recognizes that wisdom comes from studying her own heart and pursuing that 'godlike feeling which ennobles me & makes me that which I esteem myself to be' does she find her way out of the nightmare evidence of the natural and human world and discover the Platonic-Shelleyan foundation of wisdom in the pursuit of the inner beauty of the imagination. The movement is one which replicates that taken by both Prometheus and Asia in the first two acts of *Prometheus Unbound*, a movement which leaves behind questions about causation and origins and embraces the future-oriented powers of the human mind. Diotima, in conclusion, addresses her audience and presents to them their philosophical and spiritual destination: 'Your souls now growing eager for the acquirement of knowledge will then rest in its possession disengaged from every particle of evil and knowing all things …. become a part of that celestial beauty that you admire' (Shelley, *Novels*, II, 358).

The frame narrative of *The Fields of Fancy* is far from a simple rewriting of P. B. Shelley's Platonics in *Prometheus Unbound* and elsewhere. We are reminded of this immediately after Diotima ceases speaking, when the mourner-narrator directs our attention to the young woman and her companion (Shelley, *Novels*, II, 358). Whilst the P. B. Shelley figure is rapt in admiration of Diotima's Platonic teaching, the Mathilda figure has not been transported out of her grief and misery. 'Diotima', she says, 'you know not how torn affections & misery incalculable misery – withers up the soul …. If knowledge is the end of our being why are passions & feelings implanted in us that hurries us from wisdom to selfconcentrated misery & narrow selfish feeling? Is it a trial?' (Shelley, *Novels*, II, 358) The as yet unnamed Mathilda adds: 'Oh on earth what consolation is there to misery?' (Shelley, *Novels*, II, 359). Diotima can only reassert that mourning and wisdom are to be separated and for this purpose she encourages Mathilda to narrate her earthly history, a suggestion which is at first appalling to the young woman. The crucial point of this scenario, however, is established in this exchange. Does Mathilda's narration of her history lead her to a transcendence of grief and mourning through an acceptance of a philosophical quest for the Good and the Beautiful? Is Shelley's Elysian narrative context a reaffirmation or a refutation of P. B. Shelley's Platonics?

The simple answer to those questions is that *The Fields of Fancy* presents us with a circular logic in which although the separation of mourning from philosophical contemplation is reiterated as an idea and an ideal, the actual example of this transformatory process (Mathilda) remains, at the very end of her narrative, where she began. The last lines of *The Fields of Fancy* read as follows: 'Now the turf is fresh on my grave and the violets are blooming on it – I am here not with my father but listening to lessons of Wisdom which will one day bring me to him when we shall never part' (Shelley, *Novels*, II, 405). The possibility of transcending melancholia is posited here, but it is not proven.

The changes effected by the move from the frame-narration of *The Fields of Fancy* to the first-person confessional narrative of *Matilda* are numerous. Two of them are vital for the reading I am presenting here. I will deal with one in this section, and leave the other for the final section. The linear movement of the first-person narrative of *Matilda* is constantly ruptured or punctured by digressions, or what we might call narrative wanderings. After Mathilda has made her complicated statement about her text's address to Woodville, discussed above, Mathilda writes:

> But enough of this. I will begin my tale .... My fate has been governed by necessity, a hideous necessity. It required hands stronger than mine; stronger I do believe than any human force to break the thick, adamantine chain that has bound me, once breathing nothing but joy, ever possessed by a warm love & delight in goodness, – to misery.

Mathilda, in other words, does not in fact begin her tale here but produces a meditation on the evil necessity that has ruined her life. As if remembering her earlier decision to begin her history, she then writes: 'But I forget myself, my tale is yet untold. I will pause a few moments, wipe my dim eyes, and endeavour to lose the present obscure but heavy feeling of unhappiness in the more acute emotions of the past' (M, 6). Mathilda may forget herself here, in the sense of losing the forward movement of her history, but there is a sense in which in moments such as these, when narrative movement breaks down into philosophical digressions or wanderings, Mathilda actually *remembers* herself.

Throughout her narrative these moments of wandering occur, and they invariably express the theme of a negative mode of necessity which rules her and other peoples' lives. These moments appear to mirror, on a narrative level, the frequent moments in which Mathilda loses her identity in the intertextual networks which surround her. They are also connected to a recognizable theme readers might well associate with *Caleb Williams*. The theme concerns the suddenness of the protagonist's fall, as here immediately after the father's return:

> Is it not strange that grief should quickly follow so divine a happiness? I drank of an enchanted cup but gall was at the bottom of its long drawn sweetness .... I lament now, I must ever lament, those few short months of Paradisaical bliss; I disobeyed no command, I ate no apple, and yet I was ruthlessly driven from it. Alas! my companion did, and I was precipitated in his fall. But I wander from my relation – let woe come at its appointed time; I may at this stage of my story still talk of happiness. (M, 17)

In the manuscript (Dep.d.374/1) we find that originally instead of the word 'wander' Shelley had written 'return.'[118] The relation between 'wandering' and 'returning' is unsurprising once we have recognized that in a very real sense Mathilda's digressions on the negative nature of necessity are what her text is about. When is the 'appointed time' for 'woe' given that the narrator of such a tragic history writes within the subjective experience of that 'woe'? In *Matilda* Shelley radically challenges the idea of a narrative account of tragedy through constant recourse to the non-narrative experience and reality of the tragic. I will give one further example, from the section in which Mathilda describes Woodville's impending union with his lost love, Elinor. In describing their ideal love, Mathilda asks: 'Could any thing but unmixed joy flow from such a union?' The question, at this stage of her narrative, is consciously rhetorical, the reader having been presented with sufficient evidence to understand fully Mathilda's belief in the entanglement of good and evil on earth. The reader is unsurprised, then, that, before the 'appointed time' of the catastrophe of their story arrives, Mathilda wanders off into a long paragraph on the negative nature of necessity:

> there must have been a revolution in the order of things as established among us miserable earth-dwellers to have admitted of such consummate joy. The chain of necessity ever bringing misery must have been broken and the malignant fate that presides over it would not permit this breach of her eternal laws. (M, 49)

There has been so much critical commentary on the incest narrative presented in *Matilda* that it can still seem somewhat idiosyncratic to assert that this passage, and digressions like it, is the 'relation', the central vision, of Mathilda's story. The change from *The Fields of Fancy* to *Matilda* allows for a far more subtle rendition of a mourning narrative, fascinating as is Shelley's engagement with P. B. Shelley's mythopoetic styles in the former text. Crucially, however, it allows Shelley to move from a structure in which mourning and melancholia are opposed to philosophy, to a narrative structure in which, through a constant rupture of linear narrative and through wandering digressions, melancholia and mourning are made philosophical subjects themselves. *Matilda* does not pose the question whether the psychological and ethical effects of tragedy are transcendable through philosophy, rather it asserts that philosophy (especially the perfectibilist, necessitarian philosophy associated with her father and her husband) must face the philosophical importance and unavoidability of tragedy. In *Matilda*, because of its wanderings from linear narrative, mourning and melancholia are given a philosophical voice. In this respect, *Matilda* is very similar to *Frankenstein*. Employing the combination of realism and psychologized first-person narration developed by Godwin in *Caleb Williams* and *St. Leon*, and subjected to gender consciousness in Wollstonecraft's *The Wrongs of Woman: Or, Maria*, Shelley in these texts takes up the negative dimensions of the Jacobin novel and utilizes them as a means of bringing into question the abstractly rational and at times idealized aspects of Godwinian political and social philosophy. *Matilda* allows for the expression of a subjectively singular tragedy, without that subjective experience and voice being immediately transumed and transcended by rationalist, generalized doctrines. We, as readers, are not necessarily meant to agree with Mathilda's vision of the malignancy of fate (which she equates with necessity) in the world. Her vision of the world is clearly the product of the tragic events she narrates, and so by definition her vision is singular, unrepeatable, and certainly resistant to generalization. *Matilda*, however, gives voice to that negative vision and, more than that, argues for its philosophical importance. Rajan's assertion that *Matilda* presents its readers with an abjected piece of 'unusable negativity' which cannot be absorbed within the economies of public discourse (philosophical, psychological or aesthetic) is highly insightful and has significantly influenced the reading presented here. Yet it is a reading which requires revision, since it is precisely the need to economize trauma and mourning, to recognize that there may be traumatic experiences which cannot be transformed by perfectibilist or any other kind of philosophy, which is given voice in *Matilda*. We can understand this better if we move to the subject of suicide.

V.   ON SELF-MURDER

The move to the first-person narrative delivery of *Matilda* inevitably foregrounds the theme of suicide within Mathilda's story. Whilst the reader is encouraged to place her story within the Platonic contexts of the afterlife in *The Fields of Fancy*, that particular theme must be somewhat softened in its impact. In *Matilda* the idea of the afterlife is reduced to a personal belief on the part of Mathilda herself, and so her desire for death takes on a sharper and far more acute focus. The subject of suicide, which dominates Mathilda's narration of her relationship with Woodville at the end of the text, brings us back to Godwin's letters of 1818–1819.

It is useful to compare the letter from Godwin concerning the death of William, with a letter sent the previous year by Godwin, dated 27 October 1818, in response to news of Clara Shelley's death:

> You should ... recollect that it is only persons of a very ordinary sort, and of a pusillanimous disposition, that sink long under a calamity of this nature. I assure you such a recollection will be of great use to you. We seldom indulge long in depression and mourning except when we think secretly that there is something very refined in it, and that it does us honour.[119]

Again, we have the idea of the two classes of people and the warning against indulging in depression or taking melancholia to be somehow a glamorous mode of being. Again, we have Godwin's characteristic sentiment that tragedy is a real evil but eminently transcendable. Before we go the way of many other readers of such letters and mark Godwin down as an unfeeling father, we would do well to remember, as Miranda Seymour does, that Godwin had good reason to worry about his daughter's state of mind. As she puts it: 'Mary, as Godwin frequently had cause to remind her, was heir to her mother's depressive nature. Mary Wollstonecraft had made two attempts to kill herself; poor Fanny had succeeded. Following the death of William Shelley, he saw the danger signs in his daughter's letters.'[120] We should also add the fact that Harriet Shelley had also demonstrated the real possibility of young women committing suicide. Certainly, by the time Mary Shelley was writing *The Fields of Fancy* and *Matilda* her father was obviously anxious about the possibility that his daughter might elect self-murder. Seymour suggests, in fact, that rather than the theme of parental incestuous desire, what Godwin found repellent in *Matilda* was precisely its articulation of a will-to-death.[121] As Janet Todd writes: 'In *Matilda* the whole story is a kind of suicide note, addressed to the absent poet [Woodville] who will be left to contemplate her suffering and her grave.'[122] Woodville is given the task of presenting Godwin's arguments on this subject. In *Political Justice* Godwin had given some time to 'the long disputed case of suicide' (Godwin, *Political*, III, 55). We can gauge the proto-utilitarian arguments he brings against self-murder by quoting a passage he added in the 1798 revision: 'Each man is but part of a great system, and all that he has, is so much wealth to be put to the account of the general stock' (Godwin, *Political*, IV, 68).

'Are you not young, and fair, and good?,' Woodville asks Mathilda, after she has invited him to join her in drinking enough *laudanum* to annihilate them both. He goes on: 'Why should you despair? Or if you must for yourself, why for others? If you can never be happy, can you never bestow happiness' (M, 60). It is something of an irony, of course, that these words echo those of the father, as expressed to Mathilda in his own suicide-note at the very centre-point of the text. If *Matilda* is, as Todd calls it, a suicide-note, then the father's letter left for his daughter to read, after he has quit the house intent on self-murder, provides a *mise-en-abyme* structure already familiar to readers of *Frakenstein*. The father writes: 'Resolutely shake of[f] the wretchedness that this first misfortune in early life must occasion you. Bear boldly against the storm: continue wise and mild, but believe it, and indeed it is, your duty to be happy' (M, 36).

The place of suicide as a theme within *Matilda* confirms the text's critique of what Godwin himself styled his 'moral arithmetic' (Godwin, *Political*, III, 73). *Matilda* is not a defence of suicide. In fact, in this narrative of very few actual events, the father's suicide is the one event which seems gratuitous, unnecessary and, above all, violent. It is, beyond all others, the action that induces Mathilda's fall into the realm of wandering and the tragic. Suicide, as presented and discussed in *Matilda*, is the text's emblem of irremediable trauma. That Shelley experienced such traumatized feelings during the period of 1818–19 is evident from her journal and her letters. She writes from Rome, to Maria Gisborne, during the last days of little William's life: 'The misery of these hours is beyond calculation' (L, I, 99). The idea of the reality of misery beyond (moral) 'calculation' or 'arithmetic' is symbolized by Mathilda's understandable desire-for-death. Writing to Amelia Curran, immediately after she had left her dead son in Rome, Shelley stated: 'I never shall recover that blow …. the thought never leaves me for a single moment – Everything on earth has lost its interest to me' (L, I, 100). *Matilda* is an expression of the singularity of such traumatic events. It is a personal and yet highly philosophical and ethical text, which registers in powerful ways Shelley's refusal to accept that all human experience can be calculated in terms of its benefit to the 'great system' of society, or that the idealist's notion of truth can always transcend tragic experience. In her next two novels, she developed this 'realist' philosophy to ever greater fictional degrees.

3

Valperga: Or, The Life and Adventures of Castruccio, Prince of Lucca

I. A REPUBLICAN NOVEL

After *Frankenstein* and the unpublished *Matilda*, Shelley turned towards historical forms and subjects. The three main novels which chronologically succeed *Frankenstein* are, in different ways, all historical in their subject-matter. Two of these, *Valperga* (1823) and *Perkin Warbeck* (1830), are historical novels in the obvious sense of the term; *The Last Man* (1826), set in the last years of the twenty-first century, is a novel which could be said to deliver a future history. It is clear, however, that historical forms and questions, along with the opportunities the developing mode of historical fiction offered Shelley as an author, present an unavoidable context for any serious account of her career as a novelist in the 1820s. The subject of history and its influence upon individuals and societies allows Shelley to expand and ultimately confirm her 'realist' vision of human existence and to sustain the dialogue with her immediate circle which we have already seen operating in her first two major fictional works.

As Nora Crook states, we have a good deal of information about the genesis, composition and publication of *Valperga* (V, xi). Shelley wrote to Maria Gisborne from the Baths of Pisa on 30 June 1821, describing the years of research (from 1817) which the novel had necessitated: 'It has indeed been a work of some labour since I have read & consulted a great many books' (L, I, 203). It should be remembered that Pisa was a 'garrison town' during the period in which the Shelleys lived there, and that Austrian occupation was the cause of two important if unsuccessful insurrections during the period in which Shelley wrote her novel.[123] Shelley composed *Valperga* in an Italy ruled by a foreign power and fitfully erupting with republican and nationalist resistance. As Crook puts it: 'The most intense period of writing occurred during the Carbonarist uprisings in Naples and Piedmont of 1820–21, and the novel contains a number of passing references to current events.'[124] Crook, Bennett, and others have been concerned in recent years to return the novel to its politically turbulent contexts and to reassert Shelley's clear support for a mode of political republicanism and nationalism. We have already seen that she displayed a similarly positive response to the news of revolution in Spain in the same period (L, I, 140–1).

Valperga can seem a rather daunting prospect for readers coming fresh from *Frankenstein* or *Matilda*. Set in the early part of the fourteenth century, its involvement with the specificities of Italian political and social history (the conflicts between the Guelph and Ghibeline parties, the rise of a class of political overlord known as the signori, the external political influences of France and the Empire) involve today's reader in a minor version of the substantial historical education Shelley put herself through between 1817 and 1820.[125] For today's reader, of course, the task is made more challenging by the need to remember the specificities of the political and social history of the early nineteenth-century Italy within which Shelley lived and wrote. The scholarly work of Rajan and of Crook is, therefore, of immense value to contemporary readers of the novel. Both make it clear that not only does Shelley purposefully exploit the parallels between her two Italian time-frames (fictional and compositional), but in doing so she intervenes considerably within what is in itself a contested historical record to present a narrative in which a republican ideal of national unification (associated with a version of Florentine Guelph politics) is pitted against the external force of Imperialism and the internal catastrophe of partisan politics. Bennett adds to this by stating that the interpretive crux of the novel resides in the manner in which it subtly alters and revises its historical sources.[126] What is clear is that Shelley weaves an adapted account of Castruccio's historical rise to power with the purely fictional narratives of her two principal female characters, Euthanasia and Beatrice.[127] Eliding Castruccio's historical family, Shelley interpolates into his life an emotional attachment to Euthanasia stemming from his childhood. This relationship represents hope both for Castruccio as an individual and also for Tuscany and, ultimately, Italy as a whole. Castruccio's Ghibeline father, Ruggieri dei Antelminelli, and Euthanasia's Guelph father, Antonio dei Adimari, are friends, and their ability to transcend the disastrous partisan rivalry between the Ghibelines and the Guelphs is inherited as a bond and a challenge by their children. Castruccio ultimately fails that challenge and reasserts Ghibeline supremacy in his native town of Lucca and, eventually, within Tuscany. The peace between Guelph Florence and Ghibeline Lucca, which is both the condition and the consequence of the future marriage of Castruccio and Euthanasia, is betrayed by the former in his apparently inevitable ascendancy to power within the region. Along the way Castruccio meets and then emotionally betrays Beatrice, Shelley's imagined daughter of the heretic Wilhelmina of Bohemia, a character that many have seen as the dark antithesis to the philosophically and politically enlightened character of Euthanasia. Much of *Valperga* hinges, then, on the manner in which Shelley interweaves the narrative of Castruccio's historical ascendancy with the romance stories of her two fictional, female characters. This combination of fact and fiction allows Shelley to play the historical record off against counter-factual history, opening the former up to a process in which an apparently unalterable necessity confronts the question of free-will and the ability of individual human beings to resist the march of masculinist power and violence.

In November 1820, P. B. Shelley light-heartedly wrote to Peacock: 'Mary is writing a novel, illustrative of the manners of the Middle Ages in Italy, which she has raked out of fifty old books' (*Letters of Percy Bysshe Shelley*, II, 245). The description of the novel does not sound very promising. However, as Crook and Rajan have demonstrated, the 'fifty old books' reduce in their significance, as far as the novel's re-visioning of Italian history goes, to a handful: the novel's preface mentions in particular Machiavelli's 'Life' of Castruccio (1532), Sismondi's monumental *Histoire des républiques italiennes du moyen* (1807–9, 1818), and then, as additions, Niccolò Tegrimi's *Vita Castruccii Castracani* (1496) and Giovanni Villani's 'Florentine Annals' (1537) (see V, 5).

Sismondi and Machiavelli are clearly the most important sources, although Shelley's 1823 essay on Giovanni Villani, first published in *The Liberal*, attributes to that author the ability to 'guide[s] us through the unfinished streets and growing edifices of Firenze la bella, and ... transport[s] us back to the superstitions, party spirit, companionship, and wars of the thirteenth and fourteenth centuries (Shelley, *Novels*, II, p.131). Recent critics have argued convincingly that the novel as a whole speaks for Sismondi's particular brand of republicanism. As Michael Rossington notes, Sismondi's *Histoire* was banned in Napoleonic France because it offered an alternative version of republicanism to the Imperialistic variety.[128] P. B. Shelley's description of Castruccio as 'a little Napoleon' is not, then, a throw-away remark (*Letters of Percy Bysshe Shelley*, II, p.353). It can, in fact, register for modern readers a distinction between Sismondi's communal version of Italian and European republicanism (associated in *Valperga* with Florence and the novel's main female character, Euthanasia) and the proto-'Napoleonic' version relatable to Machiavelli's endorsement of Castruccio in his 'Life.' As two modern editors and translators of his works state, referring as they do to the links between *The Prince* and the *Discourses*: 'Machiavelli, the republican enthusiast, sees no necessary conflict between a republican form of government and a dictatorship.'[129] For Machiavelli, 'great actions by single individuals are required to found republics, create religions, and reform corrupt military, political, or religious institutions.'[130] These strong individual leaders, possessed with military and political prowess, are also required to protect good institutions and the ideals of republicanism. As Bennett puts it, Machiavelli's works 'advocated coercive leadership as the only means to unify Italy and, eventually, to establish republican governance constituted on the Florentine model.'[131] Shelley's novel pits two accounts of republican destiny against each other and embodies them in the familial, emotional and political relationship between Castruccio and Euthanasia. The historical record would appear to endorse Machiavelli's assertion of the inevitability of dictatorial leadership; Sismondi's vision of a communal republic remains, it would appear, just that, a vision, a possibility, an imagined future state. The novel, then, confronts vital questions encountered by post-Napoleonic Europe: is the turn of republicanism into tyranny inevitable, or, despite the evidence of recent history, is there an alternative to despotic (monarchical or Imperialistic republican) rule? *Valperga* confronts the same questions explored by P. B. Shelley in his *Prometheus Unbound*; it does so, however, with less idealism and far greater sense of the dialectical basis of any future hope for humanity.

Because of Euthanasia's clear association with Florentine republicanism and Castruccio's increasing association with despotism and tyranny, readers can perhaps be forgiven for perceiving in its narrative a rather stark opposition between a feminized force of reform and a male force of tyrannical rule. Shelley clearly employs centuries of standard 'Machiavellianism' to produce an account of tyrannical individualism, apparently on the side of historical necessity and distinctly masculine in nature. The characters of Alberto Scoto, Benedetto Pepi, Galeazzo Visconti all espouse a version of what we might call commonplace (or stereotypical) 'Machiavellianism' in which the Florentine's misattributed assertion that 'the ends justify the means' is paramount.[132] It is important to remember the republican roots and intentions of Machiavelli's actual writings, however, since on a deep level *Valperga* does not simply display a battle between feminine values and the male will to power,[133] but also explores the internal divisions and the possible destiny of the republican movement itself. Castruccio is not simply the enemy of Florentine and, ultimately, Italian republicanism; he is also, as history, in the shape of Napoleon and Republican France, had recently demonstrated, its probable destination. He is a character who displays until the last sections of the novel a division within his personality which speaks to an historical and philosophical division within the republican movement as much as it does to any division between a masculine will-to-power and a feminized socio-political idealism. Certainly in the earlier parts of the novel, the ability of Castruccio to see through the violent excesses of stock 'Machiavellianism' is unmistakeable. As the novel progresses, however, Castruccio begins to collapse into a brute agent of history. History is not simply the context and source for Shelley's narrative of Castruccio, it is also *Valperga*'s principal subject.

Shelley's novel demands of its readers a radical questioning of the nature of history and historical necessity. It does this, in significant part, by deferring the 'fall' of Castruccio into mere historical, malignant agent. As Rajan puts it: 'In an interesting redundancy, Shelley repeatedly advances the turning-point at which Castruccio's "character" is once and for all "formed" ... in a negative direction – as if deferring the moment when possibility is narrowed into destiny.'[134] The point of closure Rajan refers to comes as late as Chapter 8, Volume III. The opening paragraph of this chapter is interesting in its focus on the external appearance of Castruccio, as if the narrator no longer has access to the 'passions' he now suppresses and, subsequently, as if Castruccio, for the narrator and therefore the reader, has shifted conclusively from fictional 'character' to a 'mere' figure from the historical record (V, 288). The narrator here is reduced to reading the lines on Castruccio's face, having been, as it were, exiled from his interior thoughts and feelings. As the narrator goes on to state, Castruccio at this stage of his career has become the stock 'Machiavellian' tyrant devoid of all ethical values: 'cruelty had become an elemental feature of Castruccio's character .... He had not forgotten the lessons of Alberto Scoto; and .... his measures had perhaps been influenced by the counsels of Benedetto Pepi' (V, 288). Rajan lists a series of 'turning points' in the novel in which Castruccio's character is stated to be 'formed', we might say 'closed', only to be subsequently 're-opened.'[135] One such passage occurs at the beginning of Chapter 7, Volume II:

> During his absence Castruccio had reduced in his own mind his various political plans to a system. He no longer varied either in the end which he desired to attain, or the means by which he resolved to accomplish it. He thought coolly on the obstacles in his way; and he resolved to remove them .... The change might appear sudden, yet it had been slow. (V, 173)

The passage is full of subtle ironies and ambiguities. For most readers of *Valperga*, this 'change' in Castruccio's character hardly seems precipitant; rather, it has been announced, retracted, re-announced and then again deferred throughout the bulk of the novel. Castruccio's 'character' generates these uncertainties (has his character 'formed' quickly or slowly? has his intention to dominate Tuscany developed or always motivated his actions?) because, as a character, he embodies the inexorable nature of history at the same time that he contains the possibility of alternative historical directions. Importantly, the narrator, only a few pages later, goes on to reiterate the questions raised about Castruccio's character, this time from the perspective of Euthanasia herself: 'Whence arose this sudden change in his character? Yet, was it sudden? or, was there indeed any change?' (V, 175). It would appear that the narrator and Euthanasia are in the same position with regard to Castruccio: both need to interpret his 'character', and both find this interpretive necessity an extremely difficult task.

Rajan, employing Godwin's important essay 'Of History and Romance', along with the obvious influence on Godwin of Leibniz's theories of counter-factual history, argues that 'the text's hybrid identity as a historical *romance* ... allows us to imagine other possible Castruccios, as for Leibniz too there are other Adams who might have existed in other worlds.'[136] In this way, the history of

Castruccio's rise to power in fourteenth-century Italy can figure both the irreversibility of the historical record and the counter-factual potential within that record for alternative directions. As Rajan puts it: 'In pursuing desire through histories ex-centric to it (as Godwin also does in *Mandeville*), both writers construct a negative dialectic in which idealism must work through material that profoundly resists it.'[137] Rajan also states that the novel's attempt to imagine counter-factual histories, histories which somehow resist malignant, masculine historical necessity, is centred on the way in which Shelley interpolates into the history of Castruccio her two fictional female characters, Euthanasia and Beatrice.[138] There is a third main female character, however, and she is often neglected by the novel's commentators. Unlike the first-person narrative techniques employed in Godwin's historical novels, *Valperga* is narrated by a third-person narrator, a narrator whose relationship with Castruccio and with the two fictional female characters we have just mentioned is anything but neutral or objective.

II.   NARRATING HISTORY

Many recent readers of *Valperga* have focused on its relation to the two models for historical fiction available to Shelley, those being the historical novels of her father and of Walter Scott. By 1821 Shelley had read a great deal of Scott's historical fictions (see J, 671–2), and some of her critics have viewed that reading as a significant influence on *Valperga*. Clemit, for example, argues that Shelley's extensive reading of Scott allowed her to adopt 'an impersonal third-person narrative voice to present the main story of Castruccio's rise to power.'[139] Deidre Lynch supports that claim, and writes that all three of Shelley's historically-oriented novels of the 1820s display this concern to join Scott in the examination of 'public history' through the use of a 'neutral narrator.'[140] Although Scott did undoubtedly influence *Valperga*, the tendency to extract from that influence a 'neutral' or 'impersonal third-person' narrator for Shelley's novel is problematic.[141]

Shelley's novel contains both historically 'objective' and subjectively 'personal' perspectives within her 'hybrid' narrative voice. Rajan's attention to Godwin's essay 'Of History and Romance' is important here, since it alerts us to the Godwinian rejection of 'general history' in favour of an historical method reliant on the fictional techniques of identification and, we might say, the imaginative in-forming of historical individuals.[142] The narrator of *Valperga* constantly shuttles between an historical voice we might call in some respects 'generalized' and a series of voices which can only be related to fictional modes of imaginative representation, identification and hypothetical speculation. Such a shuttle of perspectives and voices creates, if we look for it, a quite remarkable vacillation in narrative authority throughout the novel. In particular, the narrator's relation to Castruccio is unstable and becomes increasingly alienated (or externalized) as the novel progresses. We might look at the scene (Chapter 12, Volume I) in which Euthanasia, as she sits alone in 'a favourite retreat near a spring that issued from the rock behind her castle', is courted by Castruccio as he throws down 'a bunch of myrtle' from the precipice above (V, 96). As Castruccio announces 'Euthanasia! – Victory!' from the same position as his troops will enter Valperga at the end of Volume II, the narrator inhabits her heroine's thoughts and feelings, generalizing them into the thoughts and feelings of a certain class of politically conscious and active women: 'But to be loved by such a one; to feel the deep sympathy of united affections, the delicious consciousness of being loved by one whom all the world approves, by one who fully justifies his claims to the world's esteem' (V, 97). In such a moment, both *Valperga*'s narrator and its readers are figured as female in 'character.'

Euthanasia's response to Castruccio's courtship is to state the principles from which she will not be diverted: her hatred of war and consequent desire for peace, and her allegiance to Florence and the Florentine ideals of republicanism she has learnt under the tutelage of her father. Euthanasia's anxieties over Castruccio's motives appear to affect the narrator's own understanding of and relationship to Castruccio. She (the narrator) continues:

> It had been a strange task to unveil the heart of Antelminelli, and to disentangle the contradictory feelings that influenced him at that moment. There can be no doubt that he never forgot his designs for the aggrandizement of his native city .... yet at this time his whole policy was employed in conducting a peace with [the Guelphs] .... we may perhaps form this conclusion; – that he now found it for his interest to conclude a peace with Florence; and he made the sincerity of his present purpose lend its colour to his assurances for the future. (V, 98–9)

The narrative situation here is hugely complex. Castruccio is *at the moment* sincere, and yet his ambitions are also clear and undercut that sincerity. The last sentence is characteristic of the degree of ambiguity the novel's narrative voice can produce when representing Castruccio *as a character*. What is at stake in such moments is the entire aesthetic viability of the novel, since if we simply read the historical knowledge of Castruccio's military career against Euthanasia's willingness to believe in his sincerity it becomes impossible either to take her seriously as a character (particularly one meant to symbolize rationality and politico-social enlightenment) or to understand why the narrator should present the history of their relationship in such minute detail. Such a passage presents us with what is, from a logical point of view, the impossible combination of historical and fictional perspectives, the apparent illogicality stemming from the narrator's desire that we consider the historically determined (closed) career of Castruccio at the same moment that we identify with Euthanasia's desire and hopes for her lover, the still 'open' Castruccio. This tension between an historical and a fictional time-frame, between a factually 'closed' and a counter-factually 'open' perspective, is achieved in great part by the narrator's own parallel 'relationship' with Castruccio, a relationship in which the counterfactual possibility of his taking a different, more ethically virtuous path is kept open (or at least is continually re-opened) for as long as possible, even despite the stated historical record.

The reason we continue to believe in Euthanasia's reason and authenticity is because of the fact that Castruccio is a radically divided character: he is an historical character, and he is a character existing in the same historical moment as Euthanasia. It is crucial here to recognize that, as the narrator states, Castruccio cannot simply, with any thorough accuracy, read his own mind and intentions (see V, 100–1). As the novel proceeds and Castruccio's aggression towards Florence, and ultimately Euthanasia's strategically important castle of Valperga, becomes more blatant and systematic, he becomes impenetrable to Euthanasia and to the narrator herself. As he shows Castiglione the secret entrance to the apparently invincible castle of Valperga, on the day before his forces capture it, the narrator ponders: 'Who can descend into the heart of man, and know what the prince felt, as he conducted Castiglione to the secret path, discovered by his love, now used to injure and subdue her whom he had loved?' (V, 204). In the period in which Castruccio betrays the peace with Florence (and Euthanasia) and exiles three hundred Guelph families from Lucca (Chapter 7, Volume II), the narrator again remarks: 'It were difficult to tell what his sensations were with regard to Euthanasia' (V, 183). In both these passages the narrator goes on to hypothesize Castruccio's thoughts and feelings. The point is that the reader steadily understands that these narrative representations of Castruccio's inner thoughts are just as hypothetical and speculative as are the interpretations of his character that Euthanasia and indeed Beatrice find so unavoidable. The possibility of an ethically positive interpretation runs out for all three female 'characters' by the end of the novel, so that as he prepares to execute the Guelph conspirators and to exile Euthanasia to Sicily, the narrator's and Euthanasia's sense of his possession of any substantial ethical being has dwindled away, leaving him as impenetrable as the mountain-range upon which Valperga has been fictionally interpolated: 'She looked upon Castruccio; she saw that he was moulded of an impenetrable substance' (V, 319).

Valperga's narrator and Euthanasia are both, until the last stages of his career, divided in their interpretation of Castruccio. Representative of an historical necessity favouring always the masculine will-to-power? representative of the possibility of a rapprochement between power and social justice? Castruccio is a divided figure requiring the kind of double-vision (realist and idealist) demonstrated by both narrator and her fictional heroine. This dialectical vision of Castruccio's history, and thus of the nature of history in general, is made evident early on in the novel by Euthanasia. She describes Dante's ideological significance, for a nascent Italian national identity, in terms of a dialectic ('clash and struggle') embodied within Dante's own attachment to 'a party that seemed to support tyranny' and his poetry's 'pledge' of national liberation (V, 81–2). Valperga stages that 'clash and struggle' through its complex blending of historical and romance perspectives on its chief historical agent, Castruccio. The attempt to imagine Castruccio differently, which Euthanasia, Beatrice and the narrator are equally engaged in, can be read as the novel's version of that dialectical understanding of Dante, famous supporter of tyranny and, as Euthanasia has it, spokesman for 'freedom' and 'the fallen hopes of the world.'

Many readers would no doubt object that all the novel appears to confirm at its end is the unavoidability of power over reason, and military violence over freedom. Valperga, the fictional castle so identified with Euthanasia and her republican principles of peace and freedom, is razed to the ground by the beginning of the novel's third volume, the mountain-range on which it stands apparently symbolizing the immovability of historical necessity. Valperga's often described impenetrability is proven to be no defence against the impenetrable historical force embodied, during the novel's time-frame, by Castruccio. Beatrice is increasingly described as a 'ruined temple' (V, 264), a human relic, lacking any foundation upon which to resist the forces that militate against her. When Castruccio casually announces to Euthanasia that her cousin's husband, Leodino, has been executed, 'she stood as if changed to stone', before exclaiming to Castruccio, the tyrant murderer: 'you are not a man; your heart is stone' (V, 199). It would appear that stones and rocks symbolizing the possibility of freedom and justice are invariably destroyed and supplanted by stones and rocks representing the brute force of historical necessity. Castruccio destroys three hundred towers, formerly the possession of Lucchese Ghibelines, in order to build a more impenetrable wall around his town (V, 174). He builds the awe-inspiring Agosta ('this new symbol of tyranny'), which seems precisely to supplant the now demolished castle of Valperga (V, 266–7).

Ultimately an Enlightenment imagery of philosophical and ethical foundations appears to give way to the foundationless (he leaves no family and no enduring political legacy) military career of Castruccio. The early portions of the novel dedicated to Castruccio's pupilage under the Enlightenment-figure of Guinigi make it clear that his youth included the opportunity for acquiring philosophical and ethical foundations. Guinigi states: 'We shall be much together, and will discuss many subjects; and by degrees I shall understand the foundations on which you are to build your future life.' It is clear what those foundations are meant to be: 'Guinigi had an ultimate object in view; he wished to impress on the mind of his pupil a love of peace, and a taste for rural pleasures' (V, 26). Guinigi wishes, the narrator states explicitly, 'to lay a foundation-stone for the temple of peace among the Euganean hills' (V, 26). It is Euthanasia, however, through the teachings of her father, who gains such a foundation for her identity and world-view. It appears, despite the narrator's clear endorsement of her foundational reason and love of peace and freedom, however, to leave her as vulnerable to the rock-like force of historical necessity as is her rock-built home, the castle of Valperga.

Far from presenting a dialectical 'clash and struggle' between power and republican ideals, Valperga can be read as a highly pessimistic novel in which Enlightenment ideals are trampled upon by historical forces against which they have no defence. Considered in this light, with the novel's plot-line preoccupying our thoughts, it seems difficult to deny Jane Blumberg's assessment: '*Valperga* remains the darkest and most profoundly pessimistic novel that [Shelley] ever wrote .... There is no hint in the world of *Valperga* that humanity has the potential to improve itself or to significantly better its lot.'[143] To understand why that assessment is ultimately inaccurate and the manner in which a dialectic between despair and hope operates in *Valperga* we need to get closer to the political and ethical dimensions of Shelley's complex historical, counter-factual text. We can do so by focussing on Beatrice and Euthanasia.

III.   BEATRICE: 'THE AUTHOR AND MECHANIST OF THESE CRIMES'

P. B. Shelley's 'A Philosophical View of Reform' (1819–20) is a direct and significant intertext for *Valperga*. It is a text which opens with a long celebration of Florence as a primary source for modern European culture and political emancipation (*Shelley's Prose*, 230–1). As a text, 'Philosophical View' can usefully be read alongside *Prometheus Unbound*, in that it struggles far more directly to deliver a realistic assessment of the chances for reform against the dominant powers which will inevitably resist it. P. B. Shelley writes: 'For so dear is the power that the tyrants themselves neither then, nor now, nor ever, left or leave a path to freedom but through their own blood' (*Shelley's Prose*, 231). The context of P. B. Shelley's remarks concerns the manner in which the spirit of freedom expressed in the Florentine republic of the thirteenth and fourteenth centuries (before the emergence to power of the Medici family) was defeated only to be reborn in the Renaissance, and then later in the American and the French revolution. The account of the historical trajectory of reform in P. B. Shelley's text, therefore, is one of emergence, defeat and rebirth. The essay offers a far more dialectical understanding of the historical process than the one suggested by *Prometheus Unbound*.

It is worth reminding ourselves of what Mary Shelley wrote about that 'idealized' epic poem in her notes in the second volume of her 1839 edition of her husband's *Poetical Works*. She states that for P. B. Shelley 'evil is not inherent in the system of the creation, but an accident that might be expelled' and that 'mankind had only to will that there should be no evil, and there would be none' (Shelley, *Novels*, II, 277). We might compare Mary Shelley's account of *Prometheus Unbound* with a number of moments in P. B. Shelley's 'Philosophical View' in which he articulates a fundamentally dialectical view of history in which the struggle between the forces of reform and revolution

> leave the few who aspire to more than the former and who would over-throw the latter at whatever expense to wait until that modified advantage which results from this conflict produces a small portion of that social improvement which, with the temperance and the toleration which both regard as a crime, might have resulted from the occasion which they let pass in a far more signal manner. (*Shelley's Prose*, 247)

Mary Shelley's account of *Prometheus Unbound* dwells on its metaphysical qualities (the extinction of 'evil' from human and large parts of the natural world; the idea of human and physical perfectibility); the passage from 'Philosophical View' is materialist and fundamentally 'realist' in its assessment of the chances for reform within political arenas of ideological conflict. It is important to reiterate this distinction – between a metaphysical and a materialist understanding of historical 'progress' – since when critics such as Blumberg style *Valperga*, or *The Last Man*, as wholly pessimistic they tend to conflate and confuse Shelley's critique of the metaphysical aspects of the radical culture she inherited and lived within with the question of how her novels contribute to the politics of social reform she so clearly believed in and shared with her contemporaries. Far from being 'pessimistic', *Valperga* is a novel which subtly endorses and develops P. B. Shelley's account of the historical force of reform, but it does so in a way which characteristically eliminates any metaphysical or what I am calling 'idealist' rhetoric. What produces the appearance of 'pessimism' in *Valperga* is that without a belief that human reason is simply identical to what P. B. Shelley, after Godwin, calls 'the domain of an immutable necessity', it is not inevitable that the forces of liberty and reason will ultimately triumph in history's dialectical conflict between the forces of reform and the forces of dominant power (Shelley, *Poems*, I, 380).

Readers of P. B. Shelley's poetry and prose will be familiar with the account of history presented in 'Philosophical View': the spirit of liberty rises in specific epochs and with specific events is defeated each time, and yet remains to return or be reborn in a latter day. The 'idealized' *Prometheus Unbound* and the more 'realist' 'Philosophical View' agree on what will be the final outcome, however, since reason and its products (happiness, virtue, freedom, equality) line up in the human sphere with the law of necessity, drawn from the natural sphere of cause and effect. Human beings only have to dedicate themselves to the 'immutable domain' of necessity to effect a radical change in the social and political spheres. In other words, the nightmare vision of human history in which freedom emerges only to be defeated, and re-emerges only to be re-defeated, presented by the Furies to Prometheus as an ultimate torture, is, finally, defeated by necessity, in the shape of Demogorgon. *Valperga* is similarly repetitious in its plot and its various narrative patterns, but it appears to offer no way out of that inferno of defeats.

Repetitions structure *Valperga* in ways that have not yet received sufficient critical attention. At the beginning of the novel the Ghibeline party, including Castruccio's family, are exiled from their native town of Lucca: in Chapter 7, Volume II, at pretty much the dead-centre of the novel, Castruccio has gained back power in Lucca and exiles three hundred Guelph families. In the novel's 'Conclusion', however, Castruccio's power dies with him and the Ghibeline party appear set to 'fall into their primitive insignificance when he expired' (V, 325). A similar pattern of returns and reversals structure the history of Valperga and Euthanasia: in the last two chapters of Volume I the peace between Lucca and Florence, along with the projected union between Euthanasia and Castruccio, is celebrated by an elaborate festival; at the end of Volume II, Castruccio betrays that peace and his bond with its female chief by invading the castle of Valperga; at the end of Volume III, Castruccio exiles Euthanasia to Sicily and she is lost at sea. If we add to such patterns the series of staged 'closures' of Castruccio's character we have already discussed, the novel does indeed begin to read like a thoroughly 'pessimistic' demonstration of the unavoidable defeat of hope on every occasion it appears or reappears. On this basis, the character of Beatrice seems to cement the novel's 'pessimistic' repetition of defeat and to add to that repetitiousness an uncanny, wholly metaphysical note.

Beatrice's shockingly negative and tragic history is in significant ways a series of repetitions and returns. Kept ignorant of the history of her mother, Wilhelmina of Bohemia, who in Shelley's hands is the leader of a purely female heresy, Beatrice ends up returning to the spirit of her mother despite the Bishop of Ferrara's best intentions. Attempting to save her from the falsehood of heresy, the Bishop wraps her in an impenetrable falsehood, the result of which is that Beatrice's imagination eventually turns unfounded orthodoxy into a politically dangerous and in itself heretical self-image. Beatrice as *Ancilla Dei*, spiritually favoured 'handmaid of god', is, as the Bishop well knows, a disastrous return of maternal imagination rather than the reasoned faith in which he has attempted to school her (V, 144).

The potential biographical significances of Beatrice's inherited maternal imagination have been well mined by critics and scholars. What is important here is the manner in which as one of the novel's three central characters Beatrice stands as an embodiment of a negative, 'pessimistic' response to historical necessity. The core of that embodied negativity clearly rests in Beatrice's lack of 'foundations.' Positing her identity and her actions upon her imagination, rather than her reason, Beatrice is 'guileless', prey to 'intoxicating delusions', 'the dupe of her undisciplined thoughts' (V, 144, 151, 152). She is, as the narrator, near the end of her story, states: 'poor, untaught Beatrice' (V, 246). The narrator, in the context of her devastating love for Castruccio, is very explicit, not only on Beatrice's ruinous imagination, but also on her helplessness, her lack of any ability to do other than she does: 'Poor Beatrice! She had inherited from her mother the most ardent imagination that ever animated a human soul ..... and she followed that as a guide, which she ought to have bound with fetters, and to have curbed and crushed by every effort of reason' (V, 152). The figure of the 'guide' employed here forms part of a complex network of images throughout the novel in which labyrinths, underground passages and webs challenge those caught within them to affect their exit. Significantly, when Castruccio first meets her, Beatrice possesses knowledge of a 'secret entrance', involving 'subterraneous passages', which will allow Castruccio to affect the surprise return of the Marquess Obizzo to Ferrara (the express, political objective of Castruccio's visit to that town). The Bishop's sister, the Madonna Marchesana, in the presence of Castruccio, asks the veiled Beatrice to 'light us, and lead us the way, that success may attend our steps' (V, 128; see also 279). But the irony of this scene is unmistakeable, and Castruccio's immoral, temporary indulgence of her belief in their spiritually inspired union leaves her clueless, a ruined microcosm, and a captured town: 'It was her heart, her whole soul she had given; her understanding, her prophetic powers, all the little universe that with her ardent spirit she grasped and possessed, she had surrendered, fully, and without reserve' (V, 155).

Beatrice constantly struggles between a total collapse of reason and a traumatic recognition of the reality that has indeed impacted on her.[144] Sexually betrayed by Castruccio, Beatrice becomes a wanderer, until she is sexually and psychologically raped by an apparently nameless 'wicked and powerful enemy' (V, 257). She spends three years as 'the slave of him, who was a man in form alone' (V, 258), until an uprising against this tyrant and his infernal house brings his death ('He was destroyed. I saw him die, calm, courageous and unrepenting') and Beatrice wanders again only eventually to be taken in by a Paterin recluse, who teaches her his heretical view of the universe, until he himself is captured, tortured and killed by the Inquisition. When Castruccio saves her from the Inquisition and delivers her into the apparent safety of Euthanasia's care, Beatrice is a victim of staggering degrees of trauma, with a need to interpret her experience. Like all trauma victims, however, there is something in her past experience that she finds unclaimable.[145] Something in her experience – a meaning, a rationale, an originary force or intention – wanders from her mental grasp. This 'something' is connected, via her dream, with the return of a trauma which, coming to her in the form of *déjà vu*, a proleptic dream, seems to indicate that for her trauma itself is originary, a cause rather than effect. We should remember that the first time Beatrice recounts her dream, to Euthanasia, she describes it as a memory, a return: 'The memory of a dream flashed across me' (V, 256). She goes on, before recounting it: 'Again and again I have dreamed this dream, and always on the eve of some great misfortune. It is my genius, my dæmon.' What she then recounts is not the dream but her 'memory' of it, or indeed, as has been established here, the memory of its 'memory.' Its narration to Euthanasia does not deliver up its meaning; rather, the narration is just yet another attempt on the part of Beatrice to interpret its meaning. That this attempt will fail, once again, is above all what gives the dream control over Beatrice and makes it her 'genius' and 'dæmon' (V, 256).

It is difficult to avoid the conclusion that Beatrice's dream is quite simply an expression of the traumatic nature of history; history (personal and public) understood as the unavoidable repetition of traumatic experience. Later, as she sits with the witch, Fior di Mandragola, in her cave, Beatrice is tempted to repeat her repetitious dream once again. Beatrice states: 'That is the key, the unbreakable link of my existence; that dream must either place me above humanity, or destroy me' (V, 274). When she does recount it, however, her narration includes a significant amount of detail absent from her former account to Euthanasia. This material seems to focus on doppelgängers: first, the shadowy woman in the identical boat; second, an actual meeting with her own double. What is important, however, is Beatrice's response to this reiteration of her ever changing always the same dream: 'Yes; there is something mysterious in my nature, which I cannot fathom' (V, 275). From this point on Beatrice is caught between a desperate desire to cling to the 'reality' offered to her in the shape of her 'confessor', Euthanasia, the overwhelming power of her imagination ('that evil pilot') and the inescapable reality of her dream. She states to Euthanasia: 'a very long time ago, I fancied myself a prophetess; but I awoke from that dream many years since.' But this is only after she has cried out to her 'friend': 'Save me! ... save me from madness, which, as a fiend, pursues and haunts me. I endeavour to fly him; but still he hovers near: is there no escape?' (V, 279). The figuring of madness (and by association her dream and her self-image as a prophetess) as a singular masculine 'he' is a 'clue' for the reader.

In the pre-arranged scene of the wooded amphitheatre, with its 'soft murmuring fountain', tantalizingly close to the scene of her dream, Mandragola arranges for a drugged Beatrice, to falsely prove her divine gifts, as she had in the 'Judgement of God' episode in Ferrara, this time by conjuring the presence of her beloved Castruccio. She is in fact confronted with a pair of horsemen ('she saw Castruccio and Tripalda') and the presence of the latter seems decisive in her final collapse into madness: 'The presence of Tripalda was to her the sign of diabolical interference; she believed him dead; that it was his spirit which then appeared; and, if so, it was also an unreal form, the resemblance of Castruccio alone, that she beheld. – She sunk in convulsions on the road' (V, 282). Does she or does she not see Tripalda as she collapses (sinks)? The question is significant, since it opens up a mystery the novel has woven around that character.

The narrator very subtly establishes the possibility, if not the conclusive fact, that Tripalda was indeed Beatrice's former torturer. The previous meeting between the two comes as Beatrice begins to give way to her desire to see Castruccio again, and it appears to her as 'a mere vision conjured up by her imagination': 'She thought that the vivid image of this partner of her enemy's crimes, thus coming across her while she was on the point of disobeying her confessor's injunctions, was a warning and punishment from heaven' (V, 270). Is Tripalda the 'enemy' himself or a 'partner' of that 'man in form alone'? This passage seems to confirm the latter answer; Beatrice's second encounter, under the influence of Mandragola, seems to confirm the former. Certainly, the later chapters of the novel, revolving around the conspiracy to affect Castruccio's downfall, appear to suggest that if Tripalda is not the 'enemy' himself, then as 'partner' of that man he is as guilty. Euthanasia tells him that she knows his secret and could 'tell a tale' about him to the world that would quickly bring about his destruction (V, 304). The narrator goes on to state that 'both Castruccio and Euthanasia had become in part the depositaries of [Beatrice's] secret; Euthanasia had heard his name pronounced, mingled with shrieks and despair, by the lips of the lovely maniac' (V, 306).

Why is the mystery surrounding Tripalda's identity and his precise relation to Beatrice important? The answer lies less in the attempt to ascertain positively whether he is indeed her 'enemy' or not, but rather in the significance of that final catastrophe in which she is confronted with Tripalda and Castruccio. As those around her try to revive her, the narrator describes the scene:

> Once she opened her eyes; she saw the face of Castruccio leaning over her, and she smiled. Castruccio thought that he knew that smile; but Tripalda, leaving the witch, pressed in among those who were about her. – No one who had seen him could ever forget him; she saw what she believed to be the evil genius of her life; and she again sunk into insensibility. (V, 283)

The literal referent of that last sentence is obviously Tripalda, and perhaps confirms that he was indeed the nameless 'enemy' of the Campagna di Roma. However, the association which has just been drawn, at the moment of catastrophic convergence, between Tripalda and Castruccio, inevitably leads us to see the possibility of a linguistic shifting in which the latter becomes, just as much as Tripalda, 'the evil genius of her life.' Beatrice herself has earlier referred to Castruccio as 'the master of my fate' (V, 261). Tripalda and Castruccio are interchangeable, with regard to Beatrice, since they both abuse and betray her. Throughout the novel Castruccio's potential for a more enlightened course has been marked by his relative nobility and virtue compared to inhumane, shockingly 'Machiavellian' characters such as Scoto, Pepi and Tripalda. Now, near the end of the novel, he has not simply lost any distance from these figures, he has joined them in a collective masculine entity ('evil genius', 'enemy', 'dæmon') which can easily shift its referent into the Paterin image of the dominant deity, the 'the eternal and victorious influence of evil' which Beatrice has come to believe rules the world (V, 242).

Beatrice's Paterinism is a form of Manicheism in which the principle of good struggles with and gives way to the principle of evil.[146] One of the clear sources for Shelley's exploration of this dark theology is clearly P. B. Shelley's various attempts, in particular in the 'Notes' to *Queen Mab*, to disprove monotheistic religions such as Christianity through an assertion of the principle of Necessity. As P. B. Shelley states: 'the doctrine of Neccesity teaches us, that in no case could any event have happened otherwise than it did happen, and that, if God is the author of good, he is also the author of evil; that, if he is entitled to our gratitude for the one, he is entitled to our hatred for the other' (Shelley, *Poems*, I, 380). For P. B. Shelley, the hypothesis of an omniscient God must give way to the doctrine of Necessity, the principle of cause and effect operating in the natural and the human domain. Once that transfer of power has been intellectually effected, we are in a position to employ the power of reason to direct us towards individual and social perfectibility. At that stage we are back with Mary Shelley's notes to *Prometheus Unbound*. Beatrice, however, has no rational foundation, no substantial education in the development of her reason; she has, in fact, never known anything other than the power of her own imagination, love for specific individuals (the Bishop of Ferrara, Castruccio, the Paterin heretic, ultimately Euthanasia) and the unending series of traumatic repetitions that constitute her life-story. Explaining her Paterin beliefs to Euthanasia, she states: 'God created me: am I the work of a beneficent being?' (V, 243). One can only answer as one would if asked the same question by Frankenstein's creature, in the negative. Castruccio himself, the man who even whilst conducting his brief love-affair with Beatrice bore within him 'the germ of an evil-bearing tree' (V, 151), describes Beatrice as 'a Paterin, one who believes in the ascendancy of the evil spirit in the world; poor insane girl!' (V, 241). When readers encounter Beatrice's account of the world, from the perspective of her Paterin faith, they can hardly share in Castruccio's assessment of her mental state. Beatrice says to Euthanasia: 'Look around. Is there not war, violation of treaties, and hard-hearted cruelty? Look at the societies of men; are not our fellow creatures tormented one by the other in an end-less circle of pain?' (V, 243). Castruccio, the man she continues to love until her death, is, until the final two pages of *Valperga*, the 'spirit' or even 'dæmon' of this indisputable and apparently 'end-less circle of pain' called human history. It would appear that we need to shift our attention to Euthanasia if we are to find a way of validating our assertion that *Valperga* is something more than a wholly 'pessimistic' novel.

IV. EUTHANASIA: 'THEY SPEAK ITALIAN ALSO IN SICILY'

There are many caves and caverns in *Valperga*, and most of them seem to contain within them a negative force associated with the triumph of malignant historical necessity. The connection between Beatrice's heretical view of the world, along with her mother's own female heresy, is consolidated in this series of caves and caverns.[147] Beatrice as a baby is secreted away in a leper's cavern, she meets the Paterin heretic in a cavern, and finally is taken by Bindo, the Albinois dwarf, to Mandragola in her 'witch's cave.' Most of the novel's imagery has a dialectical or antithetical quality, and it is not surprising that when Euthanasia takes it upon herself to educate Beatrice in the ways of reason she should choose, as her leading metaphor, an extended figuration of the mind (she calls it soul) as a cave. Euthanasia's enlightened education under the tute-lage of her father, Adimari, forms one of the centre-pieces of the opening chapters of the novel and acts indeed as a kind of founda-tion and orientation throughout the novel. We have seen how closely the narrative voice and the mind of Euthanasia are con-nected as the novel proceeds, and it is important to note that one of the qualities Adimari's education of his daughter gives to her is an ability to see beyond the ideological confines of the present day (V, 18); this is the basis upon which her own and the narrator's dual perspective (historical, trans-historical) coalesce. When the plot brings Beatrice and Euthanasia together, therefore, both of them betrayed by their single love, Castruccio, readers would expect that the latter would be able to convey to the former her philo-sophically, ethically and politically foundational principles. The core of this pedagogical scene comes when Euthanasia delivers her extended allegory on the 'cave of the soul.' The challenge for readers of *Valperga* is that the lesson fails.

The sources behind Euthanasia's 'cave of soul' allegory are numerous, from Plato's *Republic* through to Asia's meeting with Demogorgon in *Prometheus Unbound* and Julian's desire to find 'an entrance' to 'the caverns' of the maniac's mind in *Julian and Maddalo*.[148] What is crucial is the positioning of an 'inner cave' within the 'vast cave' of the soul. It is towards this 'inner cave' that Euthanasia directs her pupil's attention. She explains: 'This recess receives no light from outward day; nor has Conscience any authority here. Sometimes it is lighted by an inborn light; and then the birds of night retreat, and the reptiles creep not from their holes. But, if this light do not exist, oh! then let those beware who would explore this cave' (V, 263). This 'inner cave', it would appear, is not simply in itself a divided place (for some inwardly lit and so positive, for others unlit and so dangerous), it also appears to reinforce rather than heal the perceived and stated differences between a character like Euthanasia and a character like Beatrice. What possible use could Beatrice, so clearly lacking that 'inborn light', do with this description of the inner soul or mind? The moment of the novel in which, logically and dramatically, it would appear appropriate for Euthanasia to teach Beatrice, and in so doing convey to her friend her foundational reason, seems to show Euthanasia strangely stuck in her time. The allegory's medieval array of personified qualities appears to confirm a notion of innate character which for the heir of Godwin and Wollstonecraft seems dramatically outmoded, historically immature. Beatrice, quite understandably, replies to Euthanasia's lesson in the following manner: 'Talk no more in this strain .... every word you utter tells me only too plainly what a lost wretch I am. No content of mind exists for me, no beauty of thought, or poetry; and, if imagination live, it is as a tyrant, armed with fire, and venomed darts, to drive me to despair' (V, 263). Readers can only respond that Beatrice seems to have received the lesson with all due clarity and intelligence.

On a deeper level, however, Euthanasia's inability to teach Beatrice is appropriate and vitally significant in the light of the novel's ultimate direction. Beatrice is a victim. Like Mathilda before her, she is a character whose narrative attests to the real and often ineradicable presence of tragedy in human life. Beatrice's role in the novel is not to be saved or reconciled or made happy: it is, precisely, to demonstrate that for some history is an inescapable and irredeemable nightmare. Euthanasia's role is a related but different one. Euthanasia's failure as a teacher of Beatrice (she does of course give security and friendship as long as Beatrice can receive it) forces us to ask the question: what use is Euthanasia's foundational reason? The question contains within it the whole force and significance of *Valperga*. Bennett argues that, sharing a belief in the possibility of lasting social reform with her husband, Shelley through Euthanasia promotes the culturally feminine values of 'love, peace, charity.'[149] Bennett's points are in tune with a reading of *Valperga* which places it within the legacy of the Godwinian novel, in which a character symbolizing the novel's ultimate values might be defeated but still inspires its readers with the possibility of realizing those values in the future. Often, it must be said, Godwin's fictions function by presenting the story of a character who does not take the opportunities for a reasoned, socially useful life. Novels like *St. Leon*, *Fleetwood* and *Mandeville*, in that sense, present us with characters more identifiable with Castruccio than Euthanasia, and attempt to inculcate their enlightenment values to the reader via a negative example, a kind of negative image (in the photographic sense). *Valperga*, in this sense, can be said to present to the reader, in the context of an historical period in which real political opportunities for reform are lost, both negative and positive 'images.' In this regard, it is crucial to emphasize the role played in Euthanasia's life by hard, sometimes impossible ethical choices. Throughout her life, she is presented with the kind of choices predicted by her father before his death: 'he told me', she tells Castruccio, 'that either my judgement or passions must rule me, and that my future happiness and usefulness depended on the choice I made between these two laws' (V, 82). Shelley's father had gone beyond such statements, in the first edition of *Political Justice*, and had argued, in the infamous example of Fénelon and the chambermaid, that there was always a rationally correct choice to be made in any event, even if that choice were taken against one's own family members (Godwin, *Political*, III, 50). Godwin backed away from such an extreme position subsequent to the 1793 edition of *Political Justice*, but it remained a test-case for his daughter's writing, a kind of key-note (if decisively in the minor) against which she could play her more realistic tunes. Euthanasia's life turns out to be characterized by a series of such choices, particularly after Castruccio turns against Florence and decides to take power for himself in Tuscany. Her vow 'not to unite herself to the enemy of Florence' ruins any chance of happiness on the personal and private level (V, 169), but it also leads to the decision to defend the castle of Valperga against Castruccio's troops and, eventually, to join in the political conspiracy against him. Significant sections of Volumes II and III revolve around the devastating ethical dilemmas these two choices pose for Euthanasia, and much of what is admirable about her character rests on her refusal to simply exonerate herself.

The ethical validity of her choice to defend Valperga still appears to leave the novel's readers lacking a critical consensus. Lisa Hopkins, for example, reads *Perkin Warbeck* off against *Valperga* in this context and argues that the question of whether Euthanasia is right to defend her castle is 'answered resoundingly in the negative' by the latter text.[150] For Jane Blumberg: 'Euthanasia's defiance of Castruccio's demand that she surrender her castle and domain .... epitomizes her inflexible idealism', an 'inflexible idealism and nationalistic pride' which Blumberg reads as a kind of female version of Castruccio's 'relentless ambition.'[151] Although such assessments seem eccentric and are, in fact, significantly wide of the mark, they do register perhaps just how radical Euthanasia's questioning of her own actions can be. Such assessments might argue that there is positive confirmation of their position in passages like the following, which gives us Euthanasia's thoughts only days after Valperga has been taken: 'I have done infinite evil, in spilling that blood whose each precious drop was of more worth than the jewels of a kingly crown; but my evil has born its fitting fruit; its root in death, its produce poison' (V, 221). The reader has to remember that, defend her castle or not, Castruccio's ascendancy, during the period covered by the novel, is irresistible and, resisted or not, is likely to devastate the inhabitants of Valperga. Readers of the novel go astray when they believe that Euthanasia could have acted to avoid tragedy; she is living and acting within the midst of its absolute reign. Her genuine and moving self-doubt is in fact an indicator of her commitment to the very values of peace and love which the novel promotes through her and its narrator against the historical realities ultimately exemplified by Castruccio.

Euthanasia's decisions to defend Valperga and later, reluctantly, to enter into the conspiracy are taken in the context of Castruccio's growing monstrosity. They are also taken in full knowledge that these actions are desperate, regrettable acts: pure, ethical choices are not available to Euthanasia given 'things as they are.' What is crucial are the various moments, during her 'melancholic' meditations on her own actions and responsibilities, in which she considers her relation to time and history. The night before the battle over her castle, Euthanasia doubts 'the purity of her own motives' and hesitates 'on the brink of her purpose.' These doubts lead to a sustained meditation on the individual's relation to time. Her thoughts wander 'in idea through the whole universe' as she thinks: 'Why do our minds, grasping all, feel as if eternity and immeasurable space were kernelled up in one instantaneous sensation?' (V, 212). In this passage we find a characteristic emphasis on the human experience of tragedy, the very thing that is usually elided by more generalizing modes of historical writing. However, we are also introduced to Euthanasia's trans-historical vision, something that will dominate her character throughout the last, tragic stages of the novel. This aspect of her mind is crucial. It demonstrates a significant response on the part of Mary Shelley to P. B. Shelley's interest in Lockean and post-Lockean ideas of human sensation and time (duration).

A very useful intertext to remember here is the section of the 'Notes' to *Queen Mab* in which P. B. Shelley attempts to sum up the philosophical line which runs from Locke's account of time in terms of 'the *constant and regular Succession of Ideas* in a waking Man' to Godwin's speculations about the prolongation of human life in *Political Justice*. P. B. Shelley writes that 'Time is our consciousness of the succession of ideas in our mind' and goes on: 'If a mind be conscious of an hundred ideas during one minute, by the clock, and of two hundred during another, the latter of these spaces would actually occupy so much greater extent in the mind as two exceed one in quantity.' The inference we can take from this is clear: 'If … the human mind, by any future improvement of its sensibility, should become conscious of an infinite number of ideas in a minute, that minute would be eternity.' P. B. Shelley's argument is not that 'the actual space between the birth and death of a man will ever be prolonged', but, rather, that 'sensibility is perfectible' (Shelley, *Poems*, I, 405). Without necessarily prolonging the actual years of life, human beings can potentially live for an eternity by increasing the richness and the density of the ideas their minds entertain whilst alive. P. B. Shelley employs a comparison (between someone experiencing torture and someone sleeping soundly) which appears very familiar to readers of *Valperga* and Euthanasia's meditations on time: 'Thus, the life of a man of virtue and talent, who should die in his thirtieth year, is, with regard to his own feelings, longer than that of a miserable priest-ridden slave, who dreams out a century of dulness' (Shelley, *Poems*, I, p.406). P. B. Shelley associates the perfection of sensibility with 'the life of a man of virtue and talent', however, it is clear from his argument that such a prolongation of the experiential and mental duration of life can also be felt by those who are 'stretched on the rack.' Sensibility can be extended by positive and negative, ideal and tragic experience, as Euthanasia's case so clearly demonstrates. As the narrator states: 'day by day she experienced the acquisition of some new power, the discovery of some new light which guided her through the labyrinth' (V, 298).

It is not simply Euthanasia's fictional status that allows her to symbolize a counter-factual resistance to the malign historical necessity ultimately associated with Castruccio. Her ability to mentally and emotionally transcend her present moment (her expanded sensibility) gives her and the ideals she embodies a trans-historical status and thus a future-orientation. She states, in exile from her captured castle: 'Life is all our knowledge, and our highest praise is to have lived well' (V, 231). This quality is quietly but distinctly stressed at the moment Castruccio, sending her into exile, leaves her, and in her often commented upon death at sea.[152] The latter event is described in such a way (the double negatives here are significant) that, at least poetically, the possibility of her return is suggested: 'She was never heard of more .... Earth felt no change when she died; and men forgot her. Yet a lovelier spirit never ceased to breathe, nor was a lovelier form ever destroyed amidst the many it brings forth' (V, 322).

Valperga does not stint in describing how irresistible historical necessity can be; it also, through Euthanasia and the narrator, speaks for a continued resistance in the name of peace, love and social reform. Euthanasia's last reported words ('They speak Italian also in Sicily') represent a defiant adherence to her vision of a unified and free Italy (V, 321). These words take us back to the novel's early association of Euthanasia's republicanism with the position of Dante, father of the Italian language and 'the pledge of a glorious race' (V, 82). The spirit of reform embodied by Euthanasia is not presented as assured of ultimate victory or as something that could eradicate evil from the world. It rests, rather, on a continued 'enthusiasm.' The word is highlighted in the section in which Euthanasia describes her first reaction to Dante: 'I can never forget the enthusiastic joy I experienced, in finding that I was the contemporary of

[Florence's] illustrious author', 'I must date my enthusiasm for the liberties of my country, and the political welfare of Italy, from the repetition of these Cantos of Dante's poem' (V, 81). Throughout the novel it is Euthanasia who is the object of the frequently repeated word 'enthusiasm': Castruccio calls her 'wild enthusiast', the narrator refers to 'the natural enthusiasm of her character', the influence of Dante is allied to that of her father when she writes: 'These sentiments, nurtured and directed by my father, have caused the growth of an enthusiasm in my soul, which can only die when I die' (V, 241, 172, 82). A great deal could be said about the meaning of this word within the Romantic period. What is perhaps most pertinent to remember here is the manner in which for P. B. Shelley the word can function both as an indicator of an imprisonment within the ideological forms of the present or a hunger for a future-oriented reform (Shelley, *Poems*, I, 398, 421). Euthanasia's enthusiasm is of the latter kind and it is, significantly, something she shares with Guinigi, that 'strange enthusiast' who 'hoped, how futilely! to lay a foundation-stone for the temple of peace among the Euganean hills' (V, 26). This is the spirit, the state of mind, within the context of the apparently pessimistic lessons of history, *Valperga* ultimately seeks to express and inspire within its readers.

4

The Last Man

I. A PARADOXICAL TEXT?

There is little wonder that Shelley's third major novel, *The Last Man* (1826), has been read as a *roman à clef*, a deep outpouring of grief over the deaths of P. B. Shelley, Byron, and all the other losses Shelley had experienced in her still relatively short life.[153] As most critics now realize, *The Last Man* constitutes, in fact, the most wide-ranging, philosophically and politically challenging, and enigmatic of her novels after *Frankenstein*. As Bennett implies, *The Last Man*, in recent years, has begun to produce a body of critical interpretation which, in its variety and its divergence, is second only to that produced by *Frankenstein*. Bennett adds, however: 'While these interpretations reflect aspects of the novel, they are largely selective and often uncritically replicate the reception history of the novel when it was first published.'[154]

It is undoubtedly true that a great deal of critical attention has been given to *The Last Man* over the past three decades. It is also obvious that the novel presents distinct and, in some regards, unique challenges to its readers. It is, for example, not clear what kind of novel it is, or even if we can viably call it a novel.[155] As Shelley's earliest reviewers noticed, largely in a negative manner, the very narrative situation of the 'last man' *as author* poses problems about the position of the reader which are at best hermeneutically challenging and at worst parodic.[156] Sophie Thomas refers to a review in *The Monthly Magazine* of 1826 which satirically alerts readers to the fact that 'last things in general are "the last things in the world that are last."'[157] The joke here is not just on Mary Shelley's 1826 novel, but on what the writer perceived as a sub-genre of 'last man' novels and poems which had emerged since the beginning of the century. The theme of 'the last man' was conspicuously present in English literary circles from the publication in English of Cousin de Grainville's *Le dernier homme* in 1808 through the 1810s and 1820s.[158] *The Monthly Magazine* author is referring in part, then, to the sheer volume of 'last man' texts of this period, including the controversy created when Thomas Campbell argued that his 'The Last Man' was more original (in the sense of primary, first) than Byron's 'last man' poem, 'Darkness.'[159] The theme clearly was one that spoke to the anxieties and fears of writers and readers living in the aftermath of the Napoleonic Wars and the apparent restitution of the *ancien regime*. Yet Shelley's novel continues to produce wildly different interpretations when readers attempt to understand its historical, social and political significance. A number of recent critics have read the novel as a continuation of Shelley's commitment to the reformist ideals of her 'circle.'[160] Others have read the novel as a farewell to the radical Romanticism associated with P. B. Shelley and Byron, and as moving towards a distinctly a-political social vision.[161] Some critics, I will take Blumberg as an example, seem to be stuck within the novel's indeterminate, enigmatic patterns, at one moment asserting '[o]f all her novels, *The Last Man* is perhaps Shelley's most political', at another: '[d]espite her preoccupation with the political throughout the novel, *The Last Man* remains a fundamentally *anti*-political book.'[162]

The Monthly Magazine writer also has in mind the fact that the narrative situation of 'last men' texts is rationally absurd. To whom are such texts supposed to be addressed? Another contemporary review extended this ironic point into an observation on Mary Shelley's intervention into what appears to be a masculine genre. Reminding their readers that the novel's three volumes 'are the production of a female pen', one reviewer asks: 'Why not *the last woman*? she would have known better how to paint her distress at having nobody left to talk to. We are sure the tale would have been more interesting.'[163] Such a response clearly alludes to the personal circumstances of the author of the novel. The reviewer, however, also seems to object to a female garrulity conspicuously absent from the 'last man' poems of Campbell and Byron, '[t]wo of the most successful poets of the day' who 'have dared only just to touch upon it [the "last man" theme] in a few detached lines.'[164] When compared to the 'last man' poems of Byron, Thomas Campbell and Thomas Hood, Mary Shelley's novel does seem hugely expansive and hugely personal, as if she required the canvas of the entire human and geographical world to express her sense of melancholia at the losses she now endured. In her play for children, 'Proserpine', written some-time in the period (late-1819 to mid-1820) in which she composed *Matilda*, Shelley gives the earth-mother, Ceres, a frightening speech of threatened revenge if Jove does not restore her lost daughter (Shelley, *Novels*, II, p.88). It is tempting to read Shelley's novel, as recent critics have, as a realization of the threat of motherly, fem-inine revenge against masculine history.[165] Against such a reading, other gender-focused readings present us with a far less strident novel, anxious about the act of authoring, or presenting, in the form of its narrator, Lionel Verney, a combination of masculine and fem-inine perspectives and discourses.[166]

A striking example of the interpretive divisions and divergences generated by *The Last Man* can be seen in recent attempts to read the novel in terms of English colonial discourse and culture at the beginning of the nineteenth century. For some, the novel's account of plague reaching out along the lines of communication and trade established by imperialist nations such as England expresses a dis-trust of the drive towards colonization.[167] In the much discussed scene, in which Verney contracts the plague from a 'negro' child, Anne K. Mellor discovers within Shelley's writing a hope of tran-scending the confines of the Western subject in a potential embrace with the Other, the foreigner.[168] A number of other critics have discovered within *The Last Man* distinct traces of an unexplored, unconscious adherence to the racialist, colonizing perspectives of Western, imperialist discourse.[169] For Paul A. Cantor, Shelley's novel appears to be a critique of Empire at the same time that it appears to support the conservative ideology which supports it. '[T]he politics of *The Last Man* is deeply conflicted', he states.[170]

Can a single text be politically radical (or at least reformist) and conservative, stridently feminist and yet anxious and uncertain about gender issues, politically oriented and yet a-political, critical of imperialism and its inherent racialism and yet steeped in colonial and racialist rhetoric? Anne McWhir describes the novel as 'a per-sonal, even autobiographical and confessional meditation and a prophetic, encyclopaedic, philosophical vision.'[171] Discussing her introduction and editorial notes, Nora Crook has noted the manner in which McWhir foregrounds the work performed in the novel by visual images. She writes: 'The work, as she presents it, is like a picture composed of minute fragments, put together with at times obsessive care, which make sense only when one stands back and looks at the whole from a distance.'[172] How does one stand back from *The Last Man* and thus gain a panorama of its entirety, its wholeness? Does it in fact possess such a wholeness or unity? Or is it in fact made up, as the 'Author's Introduction' suggests, of a 'hasty selection' of scattered leaves, which do not add up to a coherent whole? This was the conclusion of one contemporary reviewer, who, angered by the 'Author's Introduction' and its apparent undercutting of the 'machine' (device) of the discovery of the future-telling Sibylline Leaves, called the novel a 'hetero-geneous production.'[173] If we presume that Shelley's novel does present a coherent vision, however complicated by the 'Author's Introduction' and the radical indeterminacy of the Plague itself, how are we to attain that macro-reading *The Last Man* appar-ently demands? The answer begins to emerge when we return to the biographical contexts of the novel's composition and the ques-tion of what writing in general meant, in this period, to Shelley.

II. THE RETURN OF POWER

In her letters and journal entries of 1823 to 1825, Shelley describes her mournful position, back in England, exiled from the Italy she so intensely missed. In a journal passage which it seems obligatory to cite, she states that, away from the Italian scenery that had pre-viously inspired her work, 'my mind is a ... blank – a gulph filled with formless mist –', before stating: 'The last man! Yes I may well describe that solitary being's feelings, feeling myself as the last relic of a beloved race, my companions, extinct before me –'.[174] This sentence is normally quoted in isolation. It is important to add that Shelley continues in the entry to describe her sense of waning intellectual and imaginative powers and to ascribe this state to her position back in 'this miserable country' away from Italy and thus the place she will for ever associate with her husband. She writes: 'To be here without ↑ you ↓ is to be doubly exiled – to be away from Italy, is to lose you twice.... indeed, indeed, I must go back, or your poor utterly lost Mary will never dare think herself worthy to visit you beyond the grave' (J, 477). It is likely that Shelley had already conceived of the idea of her new novel by this time, although it is also likely that she had not yet begun any sustained period of writing (LM, p.xi and L, I, p.393). When she did, however, her

spirits improved, and, as Blumberg notes, by 8 June 1824, she felt a
renewal of energy as a consequence of returning to serious writing.
She states on that day in her journal: 'I feel my powers again – &
this is of itself happiness' (J, 479; see LM, pp.xi–xii).

Part of the enigma of *The Last Man* is captured in this return
of spirits. As we know from her journal writing of the period,
Shelley frequently regained a connection to P. B. Shelley in the act
of apostrophizing him as the addressee of her writing. In the paragraph before the 8 June passage I have just cited, she typically
speaks directly to her husband, still somehow contactable through
writing, through text: 'My own love – we shall meet again – The
stars of heaven are now your country & your spirit drinks beauty
& wisdom in those spheres – & I, beloved, shall one day join you
– Nature speaks to me of you – In towns & society I do not feel
your presence – but there you are with me, my own, my unalien-
able' (J, 479). We might add to her statement that P. B. Shelley
also seemed to speak to Mary, as an apostrophized addressee,
in the act of writing. Writing is the place in which lost others can
be mourned, but it is also, for Shelley, the place in which they
return.[175]

There is a strange, uncanny reversibility in texts and in writing
for Mary Shelley; she frequently expresses a sense of the power of
writing over life, a sense which, in many ways, she shared with her
husband. This reversibility often involves the over-turning of the
normative, apparently logical relationship between events in reality
and events in texts. The logical assumption that events run in that
order, from reality to written texts, is something that throughout
Shelley's life was challenged and even undermined. A good example
comes a month before this journal passage, and one day after her
now famous 14 May description of herself as 'the last man.' It comes
in the form of news of Byron's death. Shelley writes: 'This then was
the "coming event" that cast its shadow on my last night's miserable
thoughts. Byron has become ↑ one ↓ of the people of the grave –
that innumerable conclave to which the beings I best loved belong'
(J, 477–8). She goes on to express her deep sense of loss on Byron's
death: 'What do I do here? Why ~~and~~ am I doomed to live on
seeing all expire before me? God grant I may die young – A new
race is springing about me – At the age of twenty six I am in the
condition of an aged person .... I cling to the few remaining ....
Albe, dearest Albe, was knit by long associations' (J, 478).[176] The
next entry in the journal is the one from 8 June. It is quite feasible

for Shelley to state that her own written statements about being a 'last man' were in some way an augury of the news of Byron's death. Text here, once again, comes before a physical event and reverses the apparently logical order of writing's secondariness or supplementarity in relation to 'life' As she wrote to Teresa Guiccioli on 16 May: 'every day I am more certain that God has endowed us with the power to foresee our misfortunes. But we are all Cassandras' (L, I, 421).[177]

Something about Byron's death appears to have shaken Shelley into renewed artistic endeavour and to have taken *The Last Man* from an idea to a compositional reality. For readers of Shelley's journals and letters it is difficult to avoid the impression that at least one of the motives involved in this process concerned the association she drew between Byron's voice and the lost voice of her husband. Shelley had stated in a letter of 22 November to Maria Gisborne that 'when LB. speaks I wait for Shelley's voice in answer as the natural result' (L, I, 291). In a journal entry of 19 October 1822, she writes: 'when Albe speaks & Shelley does not answer, it is as thunder without rain …. I listen with unspeakable melancholy – that yet is not all pain' (J, 439).

When Byron died Shelley not only lost a friend and central figure of her 'circle', she also lost a voice that in its very presence signified the loss of P. B. Shelley's voice and yet, in that very process, returned it, made it speak again.[178] One begins to understand better why writing *The Last Man* may have afforded a return to 'power' and enthusiasm. Obviously the return of compositional powers is invariably a positive thing, whatever the subject matter, for the professional author. Writing, for Mary Shelley, however, contained within itself a reversibility which provides the key to any adequate understanding of *The Last Man*, on the psychological and the political, the personal and the philosophical level. This reversibility involves a return to and a return of loved and mourned others; it also involves a return of the past and, in the disturbance of temporal cause and effect, a promised return to and of the future. The force of what I am calling reversibility is felt throughout *The Last Man* and it will form the basis of the reading presented here. What I am calling reversibility can, ultimately, explain why *The Last Man* has produced, like *Frankenstein* before it, such diametrically opposed interpretations. It also provides us with a major link between Shelley's earlier novels and the three 1830s novels which she published after *The Last Man*.

III. A PROPHETIC TEXT?

The 'Author's Introduction' is crucial in any reading of *The Last Man*. It angered the reviewer in the *Panoramic Miscellany* because in apparently establishing a believable fictional context for a novel set in the late twenty-first century, it then appears to undermine the plausibility of that context. An anonymous 'author' and 'friend' visit Naples on 8 December 1818, just as had Mary and P. B. Shelley (J, 242). They eventually come across the Sibyl's cave, finding an access to a 'small opening' in the disappointing larger cavern declared to be the cave of the Sibyl by their rather timid guides. The inner cave within a larger cave obviously reminds us of Euthanasia's allegory of the cave of the mind, and the connection provides Shelley's readers with an intertextual clue. Euthanasia's inner cave is a place of 'Poetry and Imagination' but it is also, potentially, a place of 'secrets', madness and 'darkling, fantastic combinations.'[179] Certainly, any suggestion that reference to the Sibyl's cave works to authorize the prophetic validity of the succeeding story should be treated with great care and caution.[180] A further reference from *Valperga*, in which Euthanasia contemplates the end of hope for Castruccio, adds to our sense of the potential unreliability of Sibylline prophecies: 'Euthanasia saw all this with the observant eye of grief, which refers all things to itself, and forms omens for its own immortality from combinations more unsubstantial than the Sybilline leaves' (V. 170). Could anything be more unsubstantial than Sibylline leaves and prophecies?

The Sibylline leaves are curiously heterogeneous, written in 'ancient Chaldee, and Egyptian hieroglyphics, old as the Pyramids .... some ... in modern dialects, English and Italian.' They are also, importantly, heterogeneous in their subject matter: 'they seemed to contain prophecies, detailed relations of events but lately passed; names, now well known, but of modern date; and often exclamations of exultation or woe, of victory or defeat' (LM, 7). The arrangement of these leaves is itself less than complete: 'We made a hasty selection of the leaves, whose writing one at least of us could understand' (LM, 7). They return whenever they can to retrieve more of the scattered text, but with no sense that there is a complete, coherent text to recover. The anonymous author then explains that the 'friend' and 'companion' eventually is 'lost' and the labour of deciphering becomes a solitary task. Although Shelley's readers would not have been aware of the fact that Mary Shelley and P. B. Shelley visited Baiae on the exact date indicated in this introduction, they may well have been aware of the manner in which this initial fictional scenario alludes to her recent editorial work on P. B. Shelley's poetry.

Posthumous Poems of Percy Bysshe Shelley was published by John and Henry L. Hunt in 1824. Shelley explained in her 'Preface' to that edition: '"The Triumph of Life" was his last work, and was left in so unfinished a state, that I arranged it in its present form with great difficulty. All his poems which were scattered in periodical works are collected in this volume.' She adds: 'I have been more actuated by the fear lest any monument of his genius should escape me, than the wish of presenting nothing but what was complete to the fastidious reader.'[181] Clearly, the Sibylline introduction of *The Last Man* conflates the experience of writing the novel with her work as editor of her lost 'companion' and 'friend', and it expresses in that way tensions in the idea of completeness or what Sophie Thomas calls 'finality': gathering together all the textual fragments (of the Sibyl's leaves, of P. B. Shelley's poetry) even if they cannot be made to cohere into a whole; finding that coherence and unity within the assembled, edited material. As Thomas states: 'Metaphors of fragmentation (and of parts, wholes, ruins, and so forth) occur with remarkable frequency in *The Last Man*. Shelley exploits the considerable power of the opposition between parts and wholes to figure forth the ideal interconnectedness of things, as well as to describe their disintegration.'[182] This is an insightful comment to which we will return in the next section.

What has frequently been noted is the positive reaction the 'author' describes in the task of incomplete restoration: 'Their meaning, wondrous and eloquent, has often repaid my toil, soothing me in sorrow.' The comment is double: its referent is both the editing of P. B. Shelley's poetry and the composition of the novel. Is the latter an attempt to create a coherence and cohesion lacking in the former? The 'author' admits: 'I have been obliged to add links, and model the work into a consistent form. But the main substance rests on the truths contained in these poetic rhapsodies.' The narrative presented in *The Last Man* is an 'adaptation and translation' of 'the frail and attenuated Leaves of the Sibyl', and yet it is also 'faithfully transcribed from my materials.' It is a faithful representation, and yet as a representation (in the 'author's' own words) it is a translation which inevitably produces 'distortion and diminution of interest and excellence.' 'Sometimes', the author worries, 'I have thought, that, obscure and chaotic as they are, they owe their present form to me, their decipherer' (LM, 8). *The Last Man* is a fiction which contains truths, and it is on that basis that the 'author', by describing their own paradoxical response to the narrative about to commence, indicates the manner in which Shelley wished her readers to read: 'Will my readers ask how I could find solace from the narration of misery and woeful change? This is one of the mysteries of our nature, which holds full sway over me, and from whose influence I cannot escape' (LM, 8). We could add to this passage that it is also part of the mystery of the Godwinian novel tradition to present us with narratives of defeat, pessimism, irrationality, anti-social misanthropy and yet still produce hope and frequently manage to generate socially progressive and reformist responses in its readers.[183]

The apparent inconsistencies of the 'Author's Introduction', which angered the *Monthly Magazine* reviewer, and have so preoccupied the attention of modern critics, represent on a global and trans-historical setting the reversibility built into the novel tradition Shelley inherited and independently developed. The reversibility of the Godwinian novel tradition is perhaps encapsulated in the relation between narrative voice and plotline (frequently negative, pessimistic and demonstrative of the dominance of power and irrationality in contemporary society), and what Godwin himself calls the 'moral tendency' of the text itself (Godwin, *Political*, V, 135–43). The latter, Godwin argues, can frequently be in opposition to, a reversal of, the apparent tendency of the narrative itself: hence, for example, the apparently pernicious lessons taught by the plotline of Milton's *Paradise Lost* are reversed by the poem's moral tendency (Godwin, *Political*, V, 138). The challenge of *The Last Man*, as the best recent critical work has demonstrated, is to understand the novel's tendency (in Godwin's hermeneutic sense).

The first stage of such an undertaking arrives when readers understand the possibility of reversibility within the text.[184] As Lynn Wells states, because of the manner in which the 'Author's Introduction' presents and positions the narrative, 'we do not read the future universal plague as unavoidable but merely as one possible outcome.'[185] The second stage concerns the attempt to understand the meaning of Shelley's fictional plague and the manner in which it appears to undermine every available political, philosophical, religious and aesthetic discourse. Current criticism appears, generally, to view the plague less as a signifier than as a force of indeterminacy or even deconstruction which undermines the traditional grounds upon which human beings have constructed meaningful political and ideological systems. This is the kind of reading which has led a good number of critics to describe the novel as ultimately a-political. Shelley's novel is not a-political; on the contrary, it demonstrates things about political and ideological systems per se. One has to stand back from its narrative intricacies somewhat to appreciate this macro-aspect of the text.

IV. A DECONSTRUCTIVE TEXT?

Volume I narrates the history of Lionel Verney's small circle, its establishment and the beginning of its collapse, within the contexts of English politics in the latter part of the twenty-first century. Verney's friendship with Adrian, Earl of Windsor, saves him and his sister, Perdita, from the social alienation and solitude in which the fall from grace of their father initially placed them. Much to the disgust of the Countess of Windsor, Verney eventually marries Adrian's sister, Idris, whilst the Byronic Lord Raymond gives up his ambitions to restore the English monarchy by marrying Idris, and follows his heart in marrying Perdita. Adrian, early in love with the Greek princess Evadne, is rejected by her and becomes a melancholic, solitary figure, until he is reintegrated into the idyllic Windsor circle through Verney's friendship. The lives of this circle become enmeshed in the imagined political transitions of the period, as Ryland, leader of the democratic forces, attempts to rid England of the threat of the restoration of the monarchy; Adrian's father had abdicated power in favour of an aristocratic form of republicanism which is now associated with Adrian himself. Raymond's conversion from his original monarchical ambitions allows him eventually not only to marry Perdita, but also to gain the position of republican Lord Protector of England. The return of Evadne, however, leads Raymond away from the Enlightenment rule of his Protectorship and back towards his earlier dreams of heroism and individual glory in the Greek Wars of Independence.

The early accounts of Adrian and Raymond remind us, in many ways, of the political dimensions of the relationship between Euthanasia and Castruccio in *Valperga*. Lord Raymond sees the world as a stage upon which to exert his ambition for power and glory: 'He looked on the structure of society as but a part of the machinery which supported the web on which his life was traced. The earth was spread out as an highway for him; the heavens built up as a canopy for him.' In contrast: 'Adrian felt that he made a part of a great whole. He owned affinity not only with mankind, but all nature was akin to him' (LM, 38). Raymond embodies an individualistic, Byronic will; Adrian, a Shelleyan sense of collectivity extending beyond human society to nature itself. There is little doubt what mode of social vision is preferred by Verney, the narrator, so closely by this stage does he associate himself with Adrian. The opposition between these two principal male characters is not as simple as it appears, however. Chapter 4 takes Raymond to the verge of political victory, his ambition to become monarch of England (through defeat of Ryland in parliamentary debate, and his intended marriage to Idris) depending only on the assertion of his will over his heart (his actual love for Perdita). As they travel towards Windsor, Raymond's intentions still opaque, Verney and Raymond discuss the nature of human ambition and will in a manner already established by the earlier oppositional descriptions of Raymond and Adrian. Raymond muses: 'Philosophers have called man a microcosm of nature, and find a reflection in the internal mind for all this machinery visibly at work around us. This theory has often been a source of amusement to me; and many an idle hour have I spent, exercising my ingenuity in finding resemblances' (LM, 54). Verney, as he often does, ventriloquizes Adrian's counter-perspective, when he responds with a description of 'an active principle in man which is capable of ruling fortune' (LM, 55). Two things are at stake in this dialogue, as it proceeds, and they are issues that are rehearsed throughout Volume I and beyond.

The first concerns Adrian's belief in 'the great whole.' Echoed again by Raymond's ironic 'microcosm of nature', the political rhetoric of wholeness, of unity, spreads in the novel far beyond Adrian's own naturalistic, Shelleyan version. As many have noted the opening chapter gives us a classic version of this holistic trope in the guise of an England which is on one level a tiny 'speck in the immense whole' and yet which, when measured in terms of 'mental power, far outweighed countries of larger extent and more numerous population' (LM, 11). Like Adrian's vision of his relation to 'the great whole', this image of England presents us with a classic example of the trope of synecdoche (the substitution of, or substitutability of, part for whole or whole for part) upon which a great deal of the traditional political and social models presented within the pages of *The Last Man* ground themselves. Synecdoche, in fact, is the trope upon which is built that primary political figure: the body politic. The often discussed reference to Burkean organicism for example, in Chapter 4, Volume II, is in many senses a simple expression of what we might call synecdochal logic (LM, 180). For Burke, the body politic can be compared to a natural organicism (and ultimately to the natural realm itself) because it possesses the same synecdochal relation of parts to the whole; the whole here remaining forever young because the parts progress through unending cycles of birth, life and death. Synecdochal logic, however, is also, in differently freighted ways, at the heart of monarchical and republican/democratic political models and discourses.[186]

When Adrian is attempting to persuade Raymond not to give up the position of Lord Protector of England, in favour of Byronic escape into the putative heroism of the Greek Wars of Independence, he in fact displays the way in which his own aristocratic republicanism shades into monarchical discourse, on the level of its rhetorical basis. Raymond asks: 'Because I am Protector of England, am I to be the only slave in its empire? My privacy invaded, my actions censured, my friends insulted? But I will get rid of the whole together ....' Adrian responds: 'Know yourself, Raymond .... A few months ago, whenever we prayed for the prosperity of our country, or our own, we at the same time prayed for the life and welfare of the Protector, as indissolubly linked to it.' He continues: 'Master yourself, Raymond, and the world is subject to you.' Raymond's response, if we are alert, necessarily reminds us of the very reasons why Adrian himself had refused to take up the position of Lord Protector, conceding it to Raymond. Raymond states: 'I cannot rule myself. My passions are my masters; my smallest impulse my tyrant' (LM, 118–19). Earlier, having returned from his melancholic isolation, Adrian responds to the idea of his ascension to power: 'I know now that I am not a man fitted to govern nations; sufficient for me, if I keep in wholesome rule the little kingdom of my own mortality' (LM, 77). Ryland's democratic rhetoric, however, is equally based on a part-for-whole synecdochal logic, oriented in his discourse to an anti-monarchical ideal of freedom and equality. In the parliamentary show-down with Raymond, Verney describes the response to Ryland's discourse, and makes clear its connection to the image of nationhood with which the novel begins: 'As he spoke, every heart swelled with pride, and every cheek glowed with delight to remember, that each one there was English, and that each supported and contributed to the happy state of things now commemorated' (LM, 49).

Ryland's political rhetoric creates a synecdochal, unified response in his auditors because it too bases its appeal on a democratically pitched version of what I am calling synecdochal logic; a logic upon which is built notions of nation, freedom and equality, but, as we have seen, also notions of the organic nature of human society, the legitimacy of monarchical and also aristocratic rule. In terms of the discourses rehearsed within the novel, we could add to this list many others, including Wordsworthian naturalism, the Malthusian idea of the self-regulatory nature of human society as a body within the natural realm, and Godwinian accounts of Necessity and human perfectibility.

The Last Man is such a challenging novel for readers wishing to determine its political significances because it demonstrates, subtly and implicitly, the manner in which all political and social ideologies are dependent, in one way or another, on the same rhetorical ideal of synecdochal cohesion and unity, an ideal which makes each one of those competing ideologies dependent on a natural language centred in the body. *The Last Man*, on this level, is a fascinating anatomy of the discursive and rhetorical foundations of traditional and contemporary political discourses, and when nature, in the form of the plague, demonstrates its ability to detach itself from such discursive systems and frameworks, each one of these discourses collapse, each image of unity and wholeness is demonstrated to have been built on purely rhetorical foundations. The great set-piece elegies for humanity and the wonders of human society that in many ways dominate Volume III are all, in vital ways, elegies to synecdochal logic, a logic that has traditionally allowed for the idea of unity, cohesiveness, and ultimately a bodily metaphorics to serve as the grounds for ideas of human identity on an individual and a collective level. Mourning the death of 'man', Verney produces also an elegy for the political ideal of the synecdochal body upon which that idea of 'man' has depended (LM, 320).

As the novel demonstrates, whilst the individual and collective body of 'man' can die, the natural world, the vast, global body on which 'man' has been born, lived and now dies, cannot. The permanency sought by all uses of synecdochal logic, be they politically conservative or radical, works only one way: it is the vehicle (the metaphor of nature) rather than the tenor (human systems and belief-structures) that is permanent. No doubt Shelley was influenced in her novel by the intellectual excitement created by the work of writers such as Cuvier who were beginning to bring to the world an image of a vast geological time-scale in which whole species could flourish and then become extinct. Byron, enthused by such ideas, had woven them into his poems *Cain* (1821) and *Heaven and Earth* (1823). Shelley ranked *Cain* 'in the highest style of imaginative Poetry. It made a great impression upon me', she wrote to Maria Gisborne in 1821 (L, I, 209). *The Last Man*, unlike its literary antecedents, presents us, as Morton D. Paley has stated, with a purely secular, natural end of human history. Social, discursive systems collapse in the novel under the weight of their own internal contradictoriness, which in itself is generated by a false assumption about the relation between such systems and the natural world. This leads us to the second issue noted in the exchange between Raymond and Verney in Chapter 4. The issue has to do with human will, human imagination, ultimately what we can call human agency.

Raymond in that chapter appears to be a man dedicated to his own individual ambitions. He appears to be a man, Byron-like, Castruccio-like, Frankenstein-like, who embodies a masculine will-to-power over others and, ultimately, over life. The vision of human life he paints in this scene, riding with Verney towards Windsor, is, nonetheless, one of a helpless passivity in the face of fate: 'I cannot set my heart to a particular tune, or run voluntary changes on my will. We are born; we choose neither our parents, nor our stations; we are educated by others, or by the world's circumstances, and this cultivation, mingling with our innate disposition, is the soil in which our desires, passions, and motives grow.' Verney here still believes that Raymond is offering an excuse for his monarchical ambitions; Raymond in fact is explaining the decision he will make to resign them in favour of a union with Perdita. The point is that the character most associated with the masculine, individualist will sees that will as dominated, even overwhelmed by circumstances. Adrian, as we have seen, is the advocate of an opposed, socially-oriented belief in synecdochal collectivity. Verney, again ventriloquizing Adrian, responds to Raymond: 'There is much truth in what you say .... and yet no man ever acts upon this theory. Who, when he makes a choice, says, Thus I choose, because I am necessitated? Does he not on the contrary feel a freedom of will within him, which, though you may call it fallacious, still actuates him as he decides? (LM, 55). Adrian eventually goes much further than Verney on this point.

At the end of Chapter 4, Adrian gives the first in a number of his 'Shelleyan' speeches on the power of the human imagination and will: 'Sleeping thus under the beneficent eye of heaven, can evil visit thee, O Earth, or grief cradle to their graves thy luckless children?' The complete identification between the fate of the natural and the human world, allows him eventually to announce: 'The choice is with us: let us will it, and our habitation becomes a paradise. For the will of man is omnipotent' (LM, 63). We can usefully, in this context, remember the opening paragraph of the novel's first chapter. Here Verney describes England as appearing 'only as an inconsiderable speck in the immense whole; and yet, when balanced in the scale of mental power, far outweigh[ing] countries of larger extent and more numerous population. So true it is, that man's mind alone was the creator of all that was good or great to man, and that Nature herself was only his first minister' (LM, 11). What is it in the idea of a synecdochal relation between humanity and nature that allows Adrian to assert the unlimited power of the human will, or prompts Verney, in the opening of his narration, to move from Imperial England to the human ascendancy over and control of nature? The answer is that synecdoche allows a part to cover the whole or to become a symbolic centre for that whole: it allows, in Ryland's ideal democracy, any one citizen to attain 'temporary sovereignty'; it allows one noble man, like Raymond, to become an indissoluble link and centre to an entire nation; it allows one small nation, such as England, to become the centre of the international world; and it allows one species on the earth, mankind, to become 'the creator of all that was good or great.' Organicist rhetoric, based on an assumption of the synecdochal relation between humanity and the natural world, forms the foundation upon which assertions of the power of human imagination and will depend. But in whatever form it is represented in *The Last Man*, this synecdochal logic, this assumption of a natural basis for human will, is shown to be simply metaphorical, figurative, ultimately ungrounded. The basis of political and social rhetoric begins to unravel in Volume I, before the plague is even a word on people's lips. Raymond, the hero of the individual, masculine will, is passive in the face of chance, fate and destiny; Adrian, the idealist spokesperson for a naturally endorsed human will, is undermined by those same forces, symbolized in his own frail, emasculated body: 'The spirit of life seemed to linger in his form, as a dying flame on an altar flickers on the embers of an accepted sacrifice', writes Verney, after Adrian has delivered his speech on the omnipotent 'will of man' (LM, 63).

The Windsor circle, acting as it does as a potential trope for national unity, begins to come apart when Raymond relinquishes his protectorate. Perdita, in the midst of this crisis, explains to Raymond: 'It was not – it is not a common infidelity at which I repine. It is the disunion of an whole which may not have parts; it is the carelessness with which you have shaken off the mantle of election with which to me you were invested, and have become one among the many' (LM, 111). By the time the plague asserts its full power humanity itself becomes anarchic, lacking a centre or collective identity and agency, 'inorganic', a 'remnant', a dying body with nothing to compare itself to but a perpetually self-renewing natural body. In this respect, Verney's vision of humanity as 'the ruins of an anthill immediately after its destruction' stands out. The plague is a great leveller, and Verney adds to the anthill image a section punctuated with the repeated refrain 'We were all equal now' (LM, 249). The 'remnant' of England still cling together as a collective body as they leave England, but they are no longer a politically and socially collective 'body.' Synecdochal logic, which builds political systems out of the figurative 'body' of nature, is no longer possible, no longer a believable trope.

The Last Man has been figured by a series of critics as a deconstructive text, or at least a novel which can be read through critical lenses informed by deconstructive philosophy and literary criticism.[187] Mark Canuel, quoting Mellor's seminal reading, writes that 'the deconstructive turn has a political dimension, for the novel "first undercuts the dominant systems of government of the early nineteenth century and then shows that all cultural ideologies are but meaningless fictions."'[188] Barbara Johnson and Audrey A. Fisch both argue that the novel performs this deconstruction of political systems and cultural ideologies in order to undermine universalizing, totalizing political and social visions. Such readings clearly have a connection to the ethically, philosophically and political 'realist' Mary Shelley I am arguing for in this book. In this context the feminine figure of the plague might be understood as that malign, tragic version of Necessity Shelley throughout her writing career had fictionally presented as a counterweight to the perfectibilist ideologies of Godwin and P. B. Shelley.

It could also be understood as Shelley's feminine answer to the dreams of totality and universality she found so characteristic of all masculine political and social discourses. Certainly, such a reading of the novel could build upon the combination of feminist and deconstructive perspectives brought together by Mellor.

In her reading, Mellor argues that *The Last Man* displays the dependence of all ideological systems on precisely the kind of naturalized rhetoric we have been exploring in this section. Whether the target be Burke, Wordsworth, Godwin or P. B. Shelley, Mellor argues, the novel demonstrates ideology's reliance on 'a heuristic fiction, a trope: the image of the body politic as a natural organism.' She continues: 'If society is an organism, then it is subject to disease .... all organisms, both individual and social, are subject to the overriding power of Nature, Chance, and Accident. The body politic can die as well as grow.'[189] Reminding her readers of the manner in which the trope of plague was employed in the work of post-Revolution writers such as Burke and Godwin, Mellor argues that in demonstrating the figurative basis of organicist arguments, Shelley produces a novel which deconstructs all ideological systems. This argument leads her to the following assessment: 'Shelley's novel is on the deepest level anti-political and anti-ideological. She suggests that all conceptions of human history, all ideologies, are grounded on metaphors or tropes which have no referent or authority outside of language.'[190]

Despite the obvious insightfulness of Mellor's reading, there is a problem. This problem partly stems from a U.S.-based understanding of deconstruction which was still dominant in the 1980s.[191] This misreading stems from a purely linguistic understanding of deconstruction which culminates in claims that it is a philosophy which inevitably leads to nihilism and the collapse of all meaning. The historically specific misunderstanding of deconstruction I am referring to is very evident in Mellor's influential reading of Shelley's novel. Mellor argues that the novel 'initiates the modern tradition of literary deconstruction', but she goes on to call the novel: 'the first fictional example of nihilism.'[192] The assessment is far too literal-minded and does not recognize that it is one thing to understand the figural nature of all human ideological systems but quite another to eradicate, on that basis, all hope of human meaning and agency. Derrida's deconstructive philosophy, despite constant charges of nihilism against it, seeks to imagine how the best human ideas (of reason, Enlightenment, responsibility, human rights, hospitality, democracy, friendship and love) can be lived and thought without recourse to the totalizing and universalizing metaphysics (in which tropes are naturalized and thus made literal) which have, traditionally, formed the foundations for ideological systems. Deconstruction does not get rid of our ideas of reason, Enlightenment, right, justice, democracy, fraternity; rather, it attempts to imagine them stripped of the totalization and universalization which has historically tried to fix them as eternal monuments of truth.[193] The target of the most persuasive forms of deconstructive philosophy, which generally means the work of Derrida himself, is the very hidden metaphysics we have seen Shelley critiquing in the apparently rationalist, Enlightenment discourse of her immediate circle. The recurrent analogy made between *The Last Man* and deconstruction is only useful if we recognize the possibility that Shelley's novel, far from simply undermining human ideological systems, uses her story of the plague to re-establish her commitment to reformist, democratic ideas, but stripped of their traditional masculinist, totalizing authority. To understand this further we need to return to the issue of reversibility within the novel.

V. NARRATING THE END

There is a scene near the beginning of *Valperga* which can usefully be remembered in the context of narration and *The Last Man*. As the young Castruccio watches the 'festival of Hell' at Florence, the bridge of Carraia collapses, killing many of the spectators. As representations of hell merge into the hellish reality of the collapsing bridge '[t]he heroism of Castruccio' fails, and he flees the scene terrified (V, 15). For art to function, for mimesis to occur, as the scene clearly demonstrates, there must be a gap and a difference between reality and representation. When that gap and difference collapse, the possibility of artistic representation, and perhaps any representation, collapses with it. Time and again in *The Last Man* Verney describes scenes in which, as the strength of the plague grows and grows, and humanity becomes ever more ravaged and ineffectual, artistic representation collapses into the tragic reality it had formerly been able to describe and therefore aesthetically transform and distance. The scene in which Verney witnesses a production of *Macbeth* at the Drury Lane is, in most of its symbolic particulars, a repetition of the scene at the beginning of

Valperga. The collective response to the speech of Macduff ('All my pretty ones? Did you say all?') again demonstrates the manner in which artistic representation breaks down as the distance between it and reality becomes unsustainable (LM, 221). What stops Verney's narrative, which after all contains the most hellish of all possible stories, from disintegrating as artistic representation into an unbearable reality? What allows the reader to read *The Last Man* with something other than sheer horror, or the pessimism so often critically ascribed to it?

The answer is the reversibility of everything Verney presents. It is notable how important intertextual references to P. B. Shelley's last, unfinished poem, *The Triumph of Life*, become as the novel progresses. All these references appear to reinforce the apparent linear direction of time and history. Adrian, after the trials endured by the English exiles in Paris, states: 'I have done my best; with grasping hands and impotent strength, I have hung on the wheel of the chariot of plague; but she drags me along with it, while, like Jaggernaut, she proceeds crushing out the being of all who strew the high road of life' (LM, 308). It would appear, then, that the plague represents historical Necessity. Adrian asks Verney: 'Would you read backwards the unchangeable laws of Necessity?' before delivering a resigned speech on that principle or force ('Mother of the world! Servant of the Omnipotent! eternal, changeless Necessity! who with busy fingers sittest ever weaving the indissoluble chain of events!') (LM, 310). This attitude towards time and history is perfectly understandable from the point of view of the characters caught up in the secular apocalypse represented in *The Last Man*. It is not, however, the experience of the reader, who is faced with a narrative which is continually being complicated by the multi-directional perspective it forces us to adopt or at least contemplate. When Raymond, for example, becomes Lord Protector and Verney describes in the following manner the Enlightened progress of the English nation under his rule, the experience of reading is not singular in its direction: 'the state of poverty was to be abolished .... The arts of life, and the discoveries of science had augmented in a ratio which left all calculation behind; food sprung up, so to say, spontaneously – machines existed to supply with facility every want of the population' (LM, 85). We read such a passage, of course, with one eye on the debates between Godwin and Malthus which had been recently reignited by the publication of the former's response to the latter's famous *Essay on Population*.[194] More importantly still, in terms of reversibility *within* the novel, we read the description in a chronological fashion at the same time that we remind ourselves that plague, if nothing else, will lay all these actions and achievements to waste. In fact, we read every event and every speech in the novel in this dual fashion. Not only do covert and overt biographical referents frequently split the significance and, as it were, direction of events (Raymond's expedition to Greece is also a reference to Byron's; Adrian's death at sea off the Italian peninsula is also a reference to P. B. Shelley's death), readers can never forget, as they read the chronological history of the characters presented in the novel, that all actions and plans, all domestic, cultural and national units will be reversed (in the sense of destroyed) by novel's end. Much of Verney's narrative seems designed to accentuate this perspectival duality and temporal reversibility. In a rather uncanny way, reading the narrative of *The Last Man* is, even for the first time, an experience of re-reading.

In our analysis of Shelley's previous fictional works we have noted the importance of narrative digressions on Necessity, mutability and the ambivalence of human experience. *The Last Man* takes this aspect of Shelley's narrative style to an extreme. What were, in those previous texts, digressions, narrative ruptures, become by Volume III the entirety of the novel. Verney increasingly breaks the reality effect of his narration to deliver meditations on the inexorable and tragic movement of the history he presents. Early on in Volume I, for example, describing the initial relationship between Adrian and Evadne, Verney, in a typically Shelleyan aside, writes: 'Alas! why must I record the hapless delusion of this matchless specimen of humanity? What is there in our nature that is for ever urging us on towards pain and misery?' (LM, 30; see also 39–40). But Verney, also, frequently describes a kind of prophetic dread of the coming catastrophe in the minds of individual characters (notably Perdita and Evadne) and in himself. As the plague reaches Windsor Castle and environs, Verney records his thoughts: 'Great God! would it one day be thus? One day all extinct, save myself, should I walk the earth alone?' (LM, 208). On looking at the children celebrating his son's birthday, Verney again records prophetic thoughts of annihilation: 'The revulsion of thought passed like keen steel to my heart. Ye are all going to die, I thought; already your tomb is built up around you' (LM, 189).

Richard S. Allbright has demonstrated the manner in which, working against those narrative elements that predict, prophesy and even speed up the road to ruin, there are built into the novel a number of elements which appear to foreground a 'turning back' or various modes of reversal. Raymond, for example, is initially thought to have been captured and killed in Greece, only for him to be rescued, before his climactic death in deserted Constantinople. Adrian loses his mental and physical strength, only to have them return to him as he takes hold of the reigns of power amid the social and political anarchy created by the arrival of the plague. Verney himself appears to reverse the narrative direction of the novel, recovering from plague and experiencing a rejuvenation of his physical and mental being. As Allbright states: 'In one of the many paradoxes that add dramatic tension to *The Last Man*, all these examples of the apparent reversal in the flow of time occur in opposition to repeated statements that time cannot be rolled back.'[195] Reversibility, then, functions on the level of plot, on the level of the novel's thematics, and in terms of the peculiarities of Verney's narrative style.[196] It is most conspicuous when, as he frequently does, Verney directly addresses the reader: 'Patience, oh reader! whoever thou art, wherever thou dwellest, whether of race spiritual, or, sprung from some surviving pair, thy nature will be human, thy habitation the earth; thou wilt read of the acts of the extinct race' (LM, 310). As various critics recognize, the reader addressed reads before the events of the novel have occurred, and in fact exists in a world in which those events may never happen. As Fisch puts it: 'The "Author's Introduction" is ... positioned as a prophecy of the ends of man, intended to warn "man" so that the end of "mankind" can be averted. No one, then, is dead yet.'[197] Whether the narrative has precisely this preventive purpose is open to debate. Such comments do alert us, however, to the fact that reversibility is not simply a narrative technique and readerly experience in *The Last Man*; it is, ultimately, the site of the novel's fundamental significance and requires consideration on that basis.

One of the most striking descriptions of reversibility in the novel comes as the inhabitants of Windsor Castle, which, like the castle of Valperga before it, has become a refuge for the victims of Necessity, leave that home forever:

> England remained, though England was dead – it was the ghost of merry England that I beheld, under whose greenwood shade passing generations had sported in security and ease. To this painful recognition of familiar places, was added a feeling experienced by all, understood by none, – a feeling, as if in some state, less visionary than a

dream, in some past real existence, I had seen all I saw, with precisely the same feelings as I now beheld them – as if all my sensations were a duplex mirror of a former revelation. (LM, 283)

The figure of the 'duplex mirror' has been noted by a number of critics as encapsulating the reversible nature of Verney's 'last man' perspective and the narrative he presents.[198] Yet the whole of this passage, including its metanarrative reflection on the consolations of the imagination, and its account of a collective experience of phenomenological reversal, is in many ways exemplary of the novel as a whole. It is significant, then, that the passage should repeat (return to) the opening of P. B. Shelley's *The Triumph of Life*, with its sustained account of the experience of *déjà vu* (*Shelley's Poetry and Prose*, pp.455–6). *The Triumph of Life* presents a poetic narrative in which 'life' is figured as an inexorable force (a 'Car', 'Chariot') of destruction, a principle of Necessity which obliterates human hopes and ideals. It is, in this sense, a text which speaks directly to the preoccupations and the representational forms of Mary Shelley's work. The poem appears to literalize the moment of darkest despair from *Prometheus Unbound*, so that the Furies' devastating assessment of human existence (*Poems of Shelley*, II, p.514) is repeated, as an apparently incontrovertible assessment of the lessons of modern and ancient history:

> And much I grieved to think how power and will
> In opposition rule our mortal day –
>
> And why God made irreconcilable
> Good and the means of good; and for despair
> I half disdained mine eye's desire to fill
>
> With the spent vision of the times that were
> And scarce have ceased to be ..... (*Shelley's Poetry and Prose*, 461)

The Last Man, like *The Triumph of Life*, presents its vision of malign Necessity on the basis of a proleptic vision, an experience of para-mnesia (*beyond* or, here more appropriately, *beside* memory, recall-ing). Both texts create such a serial disturbance in the temporal order that the narratives they present become wholly figurative, metaleptic in fact.[199] *The Last Man* creates through its multi-directional, figurative frames a fictional space in which a 'duplex' mode of writing and reading can be explored. Such a vision suits perfectly Mary Shelley's characteristic vision of human existence and the ideological contexts she inherited and within which she lived and wrote. Nowhere is this more dramatically evident than in the history of Adrian's belated acceptance of the Protectorate of England. Explaining why, in the face of the plague's total domination, he can now accept the power he has always disdained, Adrian states to Verney: 'This is my post: I was born for this – to rule England in anarchy, to save her in danger – to devote myself for her' (LM, 200). The irony of his leadership in the midst of anarchy is profound when one reflects on P. B. Shelley's life-long struggle to imagine how 'power and will', 'Good and the means of good', might be united without recourse to violence. The earlier history of Raymond's Protectorate, along with Adrian's reaction to the scenes of warfare in and around Constantinople, help to establish the fact that it is only now, when the body politic sickens and begins to disintegrate, that Adrian can ascend to power without exercising the violence normally associated with leadership.

Adrian's rule, as the subsequent scenes in London, Paris and beyond make manifest, unites 'power and will', 'Good and the means of good', because human power has been superseded by a natural power that empties human will and imagination of their previous substance. In this manner *The Last Man* manages to celebrate the political and social ideals of P. B. Shelley at the same time that it demonstrates their limitations as the product of idealism. The marriage of 'power and will', 'Good and the means of good', is the best idea to which humans can aspire; it is also an ideal which is helpless in the face of the inhuman force of Necessity. *The Last Man* mourns the loss of P. B. Shelley by raising him to a sociopolitical and a physical position which reverses the history of the poet's tragically short life (LM, 236). But the novel performs such a mourning reversal by reaffirming Mary Shelley's 'realist' objections to the extremities of idealist thought present in the work of P. B. Shelley and Godwin.

'Duplex' vision is perhaps the kind of vision we have been ascribing to Mary Shelley throughout this study so far. Her peculiar combination of reformism and realism inevitably generates a reversible perspective, in which political, social, ethical and philosophical idealism is admired at the same time that it is submitted to severe reality-testing and, in the face of limit experiences, found wanting. *The Last Man* is a vast testament to that divided vision, at once celebratory and mournful, revivifying and annihilating, hopeful and pessimistic. Shelley's wholly consistent admiration for and yet 'realist' critique of the Enlightenment 'idealism' of her father and husband finds what is perhaps its most appropriate emblem in the figure of a 'duplex mirror.' To go a little further in our understanding of how the novel intentionally advocates such a 'duplex' vision we need to pay some attention to another symbolically central image.

VI. PYRAMIDS

As part of her research for *The Last Man* Shelley appears to have sat, unseen, above the debating politicians in the House of Commons.[200] Crook, Blumberg, and McWhir have remarked on the manner in which Verney's vocation as an author is frequently associated with a vision gained from a height or from a macro- or meta-perspective. As Raymond's forces engage those of the Turks at the gates of Constantinople, for example, Verney looks on through a telescope on the top of a nearby 'mount.' Verney remarks: 'my eye removed from the glass, I could scarce discern the pigmy forms of the crowd, which about a mile from me surrounded the gate; the form of Raymond was lost' (LM, 157–8). Verney's ability to move from the microcosm of his own life and the lives of those around him to a vision of the whole globe or the entire human race is frequently evidenced, as in a much quoted passage in which he states: 'I spread the whole earth out as a map before me. On no spot of its surface could I put my finger and say, here is safety' (LM, 204). This narrative ability to view the human world from a global perspective, as 'the ruins of an anthill immediately after its destruction', is clearly related to his comments about authorship. Finding a greater connection to human society by writing 'the biography of favourite historical characters', Verney states: 'Kings have been called the fathers of their people. Suddenly I became as it were the father of all mankind. Posterity became my heirs. My thoughts were gems to enrich the treasure house of man's intellectual possessions; each sentiment was a precious gift I bestowed on them' (LM, 122). The whole passage is a meta-textual commentary, in reverse, on the eventual position Verney will have with relation to the human race and to the act of writing its final history. The passage looks forward to a future-time in which writing and the associated exercise of the imagination will be the only connection Verney has left with the vanished race of 'man.'

In that final 'last man' state, as he wanders around Rome, Verney's 'duplex' vision appears to take on a terrible literalness, his ability to temporarily repopulate the city and thus the world in his imagination now the only link left between human history and the post-pestilential era. The imagination, and its ability to reverse the temporal order, now appears to lack any conceivable mode of consolation, however, and in the climactic scene in which Verney sits by the Coliseum and imagines a 'Diorama of the ages', we are slowly led to the dead-end of the present: 'The generations I had conjured up to my fancy, contrasted more strongly with the end of all – the single point in which, as a pyramid, the mighty fabric of society had ended, while I, on the giddy height, saw vacant space around me' (LM, 359). The pyramid referred to here is both literal and figurative and stands as the ultimate symbol of the novel as a whole. The literal referent is the Pyramid of Cestius, which towers above the Protestant Cemetery within which P. B. Shelley and William Shelley were then buried, and to which Verney, as the last man, retires to read in the empty 'library' of Rome (LM, 361).[201] The spot had been immortalized by P. B. Shelley in his *Adonais*, an elegy for John Keats, also buried under the shadow of Cestius's pyramidal monument. The association of pyramids with the Protestant Cemetery is strengthened when we remember Shelleys' desire in 1819 concerning a monument for their son: 'we still encline to a pyramid as the most durable of simple monumental forms.' Shelley had asked Amelia Curran in that letter: 'What would be the size of a pyramid built of the most solid materials & covered with white marble at the price of £25 sterl – and also what would be the size of an obelisk built in the same manner & at the same price?' (L, I, 105). The little pyramid by the side of Cestius's large pyramid was never built, but the idea indicates the enigmatic significance of such a monumental shape for Shelley. When we start looking for pyramids in *The Last Man* we see them punctuating the entire novel.

Pyramids were much in fashion in the period after Napoleon's Egyptian campaign, as Jane (Webb) Loudon's Mary Shelley-inspired 1827 *The Mummy!* testifies.[202] Godwin viewed them as signs of ancient Egypt's desire for 'perpetuity', something confirmed in their 'massiness and immoveableness' (Godwin, *Political*, IV, 18). That they normally symbolized the irreversibility of time seems confirmed by Verney's figuration of himself situated, as the last man, on the 'single point' of a pyramid-shaped history, and by the description of the Sibyl's leaves as 'old as the Pyramids', in the 'Author's

Introduction' (LM, 7). As the novel progresses, they appear whenever emotional loss or literal death requires an adequate symbolic
shape. After Raymond's betrayal in Volume I, 'the flame of love'
once bright within Perdita is described in terms of 'spent embers
crowned by a pyramid of snow' (LM, 120). Raymond, responding
to Evadne's dying curse as a prophecy of his own and humanity's
doom, quotes lines from Calderon in which a pyramid image
reminds us of the cultural association between pyramids and death
(LM, 149). Eventually, Raymond and Perdita will be interred on
the top of 'a nature – hewn pyramid' to the south of the town of
Hymettus (LM, 165–6, 170). It is even possible, perhaps even feasible, that when Verney states that he 'ascended St. Peter's, and
carved on its topmost stone the æra 2100, last year of the world!',
he in fact inscribes his text not on the unreadably and perilously
high 'dome' but, rather, in the blank triangle (two-dimensional
pyramid) on the lower and accessible façade (LM, 363). This interpretation works because by this stage we are fully aware of the
manner in which the pyramid image sums up the shape of Verney's
narrative; however, by this stage we are also aware of the manner in
which the image can contain within itself an imaginative reversibility
which Verney's narrative has exemplified and which he has, by the
novel's conclusion, gifted to the reader.

This last aspect of the image is best understood in the scenes in
which the remnant of the human race leave Paris and travelling
south reach the sublime, Romantic scenery of the Alps. Reduced
to 'fourteen hundred souls' and ready for the final exodus from
Paris, the plague continues to reduce their number. Verney writes:
'A man last night had died of the plague. The quiver was not
emptied, nor the bow unstrung .... We had called ourselves the
"paragon of animals", and, lo! we were a "quint-essence of dust."
We repined that the pyramids had outlasted the embalmed body
of their builder' (LM, 309–10). When they eventually arrive at
'the foot of Jura' they are only fifty in number; when they reach
the Swiss Alps their numbers reduce to a handful, until '[n]ear the
sources of the Arveiron', the four remaining (Adrian, Verney,
Evelyn and Clara) perform 'the rites for .... the last of the species',
the last member of the pre-pestilential human race. They place this
last man at the foot of the Mer de Glace, where Frankenstein and
his creature had conducted their fierce moral conflict, and watch as
first an avalanche and then a tremendous night storm marks the
event: 'Yellow lightnings played around the vast dome of Mont

Blanc, silent as the snow-clad rock they illuminated' (LM, 329).
Having returned her characters to a place forever associated with
her first journey with P. B. Shelley and her first publication, *History
of a Six Weeks' Tour*, Shelley buries the last of the pre-pestilential
race under the shadow of a mountain, Mont Blanc, that looks like
a pyramid. The return here is also to P. B. Shelley's poem on that
mountain, first published within *History of a Six Weeks' Tour*.
Mont Blanc, for P. B. Shelley, represents a pyramidal place of death
and annihilation ('dome, pyramid, and pinnacle'), a 'city of death'
and 'flood of ruin'; and yet, as we know, P. B. Shelley's poem ends
which an apostrophizing address to the pyramidal mountain which
asserts the human ability to reverse the seemingly irreversible direction of 'power':

> And what were thou, and earth, and stars, and sea,
> If to the human mind's imaginings
> Silence and solitude were vacancy? (Shelley, *Poems*, I, 549)

The Last Man presents its readers with a pyramid-shaped narrative,
narrated from a point of singularity equivalent to that Egyptian
monument's apex. What it communicates to its improbable readers,
however, is a 'duplex' vision, creative and de-creative, celebratory
and mournful, Romantic and realist. Above that point of singularity,
if one were to look down at a pyramid's design, one would see a
point at the centre of a four-sided circumference: the perfect image,
perhaps, of synecdoche, the substitutable relation between part
and whole upon which all ideas of collectivity are founded. Shelley's
novel eradicates that collective logic at the same moment it restores
it, setting off a two-way signal between social vision and tragic
realism that plays along the base and apex of her most challenging
and profound of fictional monuments.

5

The Fortunes of Perkin Warbeck

I. A TRANSITIONAL TEXT

With Shelley's fourth major novel we enter the phase of her literary career which has traditionally been perceived in terms of a decline in creative energy, a lapse into orthodox conservatism, or simply a period in which she wrote sub-standard work for money. This view of the later works has begun to change in recent years, although the process is still in a relatively early phase. *Perkin Warbeck* is perhaps the most important of Shelley's later texts in this regard, not least because it remains under-examined and continues to provoke negative critical reactions.[203] Miranda Seymour's response to the novel is a striking example of the latter point: 'Few people', she argues, perhaps proving her point by mistitling the novel, 'have read their way through *The Adventures of Perkin Warbeck*; fewer still would argue that a long, laborious chronicle filled with unconvincing characters and turgid dialogue amounted to more than a waste of Mary's imaginative gift.'[204] That assessment of the novel is beginning to be revised by modern Shelley scholars and critics. Deidre Lynch suggests that *Perkin Warbeck* may constitute 'Shelley's most crucial novel in [the] effort to "read" the past'; Charlene E. Bunnell insists that the novel 'holds its own with the previous work of the Shelley canon'; Emily Sunstein calls it 'Mary Shelley's last novel on a grand scale'; Melissa Sites describes it as 'her most nuanced response to the challenge posed by tyranny to those advocating gradual reform.'[205]

The lack of attention *Perkin Warbeck* has received in modern criticism is perhaps also explained by the lack of an affordable scholarly edition and by the fact that Romantic critics and scholars can begin to feel somewhat outside of their legitimate domain when confronted with literature published in the latter part of the 1820s and the decade of the 1830s. Composed between 1827 and the autumn of 1829 (see PW, xiv), the novel was published by Colburn and Bentley, after John Murray, Shelley's first choice, had declined it. Accounts of Shelley which view her from a primarily 'Romantic' perspective inevitably run into difficulties when confronting work written within and in response to a period which is transitional between Regency and Victorian England. The England to which Shelley returned in 1823 was about to pass through what can rather precisely be termed, a period of transition. *Perkin Warbeck* is a fascinating response to that socio-political and cultural transition, and needs to be read and understood in that light.

The historical research Shelley carried out for her novel is comparable in its breadth and depth to the research she had lavished on *Valperga*. She mentions various historical and philosophical sources in her preface to the novel, including Bacon, Hall, Holinshed and Hume. As Doucet Devin Fischer and Bennett have demonstrated, however, Shelley's research led her much further and much wider than that. She consulted Thomas Crofton Crocker, author of *Fairy Legends and Traditions of the South of Ireland* (1825–8), on the Irish chapters.[206] She wrote to Walter Scott asking him for information for her Scottish chapters (L, II, 77–8), and John Bowring for information about and histories of Spain for the early chapters of her hero's exile (PW, xvii). She also made various requests to John Murray and others regarding texts relevant to the historical period of late fifteenth-century England. As was the case with the history of Castruccio, Shelley here is dealing with a conflictual historical record, as she makes clear in her preface:

> It is not singular that I should entertain a belief that Perkin was, in reality, the lost Duke of York. For, in spite of Hume, and the later historians who have followed in his path, no person who has at all studied the subject but arrives at the same conclusion. Records exist in the Tower, some well known, others with which those who have access to those interesting papers are alone acquainted, which put the question almost beyond doubt. (PW, 5)

The subject of her narrative is stated directly here: it concerns the well-known story of Perkin Warbeck, who, during the early years of Henry VII's reign, passed himself off as Richard, Duke of York, legitimate heir to the throne, one of the two princes imprisoned in the Tower of London by Richard III. The historical Perkin Warbeck gained support in various courts and kingdoms hostile to the new Lancastrian order in England, and was assisted in various abortive military campaigns, until he was finally captured and made to confess his true identity before being executed. As Shelley suggests, she is not the first reader of the historical record to entertain the idea that Perkin Warbeck was in fact who he claimed to be, Richard, Duke of York. As she also makes clear, the dominant historical interpretation took the opposing view. Shelley's statements in themselves embody the conflicts and debates generated by the figure of Perkin Warbeck. The very historical records upon which historians have traditionally dismissed Warbeck as an impostor seem to convince anyone who studies them of his authenticity. '[N]o person who has at all studied the subject', save of course for all those historians who have done so and come up with the opposing conclusion, 'but arrives at the same conclusion.' It would appear that, once again, a counter-factual mode of historical understanding based on the truths made available by fiction is required to resolve this apparent contradiction. That counter-factual 'truth' is embodied in Shelley's representation of the character of her protagonist.

For the majority of the novel Perkin's mere presence is sufficient to convince most people he meets that he is Richard. A good number of the scenes in the first two volumes of the novel revolve around the manner in which Richard's appearance instantaneously convinces people (his estranged mother, the sailors in the ship that bring him back from Spain, the notables of Cork city, James IV of Scotland) that he is Richard. Shelley's protagonist, on this basis, can appear to be a fictional embodiment of the Godwinian principle of sincerity or confidence; he is a truth which no one, when they confront him, can choose to deny. John Ford's 1634 play on the subject, one of Shelley's most important intertexts, was entitled *The Chronicle History of Perkin Warbeck: A Strange Truth*, and any reader coming to Shelley's own version must necessarily ask the question what the 'strange truth' of Richard's identity signifies.[207] This question cannot be adequately approached, however, without an understanding of the socio-political contexts Shelley was addressing and responding to in her novel. Why did Shelley, in the last few years of the 1820s, return to the form of the historical novel? Why did she choose to

represent, in the manner she did, the well-known story of Perkin
Warbeck, pretender to the title Richard IV?

Lidia Garbin answers these questions by turning to Shelley's
need for profit from her writing, stating: 'A predilection in contemporary taste for the kind of narrative offered by the Waverley
Novels showed her the path to follow.'[208] This approach, important as Scott's influence undoubtedly was, gives us a rather circular argument in which Shelley's return to the historical novel is
motivated by her desire to imitate Scott's brand of historical novel.
It is, I would suggest, much better to begin by turning to Shelley's
intense concern with the actual historical events of the last years
of the 1820s. Shelley's letters between 1827 and 1830 are studded
with responses to the socio-political events of the day. The years
of the composition of Shelley's novel witnessed a series of crises in
England and the Union. Boyd Hilton entitles his chapter on the
years 1827 to 1832 'The crisis of the old order', and writes of the
period: 'The next five years were characterized by ideological con-
frontations and political confusion.'[209] A financial collapse of the
stock-market and banking system in 1825 was followed throughout the nation by a prolonged period of manufacturing depression
and fierce debate over the outdated protectionist Corn Laws which
sought to keep out cheap imported grain from the Continent but
served also to cause or threaten food shortages amongst the rural
and urban population. Shelley wrote to Trelawny on 15 December
1829:

> But while fog and ennui possesses London, despair and convulsion
> reign over the country – some change some terrible event is expected –
> rents falling – money not to be got – every one poor and fearful – Will
> any thing come of it – Was not the panic and poverty of past years as
> great – Yet if parlia[ment] meet, as they say it will in January – some-
> thing is feared – something about to be done – besides fishing in
> Virginia Water and driving about in a pony phaeton. (L, II, 95)

Although written after the novel's publication, it is worth looking
here at various letters authored by Shelley at the end of 1830. On
30 December, with an eye on constitutional reform's re-emergence
as a pressing topic on the political stage, Shelley wrote one letter
to her friend Robert Dale Owen and another, enclosed within the
same envelope, to the radical feminist, Frances (Fanny) Wright,
whom she had recently befriended. To Owen she explains the contents of her letter to Wright, her thoughts on 'the triumph of the

<u>Cause</u> in Europe' and her worry that in her own country
'<u>Progressiveness'</u> and '<u>tyrant quellingtiveness</u>' are 'mingled with
<u>sick destructiveness</u>' (L, II, 122). To Frances Wright she is more
voluble, praising the spread of the 'fire' of liberation across
Europe, wondering 'Will not our Children live to see a new birth
for the world!', before coming to rest again on her own rather
more antithetically mixed nation:

> Our own hapless country …. The case seems to stand thus – The people
> <u>will</u> be redressed – will the Aristocrats sacrifice enough to tranquillize
> them – if they will not – we must be revolutionized – but they intend now
> so to do …. Our <u>sick</u> feel themselves tottering – they are fully aware of
> their weakness – long curtailed as to their rents, they humble – How will
> it all end? None dare even presume to guess. (L, II, 124)

I am not suggesting that we should read *Perkin Warbeck* directly in
terms of the build-up to the 1832 Great Reform Bill. It is generally agreed by historians of the period that a combination of factors
led to a return of the question of constitutional reform only in the
latter half of 1829.[210] But Shelley's consistent support for and hopes
concerning the constitutional reform should not be ignored either
(see L, II, 133, 138–9, 143, 146). As Linda Colley suggests, various
historic acts that were passed by parliament between 1829 and
1833 (the repeal of the Test and Corporation Act, the Catholic
Emancipation Act, the Great Reform Bill, the Emancipation Act of
1833 concerning the liberation of slaves in the British West Indies)
all point to a period of political and social transition over the
future shape of Great Britain. Colley, in her analysis of the complicated synergies and divisions which characterize the period of
British political history from 1815 onwards, states how new forms
of collectivity were required after the defeat of France.[211]

   Perkin Warbeck is a novel written in a period in which questions
concerning what it means to be British and what kind of unity was
possible within 'the Union' were the dominant questions of the day.
Colley's analysis is extremely helpful in reminding us that for Ultra-
Tories, liberalizing Whigs, and radicalized agitators, the language of
patriotism was a commonly shared vocabulary and discourse.[212]
There seems to have been something about the story of Perkin
Warbeck that suited this climate of debate over citizenship and
national identity. As the editors of *The 'Perkin Warbeck' Project*
state, five books on the subject were published between 1829 and
1832. Shelley's own novel was delayed in its publication because

of a rival novel by Alexandra Campbell entitled *Perkin Warbeck; or, the Court of James the Fourth of Scotland* (see L, II, 108).[213] That Henry VII's victory at Bosworth Field in 1485 brought an end to the devastating War of the Roses and yet was achieved by a violent act of usurpation are obvious indicators of potential historical relevance for a divided post-Regency England confronted with the task of unifying around socio-political ideas and structures forged in peacetime rather than during a protracted war. The story of Perkin Warbeck brings into that mix questions which return us to the forms of synecdochal logic explored in our analysis of *The Last Man*; they concern the manner in which national unity can or cannot form around the figure of individual leaders.

In her letters of this period, Shelley often expresses her admiration for heroic figures who dedicate and even sacrifice their lives for 'the <u>Cause</u>.' In her congratulatory letter to General Lafayette, she styles herself as 'a humble ... individual' addressing 'the Hero of three Revolutions', and goes on to relate his heroic status to that of P. B. Shelley: 'I was the wife of a man who – held dear the opinions you espouse, to which you <u>were</u> the martyr and <u>are</u> the ornament; and to sympathize with successes which would have been matter of such delight to him, appears to me a sacred duty .... I rejoice that the Cause to which Shelley's life was devoted, is crowned with triumph' (L, II, 118). In her letters to Francis Wright, Shelley pictures herself as the daughter and wife of heroic beings who, like Wright, inspire her with an 'ardent admiration ... for those who sacrifice themselves for the public good' (L, II, 4).

Shelley's response to the rise to power and unexpected death of George Canning is another fascinating example. Canning, despite his association with Queen Caroline and his rather unorthodox past, and despite his intense association with the cause of Catholic Emancipation, was asked by George IV to form a government in early 1827 after the physical collapse of Lord Liverpool. Shelley wrote excitedly to Trelawny: 'The state of public affairs is in the highest degree interesting – Canning by a coup de maitre got himself maned [*named*] Prime Minister on which the high Tories resigned .... This I think is good news for Greece – for they are all liberal' (L, I, 547). Asa Briggs writes of Canning's elevation to Prime Minister: 'it was generally said, in London at least, that the choice was the most popular with the people that had ever been known.'[214] The reason for Shelley's and the nation's positive reception to Canning was that it was believed that his would be a balanced and reforming, liberalizing government that would move politics in England and Britain beyond an outmoded opposition between Tory and Whig parties. When Canning died on 8 August, Shelley expressed her grief in terms which are potentially significant for our understanding of the novel she was at that time composing. In a letter to Teresa Guiccioli, dated 20 August, she laments her absence from Italy before writing: 'the Death of our learned Canning weighs on my heart – as if he had been a friend of mine – Did you know that he praised my Frankenstein in honourable terms in the House of Commons – extremely pleasing to me – To poor England – bereft World – what an irreparable misfortune the loss of this great man is for you' (L, I, 566).[215] In another letter, this time to John Howard Payne, two days later, Shelley returned to the subject of Canning's death: 'Do you not lament our miserable loss? You Americans lo[o]k disdainfully on our European politics, yet you must regret the Ma[n] who might have regenerated our liberty, and given to the world a gl[ ] that without him, it will never attain' (L, I, 569).[216]

Is Shelley's Richard, Duke of York, a hero who seeks to regenerate liberty and forge a more unified England? The question of national unity and how it is achieved is without doubt the central ideological issue in *Perkin Warbeck*, just as it is in the novels of Walter Scott. The enigma of Shelley's novel, and its major importance as a historical novel, is that Richard is not a hero of unification and liberalization, despite his overwhelming attractiveness and sympathetic portrayal. *Perkin Warbeck* encourages its readers to identify with a male quester who is precisely out of synch with the needs of his own nation. The politics of Shelley's novel are contained within that fact.

II.   THE RIGHT OF RIGHT

The opening paragraph of the first chapter of *Perkin Warbeck*, positioned in the immediate aftermath of the Lancastrian victory at Bosworth Field, presents us with an image of unification after bloody war which reverberates throughout the rest of the novel (PW, 7). The state of England under Henry VII is a complicated one. Henry VII is described throughout the novel as a cold, inhuman, calculating monarch for whom the maintenance of his own usurped power takes precedence over all other considerations. The narrator describes him as 'prudent, resolute, and valiant' but also 'totally devoid of generosity, and … actuated all his life by base and bad passions.' The opposite of Byron's antithetical Napoleon in *Child Harold's Pilgrimage*, Canto III, Henry has 'a mind commensurate to the execution of his plans …. He never aimed at too much, and felt instantaneously when he had arrived at the enough.' The narrator goes on, surely with Byron's description of Napoleon in mind: 'More of cruelty would have roused England against him; less would have given greater hopes to the partisans of his secreted rival. He had that exact portion of callousness of heart which enabled him to extricate himself in the admirable manner he did from all his embarrassments' (PW, 26–7). Shelley's Henry VII is not a monarch her readers are expected to, or even could, identify or sympathize with. His callous treatment of Richard's sister, Elizabeth, whom he marries in order to reinforce his grasp on power, only goes to add to his antipathetic role within the novel.

This is Shelley's Henry VII. We need to remind ourselves here of something almost always forgotten or elided in discussions of *Perkin Warbeck*. Henry VII, so callous, politically scheming and inhuman to his enemies and even his apparent allies, is associated with the force of modernity. A long passage from Volume III is required to open this point to view. The passage is given as Richard is preparing a desperate attack on the town of Exeter, knowing now that he will never be able to realize his ambition to claim his rightful throne:

> The lapse of years had confirmed Henry on his throne. He was extortionate and severe, it is true; and thus revolts had been frequent during the earlier portion of his reign; but they took their rise in a class which even in modern days, it is difficult to keep within the boundaries of law. The peasantry, scattered and dependent on the nobles, were tranquil: but artificers, such as the miners of Cornwall, who met in numbers, and could ask each other, 'Why, while there is plenty in the land, should we and our children starve? Why pay our hard earnings into the regal coffers?' and, still increasing in boldness, demand at last, 'Why should these men govern us?
>
> 'We are many – they are few!'
>
> Thus sedition sprung from despair, and assumed arms; to which Henry had many engines to oppose, bulwarks of his power. A commercial spirit had sprung up during his reign, partly arising from the progress of civilization, and partly from so large a portion of the ancient nobility

having perished in the civil wars. The spirit of chivalry, which isolates man, had given place to that of trade, which unites them in bodies. (PW, 306)

The last sentence is hugely telling, since throughout the novel Richard's legitimate claim to the throne of England has been pursued by him in the spirit of nobility and chivalry.[217] It is perhaps important to stress that the modernity (the rise of a commercial economy associated with a more integrated social system) portrayed here is a contingent consequence rather than a direct intention of Henry's reign. We can, and perhaps we must, applaud the 'progress of civilization' at the same time that we regret Henry VII's illiberal style of monarchical rule. We should also register, particularly in the context of Shelley's use of her husband's most famous political line of poetry, the fact that England then, as in Shelley's own time, so long as it is socially and economically divided, faces a perilous negotiation between the historical forces of reform and revolution. One might remember here Shelley's comments to Francis Wright. The undeniable feature of these lines, however, is their presentation of Richard's chivalric quest to regain the throne as an historically retrograde objective. Why does Shelley write a novel in which her hero, the overwhelming centre of attention and identification, wastes his life on a quest which is socially, economically and historically misguided?

The question has generated a central interpretive debate within modern critical responses to the novel. This debate has its origins, perhaps, in Muriel Spark's account. Her account of Richard's quest to regain the throne locates within it what she believes to be a foundational flaw or confusion (between nostalgia and insurrection) in his characterization.[218] Faced with such an apparently confused protagonist (part recidivist, part revolutionary), Spark finds it difficult to avoid a judgement on the novel itself as being a confused performance. She writes: '[Shelley] might even, with success, rather have presented a black-hearted villain than place her hero thus in a no-man's land of purpose.'[219] How are readers supposed to sympathetically read the history of such a politically and ethically confused 'hero'? William A. Walling makes very similar points to those of Spark when he talks about the 'ideational incoherency' both of Richard's quest and, by extension, of the novel itself. Walling's comments here centre around notions of novelistic unity, which he argues collapse in *Perkin Warbeck* due to its protagonist's confused position between nostalgic chivalry and anachronistic revolutionary action: 'Richard simply becomes an impossibly absurd hero', he writes, 'caught between two worlds, he functions effectively in neither.'[220]

This is not the manner in which Shelley's contemporaries read the novel and the character of Richard, nor is it a reading that makes much interpretive sense. Such readings do not ascribe to Shelley's fiction sufficient sense of her continuation of the Godwinian novelistic tradition, in which novels make it their business to present the apparently contradictory and aporetic nature of 'things as they are.' Novels, in this tradition, challenge their readers through contradiction and unresolved problematics to exercise their own faculties of rational judgement. This is the case that Lidia Garbin makes, in the revised version of her essay on the novel, when she writes: 'In her portrayal of Perkin/Richard, who combines ideal capabilities with bad actions, Shelley presents a human being no more incoherent than her own Frankenstein.'[221] It is not a clash between historically anachronistic forces that is dramatized in and through the character of Richard, but rather a clash between two kinds of truth, two kinds of right. Readers of this study of Shelley's fictional work will not be surprised to be informed that this clash involves a critique of a masculine, absolutist rhetoric of truth, necessity and justice (or right).

It is generally understood by the novel's modern readers that Shelley works hard in her novel to establish the authenticity of Richard's identity and claim to the throne only, as the novel proceeds, to expose his mistake in attempting to assert that monarchical, inherited right on the historical, socio-political stage.[222] Richard, from a young age, is protected by people who are not only convinced of his true identity but also of his right to claim the throne of England. The most memorable of these is Monina, daughter of Jahn Warbeck's sister. Growing up with Richard and Edmund Plantagenet in Andalusia, Monina seems reminiscent of Beatrice, only her love and devotion are dedicated to a man who, unlike Castruccio, is deserving of them. By the time of the hopeless Cornish uprising in volume three, however, Monina's devotion has come to read like a form of irrational fundamentalism. She says to him: 'the sacred name of monarch which you bear, is the pledge and assurance of pre-destined victory' (PW, 305). Monina displays unprecedented agency for a female character in an historical novel of the period, but our admiration for her is increasingly separated from any belief in

Richard's inevitable success. We admire her as a character, but grow ever distant from her beliefs about the rightness of Richard's quest.

Monina confuses right (Richard's identity and his legal claim to the throne) with necessity; but it must also be said that the right (the truth) of Richard's identity is not, neither logically nor ethically, identical to a right to claim the throne. This is the 'lesson' of Richard's experiences, but it is a 'lesson' he continually learns only to forget or draw away from or reconfigure. Richard's character is undoubtedly noble, admirable and sympathetic. As he sails away from Spain back to his own native lands, ignorant of the plot to murder him on board, Richard's qualities of humanity and leadership tower above those of Meiler Trangmar, Shelley's gothic villain. He befriends the crew, acts heroically during a storm, and even begins to melt Trangmar's mercenary heart (PW, 107). He is, literally, a born leader and he makes a little kingdom of the British ship: 'The heart of the outcast sovereign swelled within him. "I reign here, in their breasts I reign," was the thought that filled his bright eyes' (PW, 108). Landing in Cork he addresses the townspeople as their rightful monarch: 'I, named in my childhood Duke of York and Lord of Ireland, now, if rightly styled, Richard the Fourth of England, demand my lieges of Cork, to acknowledge my rights to rise in my cause' (PW, 116). At this stage, Richard's cause is the assertion of his identity, an assertion, as he makes clear here, which is for him identical to his claim for the throne. This is the blind spot which the novel slowly reveals: Richard confuses an ontological truth (his true identity) with an ethical imperative (his right to the throne). The 'rights' of Richard's 'cause' do not necessarily cohere, and from this point onwards this fact is continually demonstrated.

In a very deliberate echo of Scott's *Ivanhoe*, Richard, returned to England, attends in disguise the celebrations of the marriage of Lord Surrey's eldest daughter to Lord de Walden (PW, 193).[223] Richard had, in fact, been married in early childhood to Lord Surrey's daughter, before her young death. Surrey is one of Richard's most deeply embedded allies, but his speech to Richard laying out the reasons why he will not involve himself in his campaign against Henry VII's forces provides the novel's readers with their first extended account of the gap between Richard's 'right' of identity and the rightness of his claim to the throne:

I love not Tudor, but I love my country: and now that I see plenty and peace reign over this fair isle, even though Lancaster be their unworthy

vicegerent, shall I cast forth these friends of man, to bring back the
deadly horrors of unholy civil war? .... I will not people my country
with widows and orphans; nor spread the plague of death from the
eastern to the western sea. (PW, 195)

Richard's irritated reply is significant on a number of fronts: it
registers the masculinist ethos of the chivalric code of honour which
has formed him ('thou wouldst teach me to turn spinster, my lord')
it also dramatically demonstrates his inability at this stage to dis-
sociate the two 'rights' (of identity and inheritance) he claims to
be one: 'you would think it well done to waste life to dispossess
the usurper of your right' (PW, 196). The statement is deliberately
ambiguous, yet it is an ambiguity readers even at this stage of the
novel can resolve easily enough. It might be that Richard refers only
to his own 'life'; however, it is patently clear, as Surrey has just
explained, that the assertion of Richard's 'right' will waste the lives
of thousands. There is an ineradicable violence in the assertion of
Richard's 'right', which only comes home to Richard himself after he
has travelled to Scotland, been acclaimed the rightful heir of England
by James IV and his court, married James's cousin, Katherine Gordon,
and commenced what was meant to be the unquestionable destiny
of his life, his military arrival (with the Scottish warriors) into the
northern counties of his own kingdom of England. As the Scottish
soldiers invade and violently sack the English homes of their 'natural'
enemies, Richard is finally brought face-to-face with the rightness of
Lord Surrey's words. The narrator seems to blend her own voice
with the thoughts of Richard here: 'Richard would have stood erect
and challenged the world to accuse him – God and his right, was his
defence. His right! Oh, narrow and selfish was that sentiment that
could see, in any right appertaining to one man the excuse for the
misery of thousands' (PW, 252). It matters greatly to our understanding of Richard and the novel's ultimate design whether this
devastating realization of the violence of his assertion of 'right' is at
this moment registered by Richard himself, or in fact only by the
narrator and the reader. In the immediately following paragraph a
further shift of referent produces a significant identification which it
is necessary for us to contemplate: 'War, held in leash during the
army's march from Edinburgh, was now let loose; swift and bar-
barous he tore forward on his way; a thousand destructions waited
on him; his track was marked by ruin: the words of Lord Surrey
were fulfilled' (PW, 252). Are the words of Lord Surrey 'fulfilled' in

Richard's ears here? The question is inevitable given the issues of voice and perspective raised in the previous paragraph. The question is not one that can be resolved in a single answer, however, since it contains within it the recognition that the 'he' of these lines, literally referring to 'war' itself, can, by association, also find their referent in Richard. Through the kind of pronominal shifter we have seen Shelley employing in previous works, Richard, in an implicit reading of these lines it is difficult to avoid, becomes identical to the force of 'war.' Certainly the northern English villagers do not discriminate between Richard and the devastation that has suddenly overwhelmed them.

As Richard's troops race southward to rescue a village from the marauding Scots ('flying children, mothers who stayed to die, fathers who unarmed rushed upon the weapons of the foe') he finally gives in to the sheer horror that confronts him: 'Richard burst into tears, "'Oh, my stony and hard-frozen heart!" he cried, "which breakest not to see the loss and slaughter of so many of thy natural-born subjects and vassals"' (PW, 255). In the very expression of his agony at the consequences of the military assertion of his 'right' Richard reaffirms his foundational sense of that 'right' ('thy natural-born subjects and vassals'). As he witnesses the tragedy that his 'right' has caused, and gives expression to his horror at the consequences, does he understand that his 'right' does not guarantee, or even include, 'right'?

Modern criticism of *Perkin Warbeck* tends not to ask this question, resting largely with the 'lessons' the novel's narrative apparently conveys to its readers. That criticism tends to elide the fact that any 'lessons' imparted by the novel are conveyed through the mediation of a narrative voice which shapes and manipulates our perception of the characters and narrative events from which we derive the meaning of the text. It is accurate enough to state that at this stage of the novel we have a good many of the elements required to construct an ultimate ideological meaning from the novel. Surrey's speech against Richard's campaign was uttered from the point of view of domestic happiness. He had explained to Richard: 'I have a dear wife and lovely children, sisters, friends, and all the sacred ties of humanity, that cling round my heart, and feed it with delight; these I might sacrifice at the call of honour, but the misery I must then endure I will not inflict on others' (PW, 195). The devastation that the Scots bring upon the northern English towns is, as we have seen, described in terms of the devastation wrought on families (children, mothers, fathers). Much of the latter part of the novel concentrates on the tension between Richard's continued determination to assert the 'right' of his identity, if not his claim to the throne, and Katherine's arguments in favour of a domestic life of peace, tranquillity, but above all social utility. She says to him: 'Why may we not – why should we not live? .... what is there in the name or state of king, that should so take captive our thoughts, that we can imagine no life but on a throne?' (PW, 302). Richard's reply can only be that without the world's acknowledgement of his identity, his 'name', he is nothing, a counterfeit person. The chivalric honour of the name is something he cannot relinquish: 'Thus, my gentle love', he replies, 'you would have me renounce my birth and name .... I am a king, lady, though no holy oil nor jewelled crown has touched this head; and such I must prove myself' (PW, 302–3). The themes of the novel are, on this basis, clearly stable and readable. As Bennett argues, the novel owes far more to a debate with P. B. Shelley and Godwin than it does a 'fashionable imitation' of Scott's historical romances.[224]

Monina's father, Hernan de Faro, stands out as another of the novel's indicators of this thematic of love over violence, social unity over divisive social structures. Having gained a 'horror' of warfare, he builds a Valperga-like refuge on the top of the hills of Alcala-la-Real: 'It was perched high upon the mountain, overlooking a plain which had been for many years the scene of ruthless carnage and devastation, being in itself an asylum for fugitives – a place of rest for the victor – an eagle's nest, unassailable by the vulture's of the plain' (PW, 87). As a Moor converted to Catholicism, De Faro finds the slaughter of Moors by Catholic soldiers unbearable, and when his own wife is slain in the capture of Alcala-la-Real he leaves his native land for a sea-faring life which eventually takes him towards the 'wild western ocean' (PW, 374) and the promise of a new land beyond Europe's perpetual violence and division.

A great deal of the novel could be marshalled in support of Bennett's reading, including the manner in which the claims of the peoples of Ireland, Scotland and Cornwall are foregrounded, as a challenge to any complaisant sense of pre-existing unity within the Union. Reading *Valperga* and *Perkin Warbeck* together, Bennett argues that Shelley's

> criticism of fourteenth-century Italy differs little from her criticism of fifteenth-century England (and by implication, of nineteenth-century Europe), and that these works .... are written in the tradition of social

reform, particularly influenced – as were the efforts of so many other reformers of the time – by Godwin and Wollstonecraft.[225]

I would not wish to disagree with this assessment of the thematics of *Valperga* and *Perkin Warbeck*. We have seen enough of the latter to have confirmed such a reading. This is, or at least should not be, the end of our analysis, however. *Perkin Warbeck*, like *Valperga* before it, does not simply convey a set of socio-political themes to its readers. The point is an important one, since if the novel's thematics were the final resting place of our reading it would be difficult to avoid those assessments (from Spark and Walling, for example) that query the characterization of Richard and, by extension, the aesthetic and ideological design of the novel as a whole. The fact of the matter is that to read *Perkin Warbeck* is to be involved in a process of identification with Richard from first to last. There is a palpable sense of loss and an undeniable sense of nostalgic regret conveyed in the narration of Richard's 'fortunes' and eventual execution. Like *Valperga*, Shelley's *Perkin Warbeck* does not simply narrate an historical life of a central male protagonist, it also presents us with a complex narrative engagement (even relationship) with that human object of narration. To understand *Perkin Warbeck* it is not sufficient simply to outline its perceived thematic structure; one has to attend to the manner in which the narrator retains our admiration and emotional attachment to Richard, even in the face of his ethical mistakes and flaws.

III. NOSTALGIA AND NARRATION

Many of the narrative techniques used in *Valperga* to defer the reader's critical conclusion on the character of Castruccio are taken up again in *Perkin Warbeck* and developed in significant ways. Although less demonstratively female than *Valperga*'s narrator, it is difficult not to attach a feminine gender to this hugely important narrative presence. Much of the fascination involved in attending to the role of the narrator in the novel concerns the manner in which she mediates our understanding of and judgement on the character of Richard. There are, for example, frequent passages of contextualization, which remind the reader that we should not unthinkingly import our modern liberal values onto this earlier, more chivalric age (see PW, 61). We have to come to the history contained in this novel, and the character of a man like Richard, with a double, even duplex vision which, without losing contemporary values, can enter into a value-system now outmoded and inoperative. Time and again the narrator reminds us, through such passages, that we cannot simply dismiss Richard's chivalric value-system as an ethical error, even though, as we have seen, the novel quite clearly proves that it is. We need the double-vision of a responsible historiography if we are to authentically engage with the 'fortunes' of Richard, Duke of York.

We are also reminded on a number of occasions of the manner in which circumstances dictate the course of Richard's actions. The narrator often figures him as the helpless victim of fate; more pragmatic circumstances also conspire against him. As Richard struggles with the speech of Lord Surrey, the narrator sets the scene for the next stage of his campaign, the arrival of the fleet sent in his aid by his aunt, Margaret of Burgundy:

> Lord Surrey's deep-felt abjuration of war influenced him to sadness, but the usual habit of his mind returned .... In addition, the present occasion called for activity. The fleet, armed for invasion, prepared by his noble aunt – manned by his exiled zealous friends – would soon appear on the English coast, giving form and force to, while it necessitated, his purposed attempt. (PW, 196)

Richard here does not have sufficient time and space to assimilate the 'lesson' of Lord Surrey; he is, in fact, the central focus of a huge, internationally-sponsored operation which at this moment he could not halt if he wanted to. Added to this, the narrator makes it clear that, in opposition to Surrey's words of wisdom, the 'oily flatterer' Frion, who had formerly worked for Henry VII against the young Prince, works on Richard 'day and night to ensure that nothing [comes] near the Prince, except through his medium, which was one sugared and drugged to please' (PW, 196–7). Just as Castruccio's faulty character is put in positive relief by its proximity to characters such as Scoto, Pepi and ultimately Tripalda, so Richard is surrounded by villainous and treacherous characters, such as Trangmar, Frion, and most significantly of all, Sir Robert Clifford. His former playmate in the Tower of London, and his rescuer from Frion's early abduction attempt, Clifford becomes Richard's unshakeable nemesis, maddened by his love for Monina and consequent hatred of his apparent friend. In an undoubtedly playful piece of intertextual reconfiguration, Clifford's story of intrigue and obsessive

desire for irrational revenge mirrors the story of Godwin's Mandeville. Godwin's protagonist demonstrates a similarly abortive nature
to Shelley's villain ('Sir Robert, for sooth, is but half a man, and
never does more than half a deed' [PW, 273]) by insanely pursuing revenge against his noble counter-part, whose name is,
ironically, Clifford. There is much that can be said about the
character of Sir Robert Clifford and the manner in which he
brings Godwin's *Mandeville* into Shelley's *Perkin Warbeck*;
however, in terms of the current discussion, it is clear that as
Clifford continually plots Richard's downfall the reader's desires
are directed squarely towards his safety and immunity from such
irrational hatred.

Beyond any other technique it is the narrator's mediation of
Richard's character that colours the reader's ability to evaluate
him on an ethical level. The aftermath of the scenes in northern
England are a fascinatingly complex combination of insight and
blindness on Richard's part, accompanied by narratorial inter-
ventions which provide a form of apologia for the novel's protagonist. He writes to Katherine: 'What am I, that I should be the
parent of evil merely? Oh, my mother, my too kind friends, why
did ye not conceal me from myself?' (PW, 258). But he goes on to
state: 'Even now I think the day will come when I shall repair the
losses of this sad hour – is it the restless ambitious spirit of youth
that whispers future good, or true forebodings of the final triumph
of the right?' (ibid). He appears to have finally learnt the 'lessons' of
Surrey and Katherine herself: 'The stars play strange gambols with
us – I am richer than Tudor, and but that *thy* husband must leave
no questioned name, I would sign a bond with Fate – let him
take England, give me Katherine' (ibid). The 'but' demonstrates once
again that an apparent forward ethical movement is to be accompanied by a retrograde return to 'honour' and his 'name': 'But a
Prince may not palter with the holy seal God affixes to him – nor
one espoused to thee be less than King' (ibid). With these clear signs
of inability to accept the injustices involved in his 'right', the reader
might be tempted to dismiss Richard as an ethically flawed man. As
he prepares for a new campaign in Ireland, however, the narrator
once again steps in on Richard's behalf. Meditating on the 'fervent
imagination' of 'man', the narrator ponders on 'The creative faculty
of man's soul – which, animating Richard, made him see victory in
defeat, success and glory in the dark, the tortuous, the thorny path,
which it was his destiny to walk from the cradle to the tomb.' These

thoughts then erupt into an astonishing series of elegiac statements which demonstrate dramatically the emotional involvement of the narrator with her character:

> Oh, had I, weak and faint of speech, words to teach my fellow-creatures the beauty and capabilities of man's mind; could I, or could one more fortunate, breathe the magic word which would reveal to all the power, which we all possess, to turn evil to good, foul to fair; then vice and pain would desert the new-born world! (PW, 275)

This protracted description of the male imagination links Richard to that 'power' of mind as its exemplum, and yet the effect, which is clearly elegiac ('*had I the words*'), is also double in significance. The narrator's desire for the 'magic word' which could demonstrate how that male imaginative power can transform 'evil to good, foul to fair' is simply that, a desire. The novel has demonstrated throughout that evil cannot be transformed into good and that one mode of 'right', however intensely and genuinely imagined, does not guarantee the elimination of evil. The passage is fascinating because it manages to produce an impression of genuine elegy and mourning at the same time that it reaffirms the novel's ethical critique of Richard's absolutist notion of 'right.'

In the following paragraph the narrator pushes this combination of mourning and critique into a series of intertextual connections which make the association between Richard and P. B. Shelley very clear:

> It is not spent; he yet breathes: he is on the world of waters. What new scene unfolds itself? Where are they who were false, where those who were true? They congregate around him, and the car of life bears him on, attended by many frightful, many lovely shapes, to his destined end. He has yet much to suffer; and, human as he is, much to enjoy. (PW, 276)

There is here, for modern readers, a compelling blend of public intertexts (*The Triumph of Life*) with private ones (Mary's letters and journals after P. B. Shelley's death). Combining Richard and P. B. Shelley, the narrator begins to blend her voice with the author's private voice of mourning and apostrophe. But what is crucial to this reading is not that such passages collapse the novel into the apparently transparent realm of life-writing; they do not. Shelley's readers, we need to remember, did not have at their disposal editions of her letters and her journals. Rather, through the narrator's deeply personal relationship with her protagonist, Shelley produces a striking expression of her life-long admiration for and critique of the male idealist philosophies of her husband, her father and wider circle. Bennett's argument that the novel expresses Shelley's continued faith in Prometheanism is in this sense only half-right. In fact, the story of Richard allows her to express that unique blend of admiration for and yet realist critique of Prometheanism which is a defining feature of all her work.

Perkin Warbeck is one of Shelley's greatest expressions of her admiration (now modulated into nostalgia and mourning) and critique of the necessitarian ideology of 'right' inevitably producing 'right'. Ultimately what is so overwhelmingly attractive in the character of Richard is the very quality (his unshakeable belief in the divinely-sanctioned right of his 'right') that the novel exposes as error. But the telling word here is attraction. The peculiar nostalgic pathos generated in the novel, perhaps its most aesthetically telling feature, resides less in the character of Richard himself than in the complex relationship the narrator has with her central character. It is when we understand this aspect of the novel that the traditional reading of its concluding chapter becomes worth re-visiting.

IV. PLACING KATHERINE'S APOLOGIA

In the 'Conclusion' to *Perkin Warbeck*, 'years' after Richard's execution, Katherine meets a disguised Edmund Plantagenet and, due to his criticism of her existence within the court of Henry VII, delivers what amounts to an apologia. It is very common in Shelley criticism to read this last chapter as Shelley's own defence of her life in England from 1823 onwards.[226] The opening paragraph appears to confirm such readings, merging, from a modern perspective, the voice of the narrator with Shelley's own private voice in her letters and journals post-1822: 'Time, we are told by all philosophers, is the sole medicine for grief. Yet there are immortal regrets which must endure while we exist' (PW, 395). However much we may draw parallels between such passages and Shelley's own private voice of mourning, it is clear that readers are led in this conclusion to associate the mourning voices of the narrator and Katherine. What is crucial about Katherine as mourner is her 'living on', by which the narrator signifies a continued social agency:

'she lived on, dispensing pleasure, adored by all who approached her' (ibid). The persistent attention to her social duty, her continued sense of responsibility towards and love of others, is what is most central and significant in her address to Edmund.

Before we come to the significance of that central vision of social utility, we should make sure that we do not simplify Katherine's position. She makes it extremely clear throughout this chapter that for her Richard remains the focus of her life and identity. She says to Edmund: 'When years and quiet thought have brought you back from the tempest of emotion that shakes you, you will read my heart better, and know that it is still faithfully devoted to him I have lost' (PW, 398). Katherine's position is, in a very real way, the position of the narrator: these two female voices have expressed a critique of Richard's chivalric code without in any way reducing him as a man and as an object of love. They have both expressed the most sustained alternative to Richard's absolutist ideal of 'right'; both perceived within Richard's character a desire for unity and concern for others which offers the prospect of that alternative; and, in Katherine's apologia proper, their voices finally merge to express what it means to *live on* after the 'glorious' Promethean age has been lost with the loss of its representative man. Katherine explains: 'it is no wonder that I should love and idolize the most single-hearted, generous, and kindly being that ever trod the earth' (PW, 399). When readers of the novel discover within it a thematic pattern in which Richard's ethical error is corrected by Katherine's feminine alternative of love and social duty they do not adequately read these themes until they bring them together in Katherine's continued devotion to her lost husband. If Katherine represents the novel's ethical destination, then she does so by continuing to figure Richard, for all his faults, as the best of men. Katherine's apologia does not simply mark the loss of Richard's spirit to the world; as we have seen the narrator doing, Katherine refigures that spirit into a circumscribed but still vital ethical approach to a new, modernizing world, which is, ultimately, how we should read her continued devotion.

It is the manner in which Katherine expresses that continued devotion that is most important: she fulfils his wishes and stays with his sister, Elizabeth, helping to bring up their children.[227] She says of the young Arthur, heir to the throne: 'when I endeavour to foster the many virtues nature has implanted in the noble mind of Prince Arthur, I am fulfilling, methinks, a task grateful in the eyes of Richard, thus doing my part to bestow on the England he loved, a sovereign who will repair the usurper's crimes, and bestow happiness on the realm' (PW, 399–400). She goes on to talk of her wider social duty: 'Where I see suffering, there I must bring my mite for its relief' (PW, 400). Then, in a manner modern readers can now relate to Shelley's various descriptions of herself in the late-1820s and beyond, Katherine refers to her 'many weaknesses .... My passions, my susceptible imagination, my faltering dependence on others', before concluding:

> as it is I am content to be an imperfect creature, so that I never lose the ennobling attribute of my species, the constant endeavour to be more perfect .... I must love and be loved. I must feel that my dear and chosen friends are happier through me .... Permit this to be, unblamed – permit a heart whose sufferings have been, and are, so many and so bitter, to reap what joy it can from the strong necessity it feels to be sympathized with – to love. (ibid)

Katherine ends, then, with a reaffirmation of the Godwinian doctrine of perfectibility, only now modulated into a realistic, even pragmatic tone, a tone suited for a new age in which that perfection must be striven for by the love of imperfect people in an imperfect world. *Perkin Warbeck* develops Shelley's critical engagement with the philosophy and politics of her father and husband, but it does so in the context of mourning and in terms of a new political landscape in which Shelley's realist version of perfectibility appears increasingly attuned to the temper of the times. In a rather brilliant piece of counter-factual history, Richard Holmes, in his 'Shelley Undrowned', imagines what P. B. Shelley would have done if he had survived to eventually return to 1820s and 1830s England. Holmes's undrowned poet is still something of a political 'firework', but he also shows signs of entering into mainstream society in a liberalizing manner by taking up a seat in Parliament and becoming 'involved with the Great Reform Bill of 1832.'[228] We might add one more additional hypothetical event: the poet composing a positive review in 1830, perhaps in the flourishing journal *The Liberal*, on his wife's fourth novel, selecting for special praise its emphasis on love and unification over the totalizing certainties of an earlier, more divided age.

6

Lodore

I. CRITICAL RECEPTION

Of Shelley's last three novels, *Lodore* (1835) has attracted the most attention from modern critics and scholars. Often paired with *Falkner*, as a new phase in Shelley's fictional career, the novel presents us with what Shelley herself referred to as 'a tale of the present time' (L, II, 196).[229] The recent attention paid to *Lodore* is important, since it challenges the Victorian-inspired understanding of Shelley's literary career in which her last works are written off as inferior efforts, composed and published merely for financial reasons, evidencing a marked decline in literary strength and political conviction. That negative assessment is still alive in otherwise important work on Shelley published from the 1970s on through to the 1990s. Mary Poovey states: 'the differences between her first novels and her last three are so marked that the seven novels could almost have been written by two different persons.'[230] Jane Blumberg argues that Shelley's last three novels do not 'share the complexity, scope and ambition of the first three.' There is still no dedicated chapter for *Lodore* in important modern collections such as *Mary Shelley in Her Times* and *The Cambridge Companion to Mary Shelley*.[231]

When readers begin to look at the recent reception of *Lodore* a rather striking paradox comes into view. On the one hand, the tradition of reading the novel, not as an aesthetic achievement but simply as a text to be mined for biographical material, appears to reinforce the assessment that Shelley's later works are not in themselves worthy of serious critical engagement. The idea that *Lodore* might be particularly rich in such biographical elements goes back

to what Richard Garnett called 'Professor Dowden's fortunate discovery.'[232] Throughout this study we have recognized the presence
of psycho-biography within Shelley's fictional works. In November
1835, for example, she asked Maria Gisborne if she had read
Lodore and 'If you did read it, did you recognize any of Shelley's
& my early adventures – when we were in danger of being starved
in Switzerland – & could get no dinner at an inn in London?'
(L, II, 261). Throughout this study we have also noted the manner
in which the presence of such biographical elements tends to blind
readers of Shelley's works to the intertextual engagement (political, aesthetic, philosophical) with the works of other writers in
her circle and beyond. Conflation of the latter with the former has
been, without doubt, one of the principal reasons why Shelley's
later fictions have been misinterpreted and undervalued.

We come, then, to the paradox foregrounded by the critical reception of *Lodore*, since, as various modern readers have demonstrated, the novel involves a very explicit and sustained return to
the radical writings of her parents, particularly their work on the
subject of education. Kate Ferguson Ellis describes this feature
with admirable concision when she states: 'the novel takes up
again the thematic concerns of *Frankenstein*: it could be called
Frankenstein without the science.'[233] *Lodore* re-engages in radical
ways with the work on education and gender politics associated
with Godwin and Wollstonecraft. Writing to Charles Ollier at the
end of January 1833, Shelley attempts to describe the main out-
lines of her novel:

> A Mother & Daughter are the heroines – The Mother who after
> safrifising [sic] <u>all</u> to the world at first – afterwards makes sacrifises not
> less entire, for her child – finding all to be Vanity, except the genuine
> affections of the heart. In the daughter I have tried to pourtray in its
> simplicity, & all the beauty I could muster, the <u>devotion</u> of a young
> wife for the husband of her choice – The disasters she goes through
> being described – & their result in awakening her Mother's affection,
> bringing about the conclusion of the tale .... (L, II, 185)

It does not sound particularly radical. When we come to the story
of Lord Lodore's education of his daughter, Ethel, however, we
confront writing which is steeped in the work of Wollstonecraft
and appears to be reiterating her critique of what Shelley's narrator calls the 'sexual education' of daughters by their fathers (Lod,
218). As many of the novel's recent readers have demonstrated,

Fanny Derham is also a character emerging from a profound 'conversation with Wollstonecraft', to employ Lisa Vargo's pertinent phrase.

The paradox I am pointing to is one which is familiar to us: it involves the fact that different readers still appear to find evidence for an assessment of *Lodore* as an essentially conservative novel or as an essentially radical (or at least reformist) novel. If we focus on various aspects of the novel, such as the obvious critique of Lodore's 'sexual education' of Ethel, we can mount an argument which places the novel within the radical tradition of Wollstonecraft's critique of the less than rational manner in which daughters are educated in comparison to sons. Lodore, blasted by his experiences as a young man on the Continent and then in his disastrous marriage to a young woman (barely a 'woman' at sixteen), Cornelia Santerre, whom he had hoped to mould to his paternalistic ideals of a wife, clearly attempts to construct, in his secluded life in the pioneer settlement in the Illinois, a compensatory creature (compliant, obedient, devoted, all sympathy and sentiment) in his daughter, Ethel. The narrator's critique of Lodore's treatment of his daughter rings a distinctly Wollstonecraftian bell:

> It cannot be doubted, but that it were for the happiness of the other sex that she were taught more to rely on and act for herself. But in the cultivation of this feeling, the education of Fitzhenry was lamentably deficient .... She seldom thought, and never acted, for herself. (Lod, 19)

Contrasted to Ethel, the novel provides us with a daughter-figure, Fanny Derham, whose father has given her precisely the kind of Enlightenment education missing in Lodore's approach. The wording of the narrator's comparison between these two young women takes us back to the educational discourse explored in *Frankenstein* (see Lod, 218). Lodore *moulds* and *fashions* his daughter; Derham instructs his, empowering her to develop her own rational judgement and her self-sufficient 'soul'. Ethel is in a sense a creation of Lodore's, his dependent creature; Fanny is a rational subject, who as the novel develops demonstrates the ability not only to think for herself but, crucially, to act when all others seem immobilized by the codes and rules of social manners.

If we focus on the subject of education and gender politics, isolating Ethel and Fanny as the exemplars of conservative and Enlightenment theories and practices respectively, then we can indeed make a good case for the novel as an expression of

Shelley's continued commitment to the reformist politics and philosophies of her parents and husband. The problem comes, however, if we attempt to create a more holistic reading, since a good many other elements of the novel appear far less convincingly reformist. Fanny Derham is at best a secondary character in the novel, someone who is interpolated into and just as quickly taken out of the main picture. Despite the clear critique of her education, the ethical principles Ethel stands for in the novel as a whole, as Shelley's description in her letter to Maria Gisborne suggests, appear to be the product of that 'sexual education'. If Ethel is one of the novel's two main protagonists, if she is in a sense one of the novel's heroines, then her fundamental characteristics of sensibility and reliance on the love of a male other cannot simply be written off as the consequences of a faulty, because feminized education. Similarly, if Cornelia is, as Shelley suggests, the other principal focus of the novel, how are we to assess as anything but a conservative promotion of 'feminine virtue' her narrative of social vanity relinquished in favour of the maternal values of selfless sacrifice? Does not the novel, at its very end, reward Ethel and Cornelia for their selfless devotion to others with ideal marriages to idealized men, whilst simultaneously writing off Fanny Derham as a female Quixote, fascinating within the pages of a novel, but unable to exist in the realities of contemporary upper-class society?[234] The very last words of *Lodore* are dedicated to Fanny, but they are words which suggest that her narrative has no place within this 'tale of the present time.'

Looked at from this wider perspective *Lodore* can indeed appear a rather paradoxical text, promoting a Wollstonecraftian call for a 'Revolution in Female Manners' at the same time that it apparently endorses the bourgeois ideological picture of women as emotional, sensitive, domestic and ultimately dependent creatures. Various critics have responded to such paradoxes by focussing on the manner in which Fanny Derham's life story is deferred (one might say *othered* from the text), for another day and perhaps another novel by, perhaps, another author. These readers suggest that in *Lodore* Shelley could not, ultimately, reconcile her commitment to her mother's social and educational ideas with her own belief in and need for what Mellor calls the ideology of the bourgeois family.[235] Those wishing to endorse such a reading might well feel that support can be gained by the almost universally positive reception *Lodore* gained with contemporary reviewers. As

Sunstein notes: '*Lodore* had more success than any of her novels since *Frankenstein*.'[236] Noel Gerson, summarizing the various reviews, states: '*Lodore* .... created a sensation in its own day, and was hailed as a masterpiece of fiction. The reviewers called it one of the finest novels of the era.'[237] Leigh Hunt called *Lodore* her 'most agreeable work'.[238] He goes on to state: 'though her characters are laid in high life, and she makes the best of the conventionalities, yet she sympathises with the truly great world throughout, not merely the little great world of St. James's.'[239] Hunt is referring here to *Lodore*'s relation to the style and subject matter of the dominant novel form in the late-1820s and 1830s, and he is implying, like many of the novel's other reviewers, that Shelley's *Lodore* presents a version of that generic form that is aesthetically and ideologically superior to the majority of its contemporary examples. It is by reminding ourselves of the specific literary contexts within which Shelley produced her novel that we can begin to move beyond the apparent paradoxes we have been discussing here.

II. TALES OF FASHIONABLE LIFE

We can only come to an adequate understanding and appreciation of *Lodore* by considering its relationship to kinds of novels which gained popularity in the later 1820s and 1830s.[240] The criticism of the novel of this period, positioned between the Romantic and the Victorian eras, has traditionally been rather neglected and still generates polarized views. Gary Kelly, for example, sees great cultural and political importance, along with possibilities for social critique, in the form William Hazlitt humorously labelled 'silver-fork novels', a form also satirized by Carlyle and Thackeray.[241] Michael Wheeler, on the other hand, states: 'Carlyle can perhaps be forgiven for dismissing most of the fiction of the 1830s and early 1840s as inferior stuff, for, apart from the work of Dickens and Thackeray, this was a period of fads and fashions rather than of major developments in the novel'.[242]

Shelley knew many of the leading exponents of the 'silver-fork' novel or 'novel of fashionable life', including Mrs Catherine Gore, Benjamin Disraeli and Edward Bulwer, and although she came to distrust him as a man, it is clear that Bulwer's novels were a major influence on her in this period (see L, II, 80, 155, 199, 169n, 210).

In a letter to Ollier, in which she discusses the completed *Lodore*, Shelley writes in anticipation of what would become Bulwer's most famous novel, *The Last Days of Pompeii* (1834): 'Is Mr Bulwer's book out – can you so infinitely favor me as to lend me that – You know I admire & delight in his novels beyond all others – There is none comparable to them' (L, II., 207). Richard Cronin, in his extended discussion of Bulwer's fiction as an influence on *Lodore*, spells out the manner in which Bulwer's novels of the 1820s and early 1830s demonstrate a profound engagement with the novels of Godwin. Bulwer's place in the development of the 'Newgate novel', such as *Paul Clifford* (1830) and *Eugene Aram* (1831), clearly have their novelistic origins in *Caleb Williams* and *St. Leon*. Cronin even suggests that Bulwer's *Falkland* (1827), in which the Godwinian anti-hero persuades a married woman to elope with him only to cause her death, may have influenced the plot of Shelley's last novel, *Falkner*. What is important to note here is that Bulwer distanced his own work from the more faddish 'dandiacal' variety of novels prevalent in the period, and that his works also display a distinct relation to Shelley's own previous novels, *Frankenstein* in particular.[243] It is not just Godwin that Bulwer is responding to in this period. In *Pelham* (1828), for example, Bulwer's most famous 'silver-fork novel', the Godwinian influence is undeniable: the plot revolves around Henry Pelham's suspicion that the socially honoured and respected Reginald Glanville has in fact murdered a man named Tyrrel. Bulwer would have expected his readers to make the link to *Caleb Williams*. When we also note that the main piece of evidence in the mystery involves a miniature portrait of Glanville's lost love, retrieved by Pelham at the scene of the murder, it is just as reasonable to suppose an overt allusion to *Frankenstein*.

Cronin argues that what links novels such as *Lodore* and *Pelham* is their 'hybrid' quality, by which he means that they mix the long established sentimental novel with a newer form (called by some 'silver fork novels' or 'novels of fashionable life') in which the codes and conventions dominating aristocratic life are described at the same time they are opened to satirical commentary. Such novels, Cronin argues, develop morally ambiguous heroes, such as Pelham and Lord Lodore (even Cornelia fits the bill), which allow Bulwer and Shelley to escape 'from one of the more inhibiting conventional constraints of the novel, its placing of its characters within a single hierarchy of moral judgement.'[244] On this level one could respond that all Cronin is doing is to display the fact that

both novelists were influenced by Godwin's fundamental contribution to the development of the novel, the ethically ambiguous,
psychologically complex protagonist. Cronin's argument about the
narrative style of what he calls 'hybrid' fiction is perhaps more
important for Bulwer's influence on *Lodore*. Cronin sees a merging,
within the narrative voice of *Pelham* and *Lodore*, of a prose style
that is sentimental and one he calls 'styptic', by which he refers
to an astringent wit at the expense of the aristocratic lives being
described. Certainly, *Pelham* is a novel we could describe as double-
voiced.[245] Henry Pelham is a shallow observer and satirist of an
aristocratic society he exists within and yet which he appears to
despise, and thus, particularly as the narrative develops, his very
refusal to take that society seriously opens the possibility for genuine
sentiment and feeling for others. Cronin's attempts to demonstrate
a similar utilization of satirical wit in *Lodore* is inevitably rather
constrained, since Shelley is a very different writer from Bulwer.
However, the argument about 'hybridity' or what I want to call
double-voicedness, is crucial.

Lodore is a novel steeped in the political, social and philosophical
ideas which dominate Shelley's earlier fictional texts. It is, in that
sense, still recognizably 'Romantic.' It is also a novel which utilizes the generic forms popular at the time, in particular the narrative description of aristocratic and fashionable London life. There
is little doubt that Shelley was attempting to exploit the financial
possibilities of a popular novelistic sub-genre at a time in which a
dramatic down-turn in the emergent book industry threatened the
livelihood of all authors living by their pen, a fact famously
demonstrated by the fate of Walter Scott.[246] *Lodore*, however, is
also a novel which marries its form with its content. If it is a novel
designed to make money (L, II, 184, 280, 285), *Lodore* is also, as
Stafford suggests, 'a book preoccupied with money – and especially with the difficulties arising for those who find themselves
suddenly bereft of financial support.'[247] Cronin states: '*Lodore* is the
only novel by Shelley that fully recognizes that the study of human
personality is inseparable from an understanding of economics.'[248]
The 'silver-fork' novel is also a form which constructs itself
around the codes and conventions of aristocratic social relations
(Bulwer's favoured figure is '*ton*', a word which literally means
'tone' but which is best translated as 'style'). Shelley's novel is about
social relations and it utilizes the form of the 'fashionable novel'
to reiterate the need in society for what Godwin alternatively

called 'confidence' or 'sincerity'. If we add to this the classic 'silver-fork' plot-device of inheritance, another of *Lodore*'s principal subjects, then we have begun to recognize the opportunities presented to Shelley by the popular novel of this period. Money, economics (in all senses of the term), social relations (public and private), inheritance, legacy, or the influence of the past on the present, these are both the thematic subjects and the generic, narrative forms of *Lodore*.

In her 1830 review of Godwin's *Cloudesley*, Shelley draws an explicit comparison between the fiction of Bulwer and that of her father. Whilst praising Bulwer's novels, she also complains that Bulwer ultimately 'gives us ... himself, his experience, his opinions, his emotions.' In contrast to that dominance of authorial voice over subject matter and form, Shelley's description of Godwin's narrative art is founded on the structural, psychological and ultimately the ethical unity of his novels (Shelley, *Novels*, II, 201–9). Shelley writes of *Cloudesley*: 'We will not mar its interest by a lame abridgement. It is the peculiar excellence of Mr Godwin's writing, that there is not a word too much, and curtailment of the narrative would be like displaying the unfilled-up outline of beauty: we might feel that it was there, and yet remain in ignorance of its peculiar features' (206). The plot of *Cloudesley* cannot be paraphrased. To paraphrase Godwin's novel would be to destroy its 'beauty' but also, as Shelley well knows, its educative, enlightening mission. There is a unity (structural, ethical) to Godwin's novels which can only be realized by and in the mind of the reader as she reads and, perhaps more significantly, re-reads. We can say the same for *Lodore*, in that its utilization of the 'silver-fork' or 'novel of fashionable life' cannot be flattened out into a two-dimensional map of themes and chronological events. As if to foreground this fact, the narrative account of Cornelia's 'revelation' at the end of the novel, as Lionel Verney's had been before, is figured through the reading of a map: 'Swift, as if a map had been unrolled before her, the picture of her own passed life was retraced in her mind', 'Her ideas became more consecutive, though not less rapid and imperious. She drew forth in prospect, as it were, a map of what was to be done, and the results. Her mind became fixed, and sensations of ineffable pleasure accompanied her reveries. She was resolved to sacrifice every thing to her daughter' (Lod, 250, 252).

Lodore is a novel which, in the complexity of its emplotment and its double-voicedness, displays the influence of the Godwinian novel, in that far from being a didactic announcement of political and social points, it takes the reader through a non-consecutive experience of multiple interpretations which almost inevitably involve or, better say, 'plunge' that reader into the very issues (social prejudice and misinterpretation, an ethics grounded in economic considerations rather than authentic sentiment and love) which the novel ultimately allows its surviving characters to resolve. In the 'silver-fork novel' Shelley found a novelistic form well suited to her Godwin-inspired fictional practice in which, if the reader is willing, the surface realities of dominant social ideology give way, eventually, to a deeper more rational understanding and socio-political vision. Fiona Stafford, in the most comprehensive account of *Lodore*'s connection to the period of the Great Reform Act (passed during the period in which it was composed), has demonstrated how minutely Shelley's novel engages with the politics of her day: she states that we can call *Lodore* 'in part, at least …. an allegory of the Reform Movement.'[249] We have already seen, in the previous chapter, how engaged with questions of reform and political change Shelley was in the first few years of the 1830s. My argument in this chapter will be that *Lodore*'s political 'allegory' also exists on the level of its narrative structure and presentation.

III.   CIRCLES AND RETURNS

The complex, circular structure of the plot of *Lodore* is far more intimately connected to the novel's ultimate meaning than most critics and scholars have recognized. An excellent account is to be found in John Williams's critical biography, however. Williams states, with some accuracy: 'Shelley had used a circular strategy before, but never with this degree of sophistication; it becomes the key to the way in which she challenges orthodox expectations of style and plot with an impressive input of irony.'[250] The circular structure of *Lodore*'s plot is in fact the 'key' to any adequate understanding of the novel. My account, of course, cannot avoid being in some respects 'a lame abridgement.' There is no substitute for the experience of reading and indeed re-reading *Lodore*.

We begin, in the first chapter of Volume I, with the lonely Elizabeth (sister of Henry Fitzhenry, Lord Lodore), and the enigma of Lodore's twelve year absence from England and the social world. The opening paragraphs read very much like a 'tale of fashionable life', the absentee aristocratic landlord of Longfield contrasted to the simple villagers 'scarcely aware of the kind of desert in which they are placed' (Lod, 5).[251] The mysterious absence of Lord Lodore is heightened by the periodic newspaper accounts ('its lists of fashionable arrivals and fashionable parties') of his wife in London society, and the ironic description of Longfield village life cannot but imply some hidden secret of a scandalous and rather dramatic nature. The villagers are said to vaguely remember a visit of Lady Lodore, years back: 'She had appeared indeed but as a vision – a creature from another sphere, hastily gazing on an unknown world, and lost before they could mark more than that void came again, and she was gone' (Lod, 7–8). Chapter Two circles back some twelve years to the arrival of 'an English gentleman' (Lod, 9), clearly Lodore, 'at a settlement in the district of the Illinois in North America.' Lodore is described as a Byronic character, tormented by some secret event from the past, but slowly learning to curb his inner passions, if not his distaste for society, through his relationship with his young daughter.

In the next five chapters we are presented with the relationship between Lodore and Ethel, including the narrative critique of his educational theories. Ethel is described in a language which appears to present an exaggerated ideal of feminine sentiment: 'A creature half poetry, half love .... an enthusiastic being, who could give her life away for the sake of another, and yet who honoured herself as a consecrated thing reserved for one worship alone' (Lod, 18). This language is not only undercut by the allusions to Wollstonecraft's work ('Fitzhenry drew his chief ideas from Milton's Eve'), but also by the kind of 'styptic' irony noted by Cronin: 'Not being able to judge by comparison, Ethel was unaware of the peculiarity of her good fortune in possessing such a father. But she loved him entirely ....' (Lod, 20). The 'but' in that second sentence seems to clinch the ironic tone of the narrator's description of Ethel's condition. However, what the reader is not yet aware of is that Ethel's ability to 'give her life away' will, as the novel progresses, not only remain an aspect of an ironized paternalistic mode of education and upbringing but will also connect up to the over-riding ethical positives of the novel. Time and time again in the later parts of the novel, concerned with her trials and tribulations in her economically impecunious marriage with Edward Villiers, the narrator comes back to Ethel's ability to 'give herself away' and her consequent lack of concern over their lack of financial security. Finally, of course, it is the revelatory insight of Ethel's mother, that she in fact must 'give herself away' for the sake of her child, that will form the novel's ethical apogee and allow for the ultimate resolution of the various main characters and plots. Various image patterns are established around Ethel in this section, including the figure of 'loving in a desert', negatively established, for example, by the epigram from Charles Paul de Kock which opens chapter four: 'Les deserts sont faits pour les amants, mais l'amour ne se fait pas aux deserts' (Lod, 20).[252] After Lodore has experienced a significant intertextual moment of existential crisis with the Shelleyan question, 'How long will you be at peace?' (Lod, 21),[253] and after the answer arrives in the shape of Whitelock, Ethel's first suitor (she is 'scarcely fifteen' [Lod, 25]), Lodore, in his Byronic spontaneity, decides to quit the Illinois and return to England (Lod, 27).

Volume I, having established its initial scenarios, now moves into a series of interweaving chronological turns or re-turns. In chapters 5 and 6 we are taken through Lodore's aristocratic upbringing, his education in Eton and then Oxford, and his many years spent on the Continent in thrall to an unnamed mistress, once again marking him out as a character with undoubted Byronic credentials.[254] Between Chapters 7 and 12 we are presented with the meeting, nuptials and disastrous breakdown of the marriage between Lodore and Cornelia Santerre. To discuss in isolation the relationship between Lodore and Cornelia, and her scheming mother, Lady Santerre, is insufficient, since the reader is forced to register a host of parallels and resonances between this relationship, a decade and a half in the past, and the relationship we have just observed between Lodore and Ethel. Cornelia, for example, is only sixteen on the day she marries Lodore, thus significantly intensifying the impression that he seeks compensation in the daughter for what he did not find in his child-bride. The critical point about the marriage of Cornelia and Lodore, and again this is read in comparison to the relationship between father and daughter, is that there appears no opportunity for the establishment of confidence or sincerity. The extreme youth of Cornelia, and the ever present influence of her mother, militate against any establishment of sympathetic habits between husband and wife. Lodore's motives for marrying Cornelia, in the first place, are also squarely ironized by the narrator: 'Lord Lodore had just emancipated himself from

LODORE 149

the influence, which had become the most grievous slavery, from the moment it had ceased to be a voluntary servitude. He had broken the ties that had so long held him .... He entertained a vague wish to marry, and to marry one whom his judgment, rather than love, should select; – an unwise purpose, good in theory, but very defective in practice' (Lod, 36–7).

Lodore's past 'influence' does not remain in the past, however. In this novel, past influences inevitably return and decisively affect the present. Countess Lyzinski and her son Count Casimir (who is 'pretty exactly the same age' as Cornelia) enter into the unhappy world of Lodore and Cornelia, and as the latter inevitably flirts with Casimir, Lodore's Byronic temper leads him to strike Casimir, who is, as readers might have suspected, his son. Confessing all to a terrified Cornelia, Lodore states that they must flee England rather than allow the unnatural possibility of a duel between a father and his unwitting son. Cornelia rushes to the sanctuary of her mother, and Lodore, convincing himself of the ethical right-ness of his actions, flees England with his baby daughter. The transition, forward in time, between Chapters 13 and the section beginning with Chapter 14, gives us the open warfare between Cornelia (encouraged by her mother, Lady Santerre) and the fleeing Lodore, and, twelve years later, the returning Lodore imagining possibilities for a reunion not only of Cornelia and her child but of Cornelia and himself. We return to Lodore and his daughter, travelling toward the east coast of North America, with a sense that mysteries have been solved, and, with the introduction of the daughter of Lodore's childhood friend, Fanny Derham, a sense that the door to the future for these characters is opening and freeing them (and us) from the consequences of a repetitious series of past actions. Nothing could be further from the truth. At a dinner given by their hostess, Mrs Greville, a republican-minded American joins them. He is a man whom Lodore remembers to have been at the fateful dinner at the Russian Ambassador's twelve years previously, the night on which he had struck Count Casimir. The American tells the story of that night, purposefully goading Lodore for his aristocratic pride, and the consequence is a literal return: 'The words were still on the man's lips when a blow, sudden and unexpected, extended him on the floor' (Lod, 90). This time a duel is not counter to the natural ties of family, and assisted by a young man named Villiers, Lodore meets Mr Hatfield in combat and dies, a victim of his own rash temper.

Readers of Godwin's *Caleb Williams* will no doubt have noticed the strong intertextual return involved in this scenario. In Godwin's novel, a violent act (Falkland's murder of Tyrrel) seems connected to a number of other moments of violence and madness (the unlucky first blow of the accused man; Caleb's famous moment of madness in opening the iron chest; Tyrrel's inadvertent 'murder' of his niece, Emily Melville). As Falkland says: 'All are but links in one chain' (Godwin, *Novels*, III, 122). Lodore's repetition of a public blow not only causes his demise, it links Shelley's novel in an intertextual network, returning its readers to Godwin's diagnosis of a social system in which violence breeds violence, a system symbolized by an aristocratic code of honour shared by Falkland and his literary repetition, Lord Lodore.

Immediately before the catastrophe of the blow and subsequent duel occur, the narrator spells out the issues involved: 'A strange distortion of vision blinded this unfortunate man to the truth, which experience so perpetually teaches us, that the consequences of our actions *never die*' (Lod, 87). These narrative comments are made in the context of Lodore's forgetting of the reasons that exiled him and his unfounded belief that resolutions and reconciliations can be made. The comments appear to stand for the novel's message as a whole, in fact, since the consequences of Lodore's demise, only a few pages further on, dominate everything that follows. Lodore, in the build up to the duel, forgets about the will he had made in anger, twelve years previously, which is 'in absolute contradiction to the wishes and feelings in which Lord Lodore died'; the narrator comments, again ironically: 'so true had his prognostic been, that he had no power beyond the grave' (Lod, 96). Lodore's will allows Cornelia a certain annual income (enough to maintain her in her accustomed life) 'on the express condition, that she should not interfere with, nor even see, her child' (Lod, 96). The conditions of Lodore's will dominate the events of the second and third volumes, providing, on the surface level, what Hunt calls the 'conventionalities' of the 'fashionable novel', in other words a plot revolving around questions of financial legacy and inheritance. However, having trained ourselves somewhat in the circular returns and trans-temporal patterns and parallels which structure Volume I, we can begin to see how Shelley's novel attempts to train its readers' eyes beyond a simple anticipation of generic resolution through marriage and economic settlement.

IV. THE BEAUTIFUL WIDOW

There is a moment, in the third chapter of Volume II, which can be used as something of a meta-figure for the novel as a whole. Ethel and Lodore travel from the Illinois towards the west coast, Lodore having determined to return and reconcile himself with Cornelia and English society. At the same time, Edward Villiers and his cousin, Horatio Saville, travel in the opposite direction in search of Lodore. Horatio and Cornelia have fallen in love, and yet they cannot unite since (a fact the circular narrative of *Lodore* can make us forget) she is still a married woman. Horatio's desire is to serve Cornelia by persuading Lodore to restore Ethel to her; the importance of the scene, however, is simply in its physical representation of paths crossed and significant meetings missed. The narrator writes: 'the cousins crossed the Atlantic and arrived at New York. Thence they proceeded to the west of America, and passing Lodore and his daughter on the road without knowing it, arrived at the Illinois after their departure' (Lod, 121). We might call this crossing of paths but missing of people chiastic, and it can signify the manner in which relationships in *Lodore* appear doomed to a kind of miscognition and ultimately a crossing or reversing of authentic destinies and destinations.[255] This has already been the case with Cornelia and Lodore. By this early stage of Volume II Horatio and Cornelia seem doomed to repeat the same cycle, in which the 'cobweb'-like system of social relations disallows the possibility for the establishment of confidence and sincerity, the foundations upon which, as the narrator frequently explains, all genuine relationships must be built (see, for example, Lod, 198).

The death of Lodore does not bring Cornelia and Horatio together; the mis-figurings of the society around them and their own inability to interpret each other mean that they are unable to act upon their true natures and desires, impotent to defend themselves against social misinterpretations. Horatio, believing false reports that Cornelia is engaged to a Marquess, leaves England and in Italy marries Clorinda, a character most readers associate with the figure of Emilia Viviani. In marrying Clorinda, Horatio adds another repetition to the pattern of marriages and love relations destroyed by lack of the possibility of confidence. The relationship between Cornelia and Ethel is one in which, because of Lodore's will and Elizabeth's desire to honour her brother's anachronistic wishes, the chiastic non-coincidence of their lives seems legally determined. The moving set pieces in the Opera and House of Parliament, in which Ethel's and Cornelia's paths momentarily cross, only appear to deepen the sense that they are destined to live apart, divided by a world in which appearances dominate and distort natural inclinations.

Ethel and Edward eventually marry, only to be left bankrupt by his gambling and hopelessly decadent father. It appears that another love relationship is doomed to collapse on the rocks of a social system in which gender-relations are fragile and tenuous at best, and in which love is inevitably defeated by economic and social factors. To Shelley's first readers, it might have appeared that a conventional dénouement in which marriage is underpinned by the inheritance (often unexpected) of financial security is receding rather than approaching the longer the novel proceeds. As Edward struggles to deal with his inherited sense of the shame of debt and dependence on others, it appears that Shelley is determined to return devastation on every attempt at establishing a loving union. Of course, the happy ending is secured in *Lodore* by a device which might, when abstracted, appear eminently conservative and conventional. We will see, however, for readers attuned to the double-voicedness of the novel, how explicitly that ending is undermined by the novel's conclusion.

As the novel's circular narrative pattern reinforces the repetition (the serial return) of misinterpretation, misunderstanding and the defeat of confidence, all roads begin to lead towards Cornelia. The 1865 and 1893 American editions of the novel altered the title to *The Beautiful Widow*, thus indicating the centrality of Cornelia's character.[256] Charlene E. Bunnell states: 'the central figure is Cornelia, whose story interconnects with the lives of all others and most explicitly demonstrates the "Vanity" and hypocrisy of social expectations and manners.'[257] Bunnell is not alone in reading Cornelia as an exemplum of social vanity and pride. Mellor, to take another example, writes that 'Lady Lodore's belated concern for Ethel, after twenty years of separation, rings hollowly.'[258] We need to go back to Shelley's description of her novel to Ollier and to ask the following question: in stating that Cornelia sacrifices 'all to the world at first', is Shelley suggesting that her heroine worships ('buys into') the world of 'fashionable' values? or does she mean that Cornelia is a victim of aristocratic society's codes and 'conventionalities'? *Lodore* changes utterly as a novel depending on the answer we give to that question.

Instead of immediately attempting to answer the question, we need to note that it is something that all the novel's characters are forced to ask and ultimately answer. Cornelia is a woman who must be read (interpreted) by everyone who comes into contact with her; she is a radically inscrutable text, an enigmatic figure to say the least. The last section of the narrative, of course, presents us with a literal search for Cornelia, as if the novel-long difficulty of interpreting her character has finally been literalized into a physical, geographical quest. Commenting on the difficulties of reading Cornelia for Ethel, the narrator states: 'Whenever she saw Lady Lodore, which was rarely, and at a distance, she gazed earnestly upon her, and tried to read within her soul, whether Villiers was right, and her mother happy. The shining, uniform outside of a woman of fashion baffled her endeavours without convincing her' (Lod, 178). These lines are written as a prelude to the brief encounter in the Opera House, which begins with Ethel watching her mother receiving a 'succession of visitors' as the newly installed gas-lights of the King's Theatre appear to artificially distort the beauty of Cornelia's face. The scene leads up to the extremely affective moment in which Cornelia fixes her daughter's unfastened ear-ring (Lod, 179). It is a central scene in the novel, allowing a brief, evanescent contact between mother and daughter, before the restoration of social order, which appears to generate a repetitive history in which paths are crossed and destinations missed, identities mis-figured and mal-formed, and genuine affection transformed into its negative through misunderstandings, misrepresentations, and misinterpretations.

Edward Villiers interprets Cornelia as an inveterate creature of society. Elizabeth, who influences him in his reading of Cornelia, goes further and views her as practically criminal in her past actions and present social position. Horatio worships her and as a consequence of that devotion mistakes her real character and actual desires: 'He saw in Cornelia a beautiful creation, to admire and adore; but he was slow to perceive the tenderness of soul, which her disposition made her anxious to conceal, and he was conscious of no qualities in himself that could entitle him to a place in her affections' (Lod, 124). These lines come just before Horatio leaves England: within two pages he has married Clorinda. The tragedy, however, is that Horatio does not understand that he has completely misread Cornelia's 'wishes.'

For all the novel's major characters and for the reader, the challenge of reading Cornelia presents the most profoundly double-voiced aspect of the novel. The narrator time and again describes Cornelia as a woman whose defining 'disposition' is pride and the assertion of power over others; the novel slowly demonstrates, however, that her social identity is constructed out of necessity and a laudable will to survive. A good example comes in the narrator's comments on the passage just cited:

> There was no moment of her life in which Cornelia did not fully appreciate her lover's value, and her own good fortune in having inspired him with a serious and faithful attachment. But she imagined that this must be known and acknowledged; and that to ask any demonstration of gratitude, was ungenerous and tyrannical. An untaught girl could not have acted with more levity and wilfulness. (Lod, 125)

The last sentence is, of course, crucial. Cornelia makes all the wrong moves in her relationship with Horatio. She acts like 'a spoiled Beauty' and leaves him little to interpret positively. And yet, there are few characters in Shelley's fiction who better demonstrate the veracity of Godwin's assertion that circumstances create character. Cornelia, when Lodore marries her on her sixteenth birthday, is an 'untaught girl' requiring an education beyond her mother's Machiavellian tutorship in how to catch a husband. The narrator states: 'And here his error began; he had married one so young, that her education, even if its foundation had been good, required finishing, and who as it was, had every thing to learn' (Lod, 45). Lodore abandons Cornelia in as 'untaught' a state as he had found her. She lives for twelve years, a married woman mysteriously *sans* husband, in a society in which appearances and 'conventionalities' are everything. After Lodore's death she is, for reasons unknown to those around her, denied access to her daughter. Throughout all these stages, she has no access to education, save for the often over-rated 'school of life.' There are times in which, balancing the negative descriptions of her 'disposition', the narrator quite explicitly lays out the question of survival for Cornelia in her social situation:

> Cornelia had every motive a woman could have for guarding her conduct from reproach. She lived in the midst of polished society, and was thoroughly imbued with its maxims and laws. She witnessed the downfall of several, as young and lovely as herself, and heard the sarcasms and beheld the sneers which were heaped as a tomb above their buried fame. She had vowed to herself never to become one of these. (Lod, 116)

Cornelia's 'pride' is a character fault; it is also a wholly understandable and necessary defence against a society which will bury her alive if she makes a single wrong move. Katherine Hill-Miller argues that

'Shelley shapes the reader's sympathies in favour of Cornelia .... and creates empathy for her, even in her unregenerate state, by explaining her motivations or the extenuating circumstances of her situation.'[259] Even here, with such an insightful comment on the manner in which the novel works, the word 'unregenerate' suggests that Hill-Miller has fallen into the trap of judging Cornelia by appearances only. Shelley does not so much 'shape the reader's sympathies' as leave open the possibility that readers might recognize for themselves who and what Cornelia really is and could become given the opportunity. When readers do make that interpretive leap beyond the social sur-face they perform a break in the repetitive cycle of misreading and misrepresentation which is equivalent to interpretively seeing beyond the veneer of the 'novel of fashionable life' with all its 'conventional-ities.' Cornelia's heroic 'sacrifice' is, for the sake of her daughter, to herself walk out of that fashionable world into what she thinks will be poverty, anonymity and, within a few years, death. Shelley spends considerable time making sure that readers understand quite how heroic Cornelia's actions are. But the act itself is a break with the cyclical pattern of misinterpretation and mis-figuring which has dominated the novel until this point.

It is a common move, amongst readers of the novel, to give credit for Cornelia's 'revelation' and apparent ethical conversion to the actions of Fanny. Whilst all other characters appear locked into their social and gender positions, Fanny, with her Stoic philosophy and transcendence of social ideology, is, to employ Hill-Miller's account 'the only character who, seeing to the bottom of Cornelia's heart, guesses the motherly devotion and generosity that lie there.'[260] In deciding to inform Cornelia of the situation of her daughter, faith-fully sharing the house-prison of her husband, Fanny also appears to be the one character who has successfully read Cornelia's character. We need to remember, however, that it is actually Ethel's unswerv-ing love and devotion to her husband that creates the momentous insight (or 'break') in Cornelia's mind. The effect of seeing Ethel with her husband in their squalid house-prison is described, signi-ficantly, in terms of a straightening out of thought and through images of navigation and map-reading noted earlier. The narrator states: 'Her ideas became more consecutive, though not less rapid and imperious.' Continuing: 'Yet when she looked back, a new light shone on the tedious maze in which she had been lost; a light – and she blessed it – that showed her a pathway out of tempest and con-fusion into serenity and peace' (Lod, 252, 253).

The break with the cyclical, repetitious pattern of social figuration involves all three of the novel's central female characters, each of whom appear to possess attributes we might trace back to the novel's author, a woman who in her relation to her lost husband displayed the sensibility and fidelity of Ethel, who in her relationship with her son demonstrated the self-sacrificing qualities of Cornelia, and who, in her continued commitment to study and writing, evidenced the philosophical and scholarly qualities of a Fanny Derham. The irony is that in heroically stepping out of the generic confines of the 'silver-fork' novel Cornelia makes possible a conventional ending for everyone save Fanny. To understand the unity and indeed the political and social resonances of *Lodore* we have to come to an understanding of how the break with repetitive cycles (of violence, of misreading, of social figuration) relates to the novel's conclusion.

V.   BEYOND THE NOVEL

The double-voiced approach Shelley takes to generic form in *Lodore* is nowhere more dramatically demonstrated than in the novel's 'Conclusion.' The opening sentence is enough to signal the fact that a socially recognizable form has been utilized and is now being dispensed with: 'Thus the tale of "Lodore" is ended' (Lod, 311). The epigram from Ford's *The Lady's Trial* ('None, I trust,/ Repines at these delights, they are free and harmless:/ After distress at sea, the dangers o'er,/ Safety and welcomes better taste ashore') appears an apology for the quick-fire round-up of the final destinations of Cornelia and Horatio, Edward and Ethel, and even Elizabeth, who now 'strange to say … loves [Cornelia] even more than she loves Ethel' (Lod, 312). Any reader unaware of Shelley's double-voiced, ironic use of the novel of 'fashionable life' will in all probability find this conclusion to be proof positive of the novel's conservative qualities. Those who are aware of that aspect of *Lodore* will be alert to the signal Shelley provides, the idea of having fulfilled a generic contract ('duty') marking the conclusion of her ventriloquism of popular form: 'Thus we have done our duty, in bringing under view, in a brief summary, the little that there is to tell of the personages who formed the drama of this tale' (Lod, 313).

The novel ends with a long paragraph devoted to Fanny Derham's untold life-story. The narrator states that 'it is not in a few tame lines that we can revert to the varied fate of Fanny Derham' (Lod, 313).

Having just described her other characters' lives 'in a few tame lines', the exclusion of Fanny from the generic confines of the novel of 'fashionable life' appears to give added significance, both aesthetically and politically, to her character. Even Fanny's name, as Vargo has suggested, in reminding us of a series of women from the life of Shelley and her mother (Fanny Blood, Fanny Imlay, Fanny Wright), appears to mark her out as a figure of peculiar meaning, a character who cannot be contained within fictional perimeters.[261] Vargo has also argued for a Wollstonecraft-inspired reading of Fanny and Ethel in which the former represents reason and the latter sensibility, a reading which gains a good deal of support from the narrator's own comparison of the two daughter-figures (Lod, 218). Despite their very significant differences 'one quality created a good deal of similarity between them. There was in both a total absence of every factitious sentiment. They acted from their own hearts – from their own sense of right, without the intervention of worldly considerations' (Lod, 219).

The question that has been posed by various readers, however, is whether Shelley's othering of Fanny from the conclusion of her novel suggests a belief either in the untimeliness of the idea of a rational, independent, scholarly woman like Fanny or even an inability on Shelley's part to imagine a social and aesthetic integration for such a woman? Does Fanny, like Euthanasia before her, have to wait for her time to come, in some unspecified future? Mellor's comment is worth quoting here: 'Although a minor character, Fanny Derham leaps off the pages of *Lodore* simply because she doesn't fit into the ideology of the family overtly endorsed in the novel.'[262] In this reading, Fanny's philosophic rationalism means that at the end of the novel she quite literally leaps off the pages of the novel, into a future life beyond the novel's ideological and aesthetic field of representation. Such a reading as Mellor's, however, does not attend to the novel's double-voiced relation to the 'ideology of the family' and its representation in popular novelistic forms. Modulating into a present-tense and even a future-tense account of her life beyond the novel, the narrator explains how Fanny will inevitably be hurt and let down by the less rational, ethically weak human beings around her, before concluding:

> What the events are, that have already diversified her existence, cannot now be recounted; and it would require the gift of prophecy to foretell the conclusion. In after times these may be told, and the life of Fanny Derham be presented as a useful lesson, at once to teach what goodness

and genius can achieve in palliating the woes of life, and to encourage those, who would in any way imitate her, by an example of calumny refuted by patience, errors rectified by charity, and the passions of our nature purified and ennobled by an undeviating observance of those moral laws on which all human excellence is founded – a love of truth in ourselves, and a sincere sympathy with our fellow-creatures. (Lod, 313)

On one level this ending can be read as an even more intense and personal apologia for Shelley's own post-1822 life than the history of Katherine at the conclusion of *Perkin Warbeck*. Shelley, a scholarly, philosophical woman, outside of the economic circuit of marriage, devastated by the loss of loved ones and by the betrayal of others (especially Jane Williams), could be said to be a woman whose life literally remains unpresentable, due to the paternalistic bar placed on that narrative by her aging father-in-law, Sir Timothy Shelley. As Webster-Garrett puts it: 'It may be that the narrator cannot tell us Fanny's future because the narrator is, in fact, Fanny herself.'[263]

The question facing us here, however, is what Fanny's exclusion from the novel's series of resolutions tells us about its overall structure, its aesthetic and ideological design. Fanny is a female character whose life cannot be contained within the confines of the kind of novel which concludes in marriage. Yet the manner in which the narrator races over the histories of its various matrimonial resolutions reminds us that *Lodore* is a novel which writes against the grain of the 'conventionalities' of the marriage-plot. For the reader who has seriously engaged with *Lodore*'s narrative reversibilities and double-voicedness, the exterior world into which Fanny finally disappears is no novelty; in fact, it has been present, as the other side of the 'tale of fashionable life', throughout the novel. The stories of all three female characters, despite their different relations to the generic form within which we confront them, have all tended towards the same ethical imperatives, stated in the last words of the conclusion ('a love of truth in ourselves, and a sincere sympathy with out fellow-creatures'). This ending, interestingly, reiterates the concluding lines of Shelley's review of *Cloudesley*, and in that repetition reinforces the connection Shelley's fiction would make with a society undergoing significant political and cultural change: 'let out hearts exult,' Shelley writes of her ageing father, 'when one of the wisest men of this or any age tells us, that "the true key of the universe is love"' (Shelley, *Novels*, II, 209).

Lodore exploits the conventions of the popular novel of the day in order to reiterate a characteristic message of her literary and familial circle. If the underlying hope and desire in *Caleb Williams*, *The Wrongs of Woman, or Maria* and *Prometheus Unbound*, even Byron's *Childe Harold*, is that the nightmarish cyclical repetitiveness of history can be broken, or at least re-routed towards a better, more human destiny, then *Lodore* stands as a proto-Victorian reiteration of that hope. Despite their differing destinies and destinations, Ethel, Cornelia and Fanny all contribute to the novel's reaffirmation of that hope of reform. The novel, in fact, pushing its doubleness and reversibility to the very end, presents us with a break in cyclical history contained within the narrative itself (Cornelia's sacrifice, the reunion of mother and daughter) and another break leading us outside of that narrative (Fanny's untold future story). The othering of Fanny's future history serves ultimately to return us to the double-voiced, reversible nature of the novel it concludes.

7

Falkner, A Novel

I. A FAVOURITE NOVEL

Falkner (1837), Shelley's last novel, has traditionally been read alongside *Lodore*, frequently as a rather inferior version of the same kind of 'tale of fashionable life', focussed, as was the previous novel, on the intense relationship between a father and daughter estranged from the mainstream of society. The association drawn between *Lodore* and *Falkner* appears confirmed by the fact that composition of the latter novel was suggested by Shelley's publishers, on the strength of the success of *Lodore* (L, II, 260). In January 1836 she was writing to Charles Ollier about the novel that would become *Falkner*, stating: 'It is in the style of Lodore, but the story more interesting & even, I should think, more popular' (L, II, 263). Making the same points to Ollier in another letter, written in March of 1836, Shelley talks about how easily *Falkner* came to her: 'I wrote with a rapidity I had never done before' (L, II, 267). In the end, Shelley published *Falkner* with a rival publishing firm, Saunders and Otley, at the beginning of 1837, after what she described to Ollier as a delay caused by ill health (L, II, 280). In fact, more than the ill health of the summer of 1835 had delayed the completion of her novel, since her good friends John and Maria Gisborne had died in early 1836 and in that same period Shelley had nursed her father in his last illness. Godwin died on 27 March 1836. In a journal entry of June 1836, Shelley reflects on the tragic circumstances of what promised to be one of her most pleasurable writing experiences: 'I am now writing a novel 'Falkner' – My best it will be – I believe' (J, 548). She maintained this opinion after publication, despite contrary responses from

Trelawny and Jane Williams, in a letter of April 1837 to Leigh Hunt: 'for myself I own it is a favourite of mine' (L, II, 285).

Given Shelley's estimation of what was to be her last novel, it is somewhat surprising that so little attention has been paid to *Falkner* in the modern re-evaluation of her literary oeuvre. There is still no readily available paperback edition, no scholarly edition along the lines of the Broadview Press editions of *Frankenstein*, *Valperga*, *The Last Man* and *Lodore*, and the reader will find very few discussions of the novel in the numerous collections of essays, journal articles and indeed critical monographs on Shelley's work published over the past thirty years or so. It would appear that the assumption that *Falkner* is simply a rewriting of *Lodore* for financial purposes has subtly prejudiced modern critics and scholars against a novel Shelley herself ranked as one of her best. The assumption that *Falkner* goes over the same ground as *Lodore* has also affected what critical attention the novel has found amongst a good many of its modern readers. This assumption is beginning to be challenged and the reading presented here is meant to contribute to that much needed development. *Falkner* is, in some ways, a novel which develops the new generic mode of fiction Shelley explored in *Lodore*. It is also, in profound ways, a novel which strikes off in very different directions and, certainly, has its own unique contribution to make to Shelley's body of fictional work. It is only by examining the ways in which *Falkner* differs from *Lodore* that we will begin to see how the two novels are related as responses to the Reform era in which they were composed and published.

II.   AGGRESSIVE DAUGHTERS AND BYRONIC FATHERS

The majority of modern critical responses to *Falkner* have concentrated on the gender politics of the central father-daughter relationship. In this respect, *Falkner* appears to join *Lodore* and *Matilda* in a distinct line of texts dealing with what Mellor calls the ideology of the bourgeois family. *Falkner*, like *Lodore*, is a novel which creates multiple perspectives on a series of slowly discovered events by presenting the main plot through what Johanna M. Smith calls a series of 'flashback narratives.'[264] We begin the narrative with the orphaned Elizabeth Raby in the rather unwilling care of Mrs Baker. Elizabeth's father had been cut-off by his family, the Catholic Raby family, described as the oldest family in

England, because of his choice of wife, his 'desertion of the family religion, and determination to follow a career not permitted by the policy of his relations to any younger son' (Fal, 10). When her father and mother die, Elizabeth is thus left without any contact with her blood relations. In a tableau which clearly echoes Shelley's own relationship with her mother's grave in St. Pancras churchyard, the infant Elizabeth visits her mother's grave each day, communing with her, and when a strange man (who the reader, unlike Elizabeth, knows has come to commit suicide) seems to be profaning what for her is a sacred spot, the lives of Elizabeth and Falkner begin to become entwined.

Falkner is a character who appears to return us to the Byronic anti-hero. Noble in appearance and manner, he is tormented by what must remain a secret crime. Elizabeth saves his life by tugging at his arm as he attempts to shoot himself and Falkner finds in Elizabeth a new object of meaning. Gradually we begin to learn some of the details of the terrible secret that has brought him to the brink of suicide. Falkner has been the cause of the death of a beautiful woman whom he loved but could not have. Taking Elizabeth with him, Falkner wanders Europe and beyond, an exile from what he himself figures as his unforgivable crime. By the time they reach Baden in Germany Elizabeth is thirteen and their life of wandering away from Falkner's unbearable past is about to be disrupted by a figure from that past, a young man of sixteen, with his sneering, disagreeable father and his fascinating, for Elizabeth, melancholic character. The narrator, just before this young man's entrance into the novel, writes in a manner which clearly reminds us of the thematics of inheritance and the circular nature of history in *Lodore*:

> It is a singular law of human life, that the past, which apparently no longer forms a portion of our existence, never dies; new shoots, as it were, spring up at different intervals and places, all bearing the indelible characteristics of the parent stalk; the circular emblem of eternity is suggested by this meeting and recurrence of the broken ends of our life. (Fal, 43)

The young man, we discover, is the son of a woman who has mysteriously vanished, subsequently been divorced and labelled, by the disagreeable father, as an adulteress. The young man, Gerard Neville, refuses to believe in his mother's betrayal. As soon as Neville enters the scene, Falkner loses what 'equanimity' he had managed to gain in the preceding years: he is, unknown to anyone but himself (and the reader), the 'destroyer' of Neville's mother, and with Neville's mournful presence, he is now brought to contemplate the consequences of his actions upon someone other than himself and his 'angelic' victim (Fal, 49).

Throughout the rest of Volume I and into Volume II, as the presence of Neville haunts him, and as Elizabeth innocently wishes for a link to bind her father and her 'friend', Falkner attempts to extricate himself from what promises to be his wholly negative influence on his adopted daughter's life. He travels, Byron-like, to Greece to fight in the War of Independence, but Elizabeth refuses to leave him and waits for him on the British occupied Ionian Isles. Nursed back to life by Elizabeth, Falkner and his 'daughter' eventually return back to England. However, Elizabeth's growing affection for Neville and his own step-sister, Lady Cecil, only reaffirm for Falkner the need to disengage his fate from that of his daughter. Volume II presents us, via Lady Cecil's mediation, with Neville's story, centring on the loss of his mother, his rebellion against his despicable father and his adult quest to vindicate his mother's name. We are then, finally, presented with Falkner's own narrative of his tragic relationship with Neville's mother, Alithea, a narrative he delivers into Elizabeth's hands in the belief that Neville will demand a duel to the death. The final volume of the novel concerns the fall-out from Falkner's narrative, with Sir Boyvill's desire for Falkner to be tried as a murderer, Neville's division between love of Elizabeth and his quest to publicly vindicate his mother's name, and Elizabeth's unwavering fidelity towards Falkner, her 'more than father.'[265] Falkner, put on trial as a murderer, is finally acquitted (he had foolishly abducted Alithea, the love of his life; in her desperation to return to her son she had drowned in the stormy waters of Northumberland, near the Boyvill estate in Dromore), and a resolution between Elizabeth, Neville and Falkner comes when Neville follows Elizabeth's lead in recognizing the essential nobility and goodness of Falkner's character.

Shelley saw her novel as a celebration of fidelity, as she stated to Maria Gisborne in November 1835 (L, II, 260). It seems little wonder that the majority of the novel's modern readers have focused on the idea of the daughter's fidelity to the father as the central point of interpretive significance. Is *Falkner* demonstrable evidence of Shelley's movement in her later years to a conservative value-system of domesticated femininity? Mellor's influential reading suggests a cautious yes and no to that question. Mellor takes a psycho-biographical approach to the text which explores the 'erotics' within father-daughter relationships, a phenomenon which threatens the ideal of bourgeois family life which she views as essential to Shelley's overall position as a woman writer. This approach, which reads *Falkner* and *Lodore* through the patterns of repressed incestuous desire first explored in *Matilda*, leads Mellor to argue that underneath Elizabeth's conventionally feminine fidelity to her father lies an aggression which represents a fundamentally repressed and yet unavoidable feature of the male-dominated family unit.[266] In such a reading, despite recognizing Shelley's celebration of the ethics of fidelity and love, we end with an interpretation in which 'Falkner has been entirely destroyed by Elizabeth.'[267] Poovey's equally influential reading complements Mellor's, if providing a more complex analysis, by arguing that in novels such as *Lodore* and *Falkner* Shelley demonstrates the opportunities afforded to women writers who were prepared to accommodate their work to the conventions of conservative fiction and ideology. In this account, 'stereotypical feminine propriety', or the conventions of the 'Proper Lady', disguise female authors' more unconventional and rebellious instincts and meanings. Poovey reads *Falkner* as a novel which present us with a character, Elizabeth, embodying the passive and domesticated virtues of the proto-Victorian ideal daughter/wife, but who, through the intricacies of narrative plot and presentation, ends up demonstrating the power such women can exert over the ostensibly dominant men in their family and circle. Poovey's account, complex as it is, also delivers up an Elizabeth who exhibits a suppressed aggressiveness towards the men in her life: 'In this novel, the father figure, Falkner, is actually being humbled by a daughter for crimes committed against the mother.'[268]

Mellor's and Poovey's readings have been extended and developed by a good number of the novel's more recent readers. In Hill-Miller's important reading, for example, *Falkner* is read as inverting the father-daughter relationship displayed in Godwin's last novel, *Deloraine* (1833). This approach eventuates in another account of Elizabeth in which passivity is belied by daughterly power and even aggressiveness. 'Elizabeth's repeated insistence on saving Falkner's life', Hill-Miller writes, 'may be read as a form of veiled aggression.'[269] Kate Ferguson Ellis's approach to this issue seems to have modulated somewhat: her first essay on *Falkner* and other 'later' works contributes to the idea of daughterly aggression hidden under apparent conformity to conventional feminine values; her more recent account posits aggression on the side of a male 'desire for unlimited power and social approval' finally balanced by an empowered female assertion of the counter-value of love 'in human affairs.'[270] The crucial point for Ellis in her more recent reading is that in *Falkner* it is Elizabeth's point-of-view and Elizabeth's values that ultimately prevail. Julia Saunders makes a similar point when she focuses on Elizabeth's combination of submissiveness and empowerment. As she writes: 'In *Falkner* Shelley constructs a form of feminine power that can exist successfully within society *and* change it to answer the emotional needs of the female.' Elizabeth's power, she writes, 'is a strange one because it poses as submission .... Her presence forces [Falkner] to live against his will.'[271]

We must be careful not to presume that *Falkner* is covering the same ground in the same manner as *Lodore*. Despite appearances, there are many differences in the treatment of the father-daughter relationship in the later novel. One obvious example concerns the issue of education. Falkner's education of Elizabeth may seem to readers to repeat rather precisely Lodore's 'sexual education' of Ethel. The motive for his 'adoption' of Elizabeth can certainly be read, like Lodore's 'abduction' of Ethel, as a selfish desire for a compensatory, passive object of affection. The narrator reports his thoughts in this context: 'Should he not adopt her, mould her heart to affection, teach her to lean on him only, be all the world to her; while her gentleness and caresses would give life a charm – without which it were vain to attempt to endure existence?' (Fal, 28). The narrator then makes it very clear that his actions here are not legitimate on an ethical level, and the relation with Lodore's own thoughts and actions early on in Shelley's previous novel appear obvious and indisputable:

> We are all apt to think that when we discard a motive we cure a fault, and foster the same error from a new cause with a safe conscience. Thus, even now, aching and sore from the tortures of remorse for past faults, Falkner indulged in the same propensity, which, apparently innocent in its commencement, had led to fatal results. He meditated doing rather what he wished, than what was strictly just. He did not look forward to the evils his own course involved, while he saw in disproportionate magnitude those to be brought about if he gave up his favourite project. (Fal, 28–9)

The scenario seems rather exactly to repeat that of *Lodore* and it seems only logical to presume that a similar critique of a father's 'sexual education' of his daughter will follow. This is where the two novels differ, however, since Falkner and Elizabeth do not remain alone, but are eventually joined by a character who some critics have argued has been unjustly neglected in criticism of the novel.[272] A governess character, Miss Jervis, who cannot but remind us, in different ways, of both Claire Clairmont and Mary Wollstonecraft, hired as tutor to Elizabeth in Odessa, provides Elizabeth with an education which is both superior to Falkner's and explicitly balanced between 'masculine' and 'feminine' qualities. The narrator, interestingly, states: 'She [Elizabeth] learned from Falkner the uses of learning: from Miss Jervis she acquired the thoughts and experience of other men' (39). The reference is to Miss Jervis's tuition of Elizabeth in history and biography, but the issue of Miss Jervis's connection to 'masculine' knowledge appears to bring us back to the questions raised in *Lodore* by the character of Fanny Derham, particularly the social possibilities (or lack of them) for educationally 'masculinized' women. The narrator again directs the reader in this regard, stating:

> Nor were these more masculine studies the only lessons of Miss Jervis – needlework entered into her plan of education, as well as the careful inculcation of habits of neatness and order; and thus Elizabeth escaped for ever the danger she had hitherto run of wanting those feminine qualities without which every woman must be unhappy – and, to a certain degree, unsexed. (Fal, 40).[273]

The reference at the end of this passage is to Richard Polwhele's *The Unsex'd Females* (1798), in which Wollstonecraft had been described, on the basis of Godwin's *Memoirs*, as an irreligious, morally defective, sexually licentious woman unfit to be the 'governess of the daughter of Lord Viscount Kingsborough.'[274] Miss Jervis, like Wollstonecraft before her, is anything but 'unsexed' and the education she provides Elizabeth is, in terms of gender, balanced in precisely the manner Ethel Lodore's is not.

The very real similarities between *Lodore*'s and *Falkner*'s portrayal of a central father-daughter relationship do not necessarily, when we begin to read them in detail, lead us in the same direction. They certainly cannot simply be harmonized by recourse to a psychobiographical assumption that their ultimate referent is Shelley's relationship with her own father. That relationship was famously complicated, 'fraught' is a word which often comes to mind when reading her and his biographers. Despite that complicated relationship; it appears somewhat of a distortion to read Elizabeth's unwavering fidelity towards her surrogate father as an implicit mode of aggression towards Godwin in particular and 'the father' in general. Having read Falkner's narrative account of his 'crime' against Alithea Neville, Elizabeth, writing to Gerard Neville, states: 'I am, from this moment, more than ever devoted to his service, and eager to prove to him my fidelity' (Fal, 196). To fully read the gender politics inscribed in Shelley's novel it is far preferable to understand *Falkner* as an explicit intellectual re-engagement with Godwin's work and thought than an unconscious expression of psychological drives and desires on the part of that novel's author.

When we adopt this approach various issues take on a new, more profoundly philosophical and political significance. The reference many of the novel's readers make to the apparently 'erotic' or 'sexualized' language employed by Falkner and Elizabeth to describe their relationship can be reconnected to a life-long attempt on the part of Godwin to assert a social bond between individuals more primary than the bonds of family. The issue resonates throughout *Political Justice*, most directly in comments on the infamous example of Fénelon and the chambermaid, and gains significant fictional treatment in his novel *Cloudesley* (1830), in which the titular character, initially agreeing to adopt Julian in order to keep him in ignorance of his rightful inheritance of the Danvers' title and estates, learns to love and cherish him as a son. *Cloudesley* is a novel which celebrates what we might call the triumph of authentic feeling over the legal and habitualized demands of consanguinity, blood-relations. The narrator of that novel, summarizing Julian's thoughts, as he remembers his surrogate father, states: 'The more he analysed the character of Cloudesley, the more he admired it .... Cloudesley had been to Julian a more than father; and the never-ceasing penitence of his error that lived within him, rendered him more exemplary and unalterable, than "a just man who needed no repentance", could ever have been' (Godwin, *Novels*, VII, 286–7). The passage gives us two important contexts for an understanding of the relationship between Falkner and Elizabeth. The first of these concerns the *more than* (*father*) rhetoric employed by Godwin to figure transcendence of crime and lack of blood relation in Cloudesley's relationship with Julian. Throughout *Falkner* a similar rhetoric is employed to figure Elizabeth's feelings towards Falkner and his towards her. In response to Falkner's declared intention of leaving England after his acquittal, and his assertion that 'Daughters when they marry .... leave father, mother, all, and follow the fortunes of their husbands', Elizabeth replies: 'our position is different from that of any other parent and child. I will not say I owe you more than a daughter ever owed father – perhaps the sacred tie of blood may stand in place of the obligations you have heaped on me; but I will not reason; I cannot leave you' (Fal, 278).

Early on in the novel, the narrator has begun to make it clear that Falkner and Elizabeth share a bond which mere relation through blood cannot produce: 'The link between them of mutual benefit and mutual interest had been cemented by time and habit – by each waking thought, and nightly dream. What is so often a slothful, unapparent sense of parental and filial duty, was with them a living, active spirit, for ever manifesting itself in some new form' (Fal, 43). The many examples of the devastation to individuals caused by blood relations (and the accompanying issues of hierarchical abuses and legal inheritance and disinheritance) would appear to suggest that far from a psychological manifestation of the erotics of the bourgeois family, the achieved rather than given nature of Falkner's and Elizabeth's relationship as father and daughter represents a version of Godwin's and indeed Wollstonecraft's critique of a socio-ethics which would found itself on the apparently 'natural' ground of family relations rather than on the rational foundation of sincerity, confidence and mutual benefit. As Julia Saunders states: '[Shelley] adopts the premise that relationships should be based on more substantial values than a blind adherence to the creed that blood is thicker than water. By doing so, Shelley picks up a central theme of the social reform agenda of her parents' generation.'[275]

The second context provided by the passage from *Cloudesley* takes us further into *Falkner*'s intellectual engagement with the work of Godwin and further towards an understanding of its socio-political as well as aesthetic significance. It concerns criminality and reformations. Various readers have made the connection between the plot of *Falkner* and the assistance Shelley provided her father in 1832 as he struggled to find inspiration for the third volume of his last novel, *Deloraine*.[276] On 13 April 1832, Godwin had written a fascinating letter to Shelley which displays the extent to which he was willing to rely on her literary talents and judgement. Stuck at an early point in the third volume of his novel, and yet possessed fully of his faculties and imaginative powers ('I cannot lay my present disappointment to the charge of advancing age'), Godwin explains that he requires external aid in bringing his narrative to an appropriate dénouement: 'My mind', he writes to his daughter, 'is like a train of gunpowder, and a single spark, now happily communicated, might set the whole in motion and activity. Do not tease yourself about my calamity; but give it one serious thought. Who knows what such a thought may produce?'[277] We do not possess Shelley's reply, so we can only conjecture what 'spark' she provided Godwin. What we can say is that the third volume of *Deloraine* gives us a scenario which can be related to both *Lodore* and *Falkner*. Deloraine struggles to deal with his pursuer, Travers, a man who is determined to bring him to justice for the death of his second wife's beloved, William. Deloraine vacillates between disguise and direct confrontation with Travers, until his faithful daughter, Catherine, takes it upon herself, Fanny Derham-like, to address their pursuer directly and in all sincerity lay before him the facts of her father's life. It is this action, on the part of the daughter, that convinces Travers of the error of his ways, of Deloraine's contrition, and allows for the stable union of Deloraine, Catherine and her eventual husband Thornton. By novel's end, Catherine's daughterly fidelity towards her father raises her to a position of ethical superiority to him (cursed by his sense of personal guilt) and her husband: 'Catherine was the illustrious personage that gave radiance to the scene of our domestic life; for we all lived together. But Thornton and myself felt no uneasiness at her superiority. We were satisfied that every thing was in its due order, and willingly submitted ourselves to her benignant sway' (Godwin, *Novels*, VIII, 282).

It is tempting to imagine that the 'spark' provided to Godwin by Shelley was the very idea (the ethical agency and superiority of a daughter resolving the turbulent and circular history created by the noble but tragically flawed father) around which Shelley herself then went on to weave her final two novels.[278] It is curious, certainly, why Godwin should have felt blocked in completing the final stages of his novel. *Deloraine*, as we know, is Godwin's version of an historically factual story, mentioned as far back as *Caleb Williams*, which Godwin seems to have shared with Edward Bulwer, who himself wrote a novel version of the story in his *Eugene Aram* (1832). Godwin drew up interesting notes on the case of Eugene Aram (1704–1759), an erudite teacher who, with an accomplice, had murdered Daniel Clarke, and who had afterwards lived for thirteen years in the most respectable and socially useful fashion, until he was discovered as a murderer, brought to trial, and executed.[279] It seems clear from

Bulwer's preface to the 1840 edition of his novel that Godwin had originally planned to write a novel on the basis of the life of Eugene Aram, but had then suggested the story to Bulwer himself. *Deloraine* is Godwin's modified version of the story, but with the addition of, above all else, a daughter-figure, Catherine, who provides a feminine perspective and, crucially, a testifying or witnessing role lacking in the original story and in Bulwer's eventual fictionalization.

Falkner, as a literary character, has, like Lodore, Lord Raymond, Castruccio and even Frankenstein, frequently been figured as a 'Byronic' character. When it comes to Falkner there has been a rather irresolvable argument about whether his biographical referent is Byron or, alternatively, the Byron-imitating figure of Trelawny.[280] The echoes of both Byron and Trelawny within the character of Falkner are indisputable, but they are perhaps more localized than critics have previously allowed. If Falkner is modelled on a literary figure, then we would have to say that via Deloraine, he has his origin in the historical and subsequently literary figure of Eugene Aram. Bulwer's novel, as Lynn Pyckett has stated 'confirmed the Newgate trend, with its criminal hero, based on a real murderer.'[281] The 'Newgate novel' gained popularity in the 1820s and 1830s and then again in the 1860s; as a form concerned with criminality, but also with the unjust nature of the legal and penal system and with exploring the thin line between 'respectable' society and the so-called criminal 'underworld.' Its literary antecedents can be traced back directly to Godwin's *Caleb Williams* and other Jacobin novels, such as Thomas Holcroft's *Bryan Perdue*.[282] When Godwin came to write *Deloraine*, he was revising a genre, the 'Newgate novel', which had itself expanded on his own most famous and popular novel, *Caleb Williams*, published forty years earlier. It would be provocative but also somewhat pointless to call *Falkner* a 'Newgate novel.' What opens the novel out to a more contextually accurate assessment is when we remember that it is a novel that participates in an intertextual loop that takes us from *Caleb Williams* through Bulwer's revision of that novel in *Paul Clifford* and especially *Eugene Aram* to Godwin's own response in his last novel, *Deloraine*. Shelley's *Falkner* is a novel which places a significantly feminine perspective on a tradition of Romantic and post-Romantic novels, the principal subject of which is criminality and the question of the ethical nature of those publicly labelled as criminals.

III. REVISING HAMLET

Godwin's interest in the story of Eugene Aram is linked to ideas about legal reform. He notes:

> Let there be an Act of Pt. that, after a lapse of ten years, whoever shall be found to have spent that period blamelessly, and in labours conducive to the welfare of mankind, shall be absolved.
>
> No man shall die respecting whom it can reasonably be concluded that if his life were spared, it would be spent blamelessly, honourably, and usefully.[283]

Godwin's *Deloraine* finally exonerates a murderer, at least through his daughter's eyes if not his own, in a manner which psychologically and ethically supports such a re-evaluation of criminality. Deloraine is guilty of a murder, but he is also capable of living an honourable, blameless and useful life, as his daughter testifies. Bulwer's fictional account of Eugene Aram, despite the revisions he made to his text, similarly attempt to vindicate the character of a man involved (directly at first, by association in later versions) with a heinous crime. In *Falkner* Shelley takes this literary and legal context and focuses on the manner in which individuals in society are interpreted and named (guilty, innocent, murderer, adultress). The Eugene Aram material provided Shelley with a fresh context in which to explore her perennial concern with how the past dominates the present, and how a break in the violent cycle of history and historical returns can be achieved on a human and social level. The particular challenge to the reader of Shelley's novel lies in the fact that Falkner, ultimately, is not simply subject to a reinterpretation by others, we have to believe by novel's end that he himself *is* blameless, honourable and socially useful. How do you absolve from guilt and the charge of crime the 'destroyer' of Alithea, a woman who comes to stand symbolically and literally for the maternal and whose name comes from the Greek goddess of 'Truth'?

The question confronts every serious reader of Shelley's novel, and it is a question which inevitably leads us to the symbolic patterns that weave together the histories of the two male characters directly associated with Elizabeth: Falkner and Neville. The history of both these men appears to confirm the dark reality explored in Shelley's earlier novels: the quest for truth and justice (embodied in the figure and the name of Alithea) leads, in both their narratives, to the threat of the return of violence and the triumph of injustice and falsehood.

Falkner's character represents a challenge to the novel's readers: as we have seen, his motives for 'adopting' Elizabeth, and much of his behaviour in the first part of the novel, is fundamentally ambiguous. We might look back at the passages on his decision to 'adopt' Elizabeth, already cited, and remind ourselves that although the narrator makes it quite clear that his motives are wrong, it is also clear to the reader that there are very few alternatives, and that those that do exist seem far worse as far as Elizabeth is concerned. Compared with staying with the small-minded and rather vindictive Mrs Baker, or returning to the isolated, bigoted and essentially paranoiac Raby family, Falkner's 'adoption' of Elizabeth is unquestionably the best option. The action is ethically wrong, and yet it is by far the best one available. Falkner's story and his character continually confront the reader with this kind of moral ambiguity and, in ways which directly relate Shelley's fictional art to that of her father, force us to suspend any quick and simplifying ethical judgement.

Highlighting the cardinal issue of moral interpretation, Shelley's novel *Falkner* has, at its very centre, a narrative written by Falkner himself. The necessity of interpreting Falkner's narrative for all the novel's major characters creates a metatextual reference for the reader's ultimate interpretive responsibility. Falkner's narrative (which one feels tempted to call 'Falkner') begins in a manner which plugs directly into that intertextual loop in which *Caleb Williams* and the 'Newgate novel' form the contextual backdrop for both Godwin's and Shelley's last novels. After having declared the truthfulness of his narrative, Falkner begins with the ultimate question for his particular life: 'What is crime?' He ventures an initial answer: 'A deed done injurious to others – forbidden by religion, condemned by morality, and which human laws are enacted to punish' (Fal, 155). The definition is legalistic, but it is also wholly inadequate, given that one 'deed injurious to others' may be engulfed by many thousands of others which are beneficial to others. Are we prepared to allow for such an unforgiving, rigid and practically universalized definition of 'crime'? Who could escape from being labelled a criminal under such a definition? Such questions prepare the reader for Falkner's next move, which is to present a sustained critique of the legal and penal systems as they currently operate; a critique which it is historically accurate to call 'Godwinian' (Fal, 155). Our understanding of precisely what Falkner accuses himself of is also less than certain. He states, rather enigmatically: 'My act was the murderer, though my intention was guiltless of death' (Fal, 155).

Falkner goes on to give an account of his miserable childhood, brightened only by his relationship with Mrs Rivers and her daughter, Alithea. The history of childhood abuse from fathers and father substitutes and of schoolroom tyranny, generate both an understanding of why Falkner should become so utterly cathected onto Alithea, and also demonstrates his rebellious hatred of injustice, something which comes to the fore when he leaves to take up a post in the cavalry of the East India Company, determined to one day liberate Alithea from her tyrant of a father. In India Falkner courts native insurrection whilst simultaneously and contradictorily desiring the acquisition of power. He writes:

> I was for ever entangled in the intimacy, and driven to try to serve the oppressed; while the affection I excited was considered disaffection on my part to the rulers .... I own I often dreamt of the practicability of driving the merchant sovereigns from Hindostan .... A subaltern in the Company's service, I could never gain my Alithea, or do her the honour with which I longed to crown her. (Fal, 172).[284]

Falkner is a man who, because of his desire for Alithea, is trapped in irreconcilable motives of service to others and a need to acquire power for himself, a desire to liberate and a desire to possess the truth. He is another in the now long series of examples, in Shelley's fiction, of the male Romantic idealist undermined by the realities of self and a tragic external reality. His reaction to meeting, by chance, the husband of Alithea, on his return to England, provides inter-textual confirmations of such a reading of Falkner. Mr Neville is a misogynistic, 'cold, proud, sarcastic ... decayed dandy' (Fal, 175), years older than his beautiful and matchless wife.[285] It is Mr Neville's negative view of human existence in general ('A man .... who took pride in the sagacity which enabled him to detect worms and corruption in the loveliness of virtue') and his degraded view of women in particular that cause Falkner to hate him on the spot. Falkner states: 'For Alithea's sake I respected every woman .... and this animal dared revile beings of whose very nature he could form no conception' (Fal, 175). The animalistic and sub-human epithets spin out of Falkner as he figures Alithea's hideous husband: 'detested animal', 'grovelling and loathsome type of the world's worst qualities', 'devil' (Fal, 176), 'base-minded thing', 'an animal of another species', 'a blind, creeping worm', 'a wretch' (Fal, 179–80), and on two occasions these figures are linked to a classical trope of bondage which resonates throughout the literature of the Godwin-Wollstonecraft-Shelley circle. Falkner describes Alithea 'bound for life to a human brute', and, in an apostrophic address to her, states: 'You are tied to a foul, corrupting corpse' (Fal, 176).

Falkner's figuration of the live Alithea tied to the 'corrupting corpse' of her despicable husband has its origins in Virgil's description of Mezentius, Etruscan King of Caere, who, as Mandeville explains in Godwin's novel of that name 'tied a living body to a dead one, and caused the one to take in, and gradually to become a partner of the putrescence of the other' (Godwin, *Novels*, VI, 141).[286] Wollstonecraft had employed the image in *The Wrongs of Woman* to figure the enslavement created by the institution of marriage (Wollstonecraft, *Works*, I, 154). Shelley herself employs the figure on a number of occasions, but here in Falkner's narrative it serves to bring a highly resonant figure of slavery and corruption into Falkner's response to the idea and the reality of Alithea's marriage. Imagining Alithea bound to this 'corpse' of a man shatters Falkner's entire sense of order and meaning: 'the devil usurped at once the throne of God, and life became a hell' (Fal, 176). Falkner, therefore, decides to liberate Alithea, and in so doing bring meaning, justice and order back to the world: 'I resolved to tear the veil which her gentleness and sense of right had drawn before the truth' (Fal, 179). His act of attempted liberation of the truth, and Alithea, in its very effort to liberate (and so restore to the world) it and her, violates the very truth Alithea embodies and turns her, through the violence of his abduction, into a corpse, buried in a secret, unmarked grave, to which he is forever existentially bound. Falkner encourages Alithea in his plan of liberation in a language which is profoundly Wollstonecraftian and essentially revolutionary: 'I was shocked to see so much of the slave had entered her soul. I told her this; I told her that she was being degraded by the very duties which she was devoting herself, body and soul, to perform; I told her that she must be free' (Fal, 180). This discourse misses the truth it would liberate, however, by eradicating the very value that allows Alithea to live up to her name. She asks Falkner, reasonably, to be her 'friend', and goes on: 'A mother is, in my eyes, a more sacred name than wife. My life is wrapped in my boy, in him I find blameless joy, though all the rest pierce my heart with poisoned arrows' (Fal, 182).

We cannot but have sympathy with Falkner's desire to liberate Alithea from her matrimonial dungeon. We also understand and

ethically register how misguided and ultimately tragic his attempt
at that liberation is. Falkner's plan is pragmatically botched when
mother and son are separated in the execution of his 'design.'
Falkner's attempt to relocate Alithea, to liberate her from 'the
man without a soul, the incarnate Belial' (Fal, 184), and so restore
justice to his and her world, is at one and the same time insanely
misjudged and yet ethically honourable and understandable (Fal,
184–5). Falkner wants to liberate Alithea from her slavery, but he
also wants to possess her for himself, and the tragedy results from
the contradiction of motive (Fal, 186). At the moment before
Osborne, his accomplice, arrives with the carriage, Falkner had
determined to give Alithea up, return her to her home and 'part
with her for ever.' But here, and in the events which lead to the loss
of Alithea's son and then ultimately her life, Falkner is helpless to
stop the tragic chain of circumstances his actions have set in train.

Falkner presents us with another embedded narrative, related
to the history of another man who seeks to liberate and restore
the truth. Gerard Neville's quest is of course uncannily parallel
to Falkner's, in that it is aimed at restoring Alithea to her rightful public position as innocent embodiment of truth and human
virtue. It is a quest which is not only demonstrably virtuous in its
intent, but also involves the kind of rebellion against a worldly
father, Sir Boyvill, we have already observed in Falkner's own story.
Neville's quest is frequently figured in terms of Shakeapeare's
Hamlet.[287] Sir Boyvill's accusation of lunacy on his son's part (Fal,
90), Neville's inclination to leap into the grave of his mother in the
scene in which Alithea's body is finally discovered (Fal, 215), and his
own self-figuration as the avenging son, all point towards a significant use of Shakeapeare's play within the overall signifying structure of the novel. It is interesting, in fact, to note that allusions to
Hamlet also attach themselves to Falkner, and in so doing symbolically relate his and Neville's rebellion against tyrannical father-
figures. When Falkner is beaten by his father, on hearing the news
that his older brother is to marry and so seal his possession of the
family name and estates, Falkner states: 'I sat down and wept, and
crept away to the fields, and wondered why I was born, and longed
to kill my uncle, who was the cause to me of so much misery' (Fal,
158). The murderous impulse towards the uncle is a displaced desire
on the young Falkner's part to kill the father, something *Hamlet*
allows us easily to recognize given that in that play the uncle and the
father become (il)legally one. Neville's account of the meaning of

Shakespeare's play is riddled with displacements and reversals. He states to Elizabeth: 'I have read that play ... till each word seems instinct with a message direct to my heart – as if my own emotions gave a conscious soul to every line .... I would vindicate a mother – without judging my father – without any accusation against him, I would establish her innocence' (Fal, 87). Neville's description of himself as a modern day Hamlet is, quite clearly, shot through with contradictions, the fundamental one of which being that he desires to play the role of the revenge hero without violence, without accusation and ultimately without tragedy. How does one adopt the role of Hamlet without stepping into a revenge tragedy? The question is, of course, one that haunts Hamlet himself. How is justice and right to be brought back into the world without a violation of justice and right? This appears to be the question generated by the absent and yet ever present figure of Alithea.

Neville, unwittingly, in his attempt to vindicate his mother, is in danger of repeating (returning to and making return) the devastating consequences of the father's (Falkner's) original 'crime'. He says to Elizabeth: 'I will yield to no impediment – be stopped by no difficulty – not even by my father's blind commands' (Fal, 87). Falkner's narrative will allow Neville to vindicate Alithea's name, but it appears necessary that this public, legal, ethical corrective be performed at the expense of his own name and indeed his own life. What Neville does not realize until after reading Falkner's narrative, indeed not until Elizabeth has shown him the way at the very end of the novel, is that the model of Hamlet, the avenging son, is wholly inappropriate, since it links vindication and justice inextricably with punishment and vengeance. Even his father, Sir Boyvill, who has acted in a spirit of revenge (against Alithea and then against Falkner) throughout the novel, acknowledges, on his death bed, that revenge and punishment are unjust forces when applied to Falkner's case. Falkner is finally acquitted of murder, in the public trial at Carlisle, in what appears to be Shelley's version of Godwin's hypothetical Act of Parliament (Fal, 286).

What allows for the novel's resolution is not simply a public trial and acquittal, but what, for the majority of the novel, appears an improbable, even an impossible convergence; that is, the final coincidence of three examples of fidelity: Neville's to his mother; Elizabeth's to her adopted father; often against his own instincts and faulty logic, Falkner's to Elizabeth. Just as Alithea allegorically stands for the truth contained in the notion of fidelity, so Elizabeth acts for and as that truth. The male realm of the law, of legal naming (guilty, innocent), is symbolically reformed in *Falkner* by feminine values absent in the male public domain.

IV.   FIDELITY AND REFORM

Elizabeth, then, is the ultimate hero of *Falkner*. As Bennett puts it: '*Falkner* ... has a genuine hero – and he is a she.'[288] Elizabeth's value-system is symbolized by the concept of fidelity, which we have read as a social and ethical value which replaces a masculine ideology of public naming and shaming, of vindication through revenge, of the establishment of right and justice through the violence of punishment and criminalization.[289] As Neville explains to Falkner, who still believes that for Elizabeth to gain the husband of her choice he must leave them, banish himself: 'No! Elizabeth herself. She alone can decide for us all, and teach us the right path to take' (Fal, 298). The union of Elizabeth and Neville cannot come at the expense of Falkner, since that would merely, once again, repeat the circular pattern of justice and truth gained through violence, alienation and loss. The power of fidelity breaks the repetitive history of justice through violence, a violence apparently determined through social mores and conventions: legal, familial, religious or all three. Elizabeth, with her lack of connection to dominant aristocratic and bourgeois English society, speaks and acts for a justice and a truth that does not betray itself through complicity with such violence. The narrator makes it very clear, in the final scene of reconciliation and resolution, how unconventional and improbable this threesome is (Fal, 299).

To transform Elizabeth into a subconsciously aggressive daughter, taming a Byronic, destructive father, may appear reasonable if we read *Falkner* through the lens of *Matilda*. But to do so takes us away from the socio-political, philosophical and ethical understanding the novel so intricately and consistently attempts to inculcate within its readers. Like *Lodore* before it, *Falkner* speaks to a decade in which reform was the central political and social issue, and it asserts the culturally feminine values upon which, according to Shelley, any viable model of reform (individually and socially) must be built. What the trial and acquittal of Falkner does is to affirm on a social level what Elizabeth has asserted all along, that the Falkner she knows and loves is the authentic one. Elizabeth's form of fidelity stands superior to the public process of vindication and criminalization; it also stands superior to the metaphysical quest for the truth embodied in Falkner and Neville. Both ways of gaining access to the truth lose it, and even pervert it, by and through their unrealistic, unrealizable totalization of ethical values. Elizabeth's form of fidelity signifies an understanding of truth and justice achieved on a human level, a level which transcends the violent, black or white, distribution of ethical names. It speaks for a realistic assessment of the reform of individuals and of society which is wholly consistent with Shelley's aesthetic, philosophical and political contribution as an author. It was an assessment which continued beyond her last novel.

Afterword: Beyond the Novels

The period between 1830 and 1844 was the most prolific and productive of Shelley's writing life. We have looked at the three novels associated with this period, Shelley also continued to publish short stories during the 1830s. The period, however, saw the publication of a greater volume of non-fictional works. In 1838 Sir Timothy Shelley finally relented and, still barring a memoir of the poet, allowed Shelley to publish an edition of P. B. Shelley's poetry.[290] The four volumes of *Poetical Works* were published through 1839 and, as she stated, cost her considerable labour and threatened her health (L, II, 318).[291] As most readers of P. B. Shelley's poetry know, Shelley got round Sir Timothy's ban on a memoir of the poet, by writing significant notes to the major poems and for each year before the shorter poems, and as this study has demonstrated she not only gave valuable biographical and intellectual information about the poet but, in a sense, presented her own critical response to her husband's work and many invaluable indications of her own politics and aesthetics. At the end of 1839, she published a companion volume, *Essays, Letters from Abroad, Translations & Fragments*.

From 1834 Shelley was involved in producing a series of volumes for *The Cabinet Cyclopædia*, a series run by Dr Dionysius Lardner. Shelley's *Literary Lives* span five large volumes, published between 1835 and 1839, and cover the lives of literary men and women of Italy (two volumes), France (two volumes), Spain and Portugal (one volume).[292] Shelley's *Lives* are a massive and definitive corrective to the Victorian myth of her decline into conservatism and political quietism, containing numerous discussions of European politics from the early modern period through to the epoch of the French

Revolution and beyond. The *Lives* are a resounding testament to her belief in the need for social reform and her wariness of all forms of violence and totalizing modes of thinking and action. Discussing the risorgimento, in her life of Alfieri, she writes that in the Italy of her day 'the voice of liberty' and its 'language is now felt and understood from one end of the country to the other, and the day must come when the oppressors will be unable to oppose the veto of mere physical force to the overpowering influence of moral courage' (LL, I, 255).

Shelley's last work, *Rambles in Germany and Italy in 1840, 1842 and 1843*, was published in 1844, the year in which Sir Timothy Shelley died ('at last'). Written with the help of the eventually blackmailing Ferdinando Gatteschi, a political exile and follower of the revolutionary leader Mazzini, *Rambles* is a deeply political work, supporting the risorgimento and, in the second volume, dedicating an entire chapter (or 'letter') to the history of the Carbonari movement. Her disapproval of secret societies such as the Carbonari, and yet her understanding of the political and social exigencies which at times necessitate secrecy and covert action, are characteristic, and registering the regretability of its continued existence she still finds a way of guiding its history towards her own reformist values (R, 322–3). The closing observations of this chapter cannot but remind her readers of a novel, *Valperga*, she had published over two decades earlier:

> The Carbonari first taught the Italians to consider themselves as form- ing a nation. It is to be hoped they will never forget the lesson. When the Roman considers himself, in his heart, the countryman of the Milanese – when the Tuscan looks upon Naples as also his country – then the power of the Austrian will receive a blow, which it has hitherto warded off, from which it will never recover. (R, 323)

Confirming Shelley's sustained commitment to her own brand of reformist politics, *Rambles* also seems a fitting last work in its moving descriptions of Shelley's return to the European cities, towns and countryside she had visited and lived in with her husband so many years previously.

On revisiting Rome, Shelley gives us one last look at this central scene of world history and private associations. Looking out from the Coliseum towards the Pyramid of Cestius ('The treasures of my youth lie buried here') she writes: 'the tomb of Cestius, gleam- ing at a distance, is a resting-place for the eye – and various trees seem placed expressly to give the scene the air of a landscape sitting for its picture' (R, 348). Looking longingly at the pyramidal sign of her husband's and son's burial place, but perhaps also looking down from the final point of her own, astonishing literary career, Shelley here returns us to that melancholic voice so misunderstood by her Victorian and post-Victorian biographers. Within a few pages, however, she is comparing the brutality of the Roman suppression of the early Christians with the reported atrocities of the British troops in the First Affghan War: 'I used to pride myself on English humanity; but the boast is quenched in shame, since I read, last winter, the accounts of the cruelties practised in the Affghan war.' And she adds, in a piece of political writing which has the concision and repeatability of P. B. Shelley's best political prose: 'We were injured, and, therefore, we revenge; such also was the tenet of old Rome' (R, 350).[293] Understanding the relation between the two voices presented in these pages (one melancholic; the other political, openly critical of injustice) is the challenge which confronts those readers today who would adequately understand who Mary Shelley was and, most importantly, the full significance of what she wrote.

Notes

INTRODUCTION

1. See Graham Allen, 'Beyond Biographism: Mary Shelley's Mathilda, Intertextuality, and the Wandering Subject', in *Romanticism*, 3.2 (1997), pp.170–84.

2. Emily W. Sunstein, *Mary Shelley: Romance and Reality* (Baltimore: The Johns Hopkins University Press, 1989), pp.387–403.

3. Sunstein, p.387.

4. The biographies are, respectively: C. Kegan Paul, *William Godwin: His Friends and Contemporaries*, 2 Vols. (London: Henry S. King & Co., 1876); Edward Dowden, *The Life of Percy Bysshe Shelley*, 2 Vols. (London: Kegan Paul, Trench & Co., 1886); and Mrs Julian (Florence) Marshall, *The Life and Letters of Mary Wollstonecraft Shelley*, 2 Vols. (London: Richard Bentley and Sons, 1889).

5. Sunstein, p.387.

6. Florence Marshall, *The Life and Letters of Mary Wollstonecraft Shelley*. Vol. II, p.322.

7. Mary Poovey, *The Proper Lady and the Woman Writer – Ideology as Style in the Works of Mary Wollstonecraft, Mary Shelley and Jane Austen* (Chicago and London: University of Chicago Press, 1984).

8. 'Introduction', in *Lives of the Great Romantics* 3. John Mullan (Gen. Ed.), *Mary Shelley*, Vol. III. ed. Betty T. Bennett (London: Pickering and Chatto, 1999), pp.ix–xxi.

9. Bennett, *Lives* 3, III, p.xvi.

10. Timothy Webb, 'Religion of the Heart: Leigh Hunt's Tribute to Shelley', in *Keats-Shelley Review*, 7 (1992), pp.1–61.

11. See Bennett, *Lives* 3, III, p.xiii.

12. William St Clair, *The Godwins and the Shelleys: The Biography of a Family* (London and Boston: Faber and Faber, 1989), p.419.

13. See Shelley, *Novels*, II, p.148, J, p.11, and Mellor, *Mary Shelley*, p.23.

14. See Robert Gittings and Jo Manton, *Claire Clairmont and the Shelleys, 1789–1879* (Oxford and New York: Oxford University Press, 1992).

15. Bennett, *Lives* 3, III, p.xix.

16. See David Wright (ed.), *Records of Shelley, Byron, and the Author* (Harmondsworth: Penguin, 1973), p.21. See also David Crane, ed. *Recollections of the Last Days of Shelley and Byron* (London: Robinson, 2000); J. E. Morpurgo, ed. *The Last Days of Shelley and Byron: Being the Complete Text of Trelawny's Recollections edited, with additions from contemporary sources* (New York: Anchor Books, 1960).

17. Bennett, *Lives* 3, III, p.xviii. See Sunstein, p. 393.

18. See Gittings and Manton, pp.81–4.

19. Edward Trelawny, *Adventures of a Younger Son*, William St Clair, ed. (London: Oxford University Press, 1974).

20. William St Clair, *The Reading Nation in the Romantic Period* (Cambridge: Cambridge University Press, 2004), p.357.

21. *Other*, p.4. See also Esther Schor, 'Introduction' in *Companion*, pp.1–2.

22. For Scott's review, see Donald Reiman, ed. *The Romantics Reviewed: Contemporary Reviews of British Romantic Writers*, Part C, *Shelley, Keats, and London Radical Writers*, 2 Vols (New York and London: Garland Publishing, 1972), Vol. I, pp.73–80.

23. St Clair, *The Reading Nation*, p.358.

24. See Marilyn Butler *Jane Austen and the War of Ideas* (2nd edn.) (Oxford: Oxford University Press, 1987).

25. Reiman, *Romantics Reviewed*, C. II, p.765.

26. St Clair, 'Frankenstein' in *The Reading Nation*, pp.357–73. An earlier version of this essay can be found in William St. Clair, 'The Impact of *Frankenstein*', in *Times*, pp.38–63.

27. St Clair, *The Reading Nation*, p.360.

28. St Clair, *The Reading Nation*, p.365.

29. St Clair, *The Reading Nation*, p.367.

30. St Clair, *Reading Nation*, pp.644–9.

31. Reiman, *Romantics Reviewed*, C. II, p.819.

32. ibid, p.823.

33. Richard Church, *Mary Shelley* (London: Gerald Howe, 1928), p.90.

34. See 'The Anniversary', in *Knight's Quarterly Magazine*, III (August 1824) in Reiman, *Romantics Reviewed*, C. II, p.498.

35. See Bennett's introduction to *Frankenstein* in F, p.xli.

36. For an excellent concise overview see Pamela Clemit, 'Mary Wollstonecraft Shelley' in *Literature of the Romantic Period: A Bibliographical Guide*, Michael O'Neill, ed. Oxford: Clarendon Press, 1998, pp.284–97.

37. See Nora Crook 'Sleuthing towards a Mary Shelley Canon', in *Women's Writing*, 6:3 (1999), pp.413–24.

38. Bennett and Curran, 'Introduction' in *Times*, p.x.

39. See Karsten Klejs Engelberg, *The Making of the Shelley Myth: An Annotated Bibliography of Criticism of Percy Bysshe Shelley, 1822–1860* (Meckler: Mansell Pubs, 1988), p.ix.

40. *Fictions*, pp.xix–xxvi. As Crook is aware, such maps elide earlier works: see Muriel Spark, *Mary Shelley* (London: Constable, 1988), a revised version of *Child of Light: A Reassessment of Mary Shelley* (Hadleigh, Essex: Tower Bridge Pubs., 1951); Elizabeth Nitchie, *Mary Shelley: 'Author of Frankenstein'* (New Brunswick: Rutgers University Press, 1953) and her edition of *Mathilda, Studies in Philology*, 3, October 1959 (Chapel Hill, North Carolina: The University of North Carolina Press, 1959); Jean de Palacio, *Mary Shelley dans son oeuvre: Contributions aux etudes shelleyennes*. (Paris: Editions Klincksieck, 1969).

41. Crook, *Fictions*, p.xix.

42. Crook, *Fictions*, p.xix.

43. George Levine, 'The Ambiguous Heritage of *Frankenstein*', in *Endurance*, p.3.

44. Kate Ellis, 'Monsters in the Garden: Mary Shelley and the Bourgeois Family', pp.123–42; U. C. Knoepflmacher, 'Thoughts on the Aggression of Daughters', pp.88–119; Ellen Moers, 'Female Gothic', originally published in *Literary Women* (Garden City: Doubleday, 1976).

45. Crook, *Fictions*, p.xix.

46. Crook, *Fictions*, p.xx.

47. These collections include, *Fictions*; *Times*; *Romanticism*, 3.2 (1997), and *Women's Writing*, 6.3 (1999).

48. Crook, *Fictions*, p.xx.

49. See Graham Allen, *Intertextuality* (London: Routledge, 2000).

50. Editions, with contextual and critical material, include the following: Johanna M. Smith's 1996 Bedford Books edition of the 1831 edition; J. Paul Hunter's 1996 Norton edition of the 1818 text; D. L. Macdonald and Kathleen Scherf's 1999, second edition of the Broadview edition of the 1818 text (with substantive variants appended). Books which survey the history of adaptation and the critical reception of the novel include the following: Donald F. Glut, *The Frankenstein Legend: A Tribute to Mary Shelley and Boris Karloff* (Netuchen, N. J.: The Scarecrow Press, 1973); Steven Earl Forry, *Hideous Progenies: Dramatizations of 'Frankenstein' from the Nineteenth-Century to the Present* (Philadelphia: University of Pennsylvania Press, 1990); Fred Botting, ed. *Frankenstein: Mary Shelley* (New York: St. Martin's Press, 1995); Radu Florescu, *In Search of Frankenstein: Exploring the Myths Behind Mary Shelley's Monster* (London: Robson Books, 1996); Berthold Schoene-Harwood, ed. *Mary Shelley. 'Frankenstein': A Reader's Guide to Essential Criticism* (Cambridge: Icon Books, 2000); Timothy Morton, ed. *A Routledge Sourcebook on Mary Shelley's 'Frankenstein'* (London and New York: Routledge, 2002).

51. This is in no way to diminish the contributions of such critics as Pamela Cemit, Nora Crook, Paula R. Feldman and Diana Scott-Kilvert, Charles E. Robinson, and others.

52. Mitzi Myers 'Mary Wollstonecraft Godwin Shelley: The Female Author between Public and Private Spheres', in *Times*, pp.160–72 (p.264n).

53. The story of how Ferdinando Gatteschi waged a sustained, if ultimately unsuccessful, campaign of blackmail against Shelley is contained in the third volume of the letters.

54. Readers should be aware that the terms 'idealism' and 'realism' are employed here in their more commonplace rather than philosophical sense. 'Idealism' could on this basis be defined in terms of a belief in the power of reason and its products (ideas) to transform external reality; 'realism' might be defined as a skepticism regarding the transformative powers of reason.

1. *FRANKENSTEIN; OR, THE MODERN PROMETHEUS*

55. Fred Botting, *Making Monstrous: 'Frankenstein', Criticism, Theory* (Manchester and New York: Manchester University Press, 1991). See also David Ketterer, *Frankenstein's Creation: The Book, The*

Monster, and Human Reality (Victoria, B. C.: Victoria University Press, 1979), pp.9–16.

56. Chris Baldick, *In Frankenstein's Shadow: Myth, Monstrosity and Nineteenth-Century Writing* (Oxford: The Clarendon Press, 1987).

57. Versions of *Frankenstein* include the 1818, 1823 and 1831 editions, plus the Draft Notebook version, the surviving Faircopy Notebooks, plus the *Thomas* edition with significant revisions Mary Shelley left in Italy when she returned to England in 1823. See FN, Part 1, pp.xxv–xxvii. In this reading, I will concentrate on the 1818 version, but will also draw on material from the Draft and Faircopy along with the later versions when necessary.

58. For a more theoretically and philosophically inflected approach to friendship in *Frankenstein*, see Graham Allen, '"Unfashioned creatures, but half made up": Beginning with Mary Shelley's Spectre' in *Angelaki* 12:3 (2008), forthcoming.

59. The letter is dated 8 June 1812; see Florence Marshall, I, p.28.

60. See, for example, Katherine C. Hill-Miller, *'My Hideous Progeny': Mary Shelley, William Godwin, and the Father-Daughter Relationship* (Newark: University of Delaware Press, 1995).

61. Jean-Jacques Rousseau, *Émile*, Barbara Foxley (trans.) (London: Dent, 1993).

62. Rousseau, p.169.

63. Rousseau, p.100.

64. See Alan Richardson, *Literature, Education and Romanticism: Reading as a Social Practice, 1780–1832* (Cambridge: Cambridge University Press, 1994).

65. This opposition between 'things as they should be' and 'things as they are' was an explicit rhetorical device in the radical literature of Jacobin literature of the 1790s and beyond, see Godwin's *Things as They Are; or The Adventures of Caleb Williams* (first published in 1794, revised in four further editions: 1796, 1797, 1816, 1831).

66. See 'Life of William Godwin', in LL, IV, pp.31–9. See also Wollstonecraft, *Works*, IV, p.469 and Godwin, *Novels*, VI, p.58.

67. John Locke. *Some Thoughts Concerning Education. The Clarendon Edition of the Works of John Locke.* John W. and Jean S. Yolton (eds) (Oxford: Clarendon Press, 1989) p.109.

68. The sentence is traditionally attributed to Aristotle. It is cited by Montaigne in his essay 'Of Friendship' and is used as a leitmotif throughout Derrida's book on the politics of friendship.

69. In the Thomas copy an unknown hand queries the father's knowledge: 'you said your family was not scientific' (F, p.27).

70. C. F. C. Volney, *The Ruins: or A Survey of the Revolutions of Empires* (1791) (London: J. Johnson, 1796). See Clemit, *The Godwinian Novel*, p.151.

71. The Geneva-Rousseau context for the Frankenstein family is not, however, as simple an indicator as it might at first appear: see Crook's notes in F, p.21.

72. Anne McWhir, 'Teaching the Monster to Read: Mary Shelley's Education and *Frankenstein*', in *The Educational Legacy of Romanticism*, ed. John Willinsky (Waterloo, Ontario: Wilfrid Laurier University Press, 1990), pp.73–92 (p.79, p.74).

73. See Geoffrey H. Hartman, 'Romanticism and Anti-Self-Consciousness', in *Beyond Formalism: Literary Essays, 1958–1970* (New Haven and London: Yale University Press, 1970), pp.298–310.

74. See also Godwin, *Political*, III, p.11.

75. See James Reiger (ed.), *Frankenstein* (Chicago: The University of Chicago Press, 1982); David Ketterer, *Frankenstein's Creation*; Anne K. Mellor, *Mary Shelley*; and, for the best overview, Robinson's introduction to FN. See also Zacharay Leader, *Revision and Romantic Authorship* (Oxford: Clarendon Press, 1996), pp.167–205.

76. David Marshall, *The Surprising Effects of Sympathy: Marivaux, Diderot, Rousseau, and Mary Shelley* (Chicago and London: University of Chicago Press, 1988), p.208.

77. Marshall, p.208.

78. Marshall, p.227.

79. See Joyce Zonana, '"They Will Prove the Truth of My Tale": Safie's Letters as a Feminist Core of Mary Shelley's *Frankenstein*', *The Journal of Narrative Technique* 21 (1991), pp.170–84.

80. Zonana, p.170.

81. Zonana, p.173.

2. MATILDA

82. Nitchie, *Mathilda*. Clemit gives the compositional dates as 4 August to 12 September for *The Fields of Fancy* and states that although Shelley dated *Matilda* 9 November 1819 it 'was probably completed in February 1820' (M, p.2).

83. For Godwin's comments, see *Maria Gisborne & Edward E. Williams, Shelley's Friends: Their Journals and Letters*, Frederick L. Jones, ed. (Norman: University of Oklahoma Press, 1951), p.44.

84. See Mellor, *Mary Shelley*, pp.191–200; U. C. Knoepflmacher, 'Thoughts on the Aggression of Daughters', pp.88–119; Susan Allen Ford, '"A name more dear": Daughters, Fathers, and Desire in *A Simple Story, The False Friend*, and *Mathilda*', in *Re-visioning Romanticism: British Women Writers, 1776–1837*, Carol Shiner Wilson and Joel Haefner (eds) (Philadelphia: University of Pennsylvania Press, 1994), pp.51–71; Caroline Gonda, *Reading Daughters' Fictions, 1709–1834: Novels and Society from Manley to Edgeworth* (Cambridge: Cambridge University Press, 1996), pp.163–9; Katherine Hill-Miller, pp.101–27.

85. See Graham Allen 'Beyond Biographism', op. cit., pp.170–84; Lauren Gillingham, 'Romancing Experience: The Seduction of Mary Shelley's *Matilda*', in *Studies in Romanticism* 42.2 (2003), pp.251–69; Diane Long Hoeveler, 'Screen-Memories and Fictionalized Autobiography: Mary Shelley's *Mathilda* and "The Mourner"', in *Nineteenth-Century Contexts*, 27.4 (2005), pp.365–81.

86. The texts of *The Fields of Fancy* and *Matilda* are held in the Abinger Collection of Shelley papers in the Bodleian Library, The University of Oxford, and are classified as MS Dep. d. 374/2 and parts of Bodleian MS Dep. Shelley d. 1. The version entitled 'Mathilda' is in Abinger Dep. d. 374/1. Shelley uses the spelling 'Mathilda' for her female protagonist; however, she referred to the title of her work as *Matilda* (see M, p.2).

87. See Terence Harpold, '"Did you get *Mathilda* from Papa?": Seduction Fantasy and the Circulation of Mary Shelley's *Mathilda*', in *Studies in Romanticism*, 28 (1987), pp.49–67.

88. Elizabeth Nitchie, 'Mary Shelley's *Mathilda*: An Unpublished Story and Its Biographical Significance', in *Studies in Philology* XL.3 (1943), pp.447–62 (pp.447–8).

89. Nitchie, ibid, p.454.

90. For a different approach see Jane Dunn *Moon in Eclipse: A Life of Mary Shelley* (London: Weidenfield and Nicolson, 1978), pp.201–2.

91. Quoted in Florence Marshall, I, pp.254–6.

92. Pamela Clemit, 'From *The Fields of Fancy* to *Matilda*: Mary Shelley's Changing Conception of Her Novella', in *Romanticism* 3.2 (1997), pp.152–69 (p.163).

93. Clemit, ibid, p.152.

94. Clemit, ibid, p.152.

95. See Judith Barbour, "'The Meaning of the tree": The Tale of Mirra in Mary Shelley's *Mathilda*', in *Iconoclastic*, pp.98–114 (p.111); Katherine Hill-Miller, pp.126–7; Sunstein, p.175.

96. Nora Crook has suggested to me that this text may have been a Keeping-Copy from which Mary would have needed to have created a new Fair-Copy for publication. See Clemit's discussion in 'From *The Fields of Fancy* to *Matilda*,' p.168.

97. Betty T. Bennett, *Mary Shelley: An Introduction*, p.51.

98. Muriel Spark, pp.71, 150.

99. Jane Blumberg, *Mary Shelley's Early Novels: 'This Child of Imagination and Misery'* (London: Macmillan, 1993), p.225.

100. Julia Kristeva *Powers of Horror: An Essay on Abjection*, Leon S. Roudiez (trans.) (New York: Columbia University Press, 1982).

101. Tilottama Rajan, 'Mary Shelley's *Mathilda*: Melancholy and the Political Economy of Romanticism', in *Studies in the Novel*, 26.2 (1994), pp.43–68. See also Rajan, *The Supplement of Reading: Figures of Understanding in Romantic Theory and Practice* (Ithaca and London: Cornell University Press, 1990).

102. See Peter L. Thorslev, 'Incest as Romantic Symbol', in *Comparative Literature* 2 (1965), pp.41–58; Eugene Stelzig, '"Though It Were The Deadliest Sin To Love As We Have Loved": The Romantic Idealization of Incest', in *European Romantic Review* 5.2 (1995), pp.230–51. See also Barbara Groseclose, 'The Incest Motif in Shelley's *The Cenci*', in *Comparative Drama* 19.3 (1985), pp.222–39.

103. See Mellor, *Mary Shelley*, pp.191–201. See also Audra Dibert Himes, '"Knew shame, and knew desire": Ambivalence as Structure in Mary Shelley's *Mathilda*', in *Iconoclastic*, pp.115–29; Ranita Chatterjee, '*Mathilda*: Mary Shelley, William Godwin, and the Ideologies of Incest', in *Iconoclastic*, pp.130–49; Margaret Davenport Garrett, 'Writing and Re-writing Incest in Mary Shelley's *Mathilda*', in *The Keats-Shelley Journal*, XLV (1996), pp.44–60.

104. P. B. Shelley wrote the majority of the play by July 1819. See *The Poems of Shelley*, II, p.714.

105. See Shelley, *Poems*, II, p.47.

106. See 'Relation of the Death of the Family of the Cenci' in LL, IV, pp.296–308; also available in *The Bodleian Shelley Manuscripts*, X, Charles E. Robinson and Betty T. Bennett (eds) (New York and London: Garland Publishing, 1992), pp.161–272.

107. Mary Shelley read Ovid in April and May 1815 (see J, p.665); she began to translate Alfieri's plays in September 1818 (J, p.226).

108. Mary Shelley, for example, found no problem in the idea of publishing the horrific details of the execution of Lucretia, Beatrice and Bernardo Cenci (LL, IV, pp.306–7).

109. Shelley wrote a play for children on the Proserpine myth immediately after completion of *Matilda* in early to late 1820: see Shelley, *Novels*, II, pp.69–111. The Shelleys were involved in a prolonged study of Dante's *Purgatorio* and then *Paradiso* throughout 1819. See Jean de Palacio, pp.44–7; Robert Ready, 'Dominion of Demeter: Mary Shelley's *Mathilda*', in *The Keats-Shelley Journal*, LII (2003), pp.94–110.

110. Katherine Hill-Miller, p.107.

111. Francois Fénelon, *Telemachus, Son of Ulysses*, ed. Patrick Riley (Cambridge: Cambridge University Press, 1994).

112. See Charles E. Robinson, 'Mathilda as Dramatic Actress', in *Times*, pp.76–87 and Charlene E. Bunnell, '*Mathilda*: Mary Shelley's Romantic Tragedy', in *The Keats-Shelley Journal*, XLVI (1997), pp.75–96.

113. See Rajan, 'Mary Shelley's *Mathilda*', p.61.

114. 'The Fields of Fancy', in Shelley, *Novels*, II, pp.351–411.

115. See Pamela Clemit, 'From *The Fields of Fancy* to *Matilda*', pp.5–6; Charles E. Robinson, 'Mathilda as Dramatic Actress', pp.30, 34; Elizabeth Nitchie, 'Mary Shelley's *Mathilda*', p.42; Margaret Davenport Garrett, 'Writing and Re-writing Incest in Mary Shelley's *Mathilda*', pp.51–2, 56–7; Tilottama Rajan, 'Mary Shelley's *Mathilda*', pp.64–70.

116. P. B. Shelley, according to Mary, began his translation on 7 July 1818 and finished it on 17 July: see J, pp.217–19.

117. The first three acts of *Prometheus Unbound* had been composed by P. B. Shelley by the spring of 1819. See *Poems of Shelley*, II, pp.456–65.

118. See Graham Allen, 'Beyond Biographism', p.180.

119. Quoted in Jane Dunn, *Moon in Eclipse*, p.178; also in Florence Marshall, I, p.229.

120. Miranda Seymour, pp.234–5.

121. Miranda Seymour, p.236.

122. Janet Todd, 'Introduction' to Mary Wollstonecraft, *Mary* and *Maria*, Mary Shelley, *Matilda*, Janet Todd, ed. (Harmondsworth: Penguin Books, 1992), p.xxiv.

3. *VALPERGA: OR, THE LIFE AND ADVENTURES OF CASTRUCCIO, PRINCE OF LUCCA*

123. See John Williams, *Mary Shelley*, p.78.

124. Nora Crook, '"Meek and Bold": Mary Shelley's Support for the Risorgimento', in *Mary Versus Mary*, Lilla Maria Crisafulli and Giovanna Silvani (eds) (Napoli: Liguori Editore, 2001), pp.73–88 (p.76).

125. For a description of the figures of the '*condottiere* (or adventurer)' and the *signore* see *Valperga*, ed. Tilottama Rajan (Peterborough, Ontario: Broadview Press, 1998), p.28.

126. Betty T. Bennett, 'The Political Philosophy of Mary Shelley's Historical Novels: *Valperga* and *Perkin Warbeck*', in *The Evidence of the Imagination: Studies of Interactions between Life and Art in English Romantic Literature*, Donald H. Reiman, Michael C. Joyce and Betty T. Bennett (eds) (New York: New York University Press, 1978), pp.354–71 (pp.356–7).

127. The name Beatrice, obviously, connects back to Dante and Beatrice Cenci. Euthanasia comes from the Greek ('noble death', good death'): see V, p.16. The name also reminds us of the Greek, philosophical notion of 'the good life' or the life which is conducive to happiness, *eudæmonia*. Joseph Lew argues that Shelley drew her name from David Hume: Joseph Lew, 'God's Sister: History and Ideology in *Valperga*', in *Other*, pp.159–81 (p.162). In actual fact, as Rajan and Crook have shown, Shelley has Godwin's response to Hume in mind in naming her character. In *Political Justice* Godwin had argued that as 'weakness and ignorance' declined, so too would 'government.' The result would be 'the true euthanasia of government' (Godwin, *Political*, IV p.114; see V, p.16). Rajan finds also a covert reference to the principal female character, Asia, in P. B. Shelley's *Prometheus Unbound*. Rajan, *Valperga*, p.447.

128. Michael Rossington, 'Future Uncertain: The Republican Tradition and Its Destiny in *Valperga*', in *Times*, pp.103–18 (p.111).

129. *The Portable Machiavelli*, Peter Bondanella and Mark Musa (eds) (Harmondsworth: Penguin, 1979), p.37.

130. *The Portable Machiavelli*, pp.23–4.

131. Betty T. Bennett, 'Machiavelli's and Mary Shelley's Castruccio: Biography as Metaphor', in *Romanticism*, 3.2. (1997), pp.139–51 (p.142).

132. See *The Portable Machiavelli*, p.21.

133. See Mellor, *Mary Shelley*; Mellor, *Romanticism and Gender* (New York and London: Routledge, 1993) and Mellor, ed. *Romanticism*

and Feminism (Bloomington and Indianapolis: Indiana University Press, 1988). See also Daniel E. White, 'Mary Shelley's *Valperga*: Italy and the Revision of Romantic Aestheticism', in *Fictions*, pp.75–94.

134. Rajan, *Valperga*, p.34. See also Rajan, 'Between Romance and History: Possibility and Contingency in Godwin, Leibniz, and *Valperga*', in *Times*, pp.88–102 (p.97).

135. Rajan, *Valperga*, p.42.

136. Rajan, *Valperga*, p.34.

137. Rajan, *Valperga*, p.33.

138. Rajan, 'Between Romance and History', p.96.

139. Clemit, *The Godwinian Novel*, p.176.

140. Deidre Lynch, 'Historical Novelist' in *Companion*, pp.135–50 (p.136).

141. Stuart Curran, '*Valperga*' in *Companion*, pp.103–15 (p.114). See also Gary Handwerk, 'History, trauma, and the limits of the liberal imagination: William Godwin's historical fiction', in Tilottama Rajan and Julia M. Wright (eds), *Romanticism, history, and the possibilities of genre* (Cambridge: Cambridge University Press, 1998), pp.64–85.

142. See Jon Klancher, 'Godwin and the genre reformers: on necessity and contingency in romantic narrative theory', in *Romanticism, history, and the possibilities of genre*, pp.21–38.

143. Blumberg, *Mary Shelley's Early Novels*, p.76.

144. See, Johanna M. Smith, *Mary Shelley*, pp.74–5. Blumberg, *Mary Shelley's Early Novels*, pp.99–113. See also William D. Brewer, *The Mental Anatomies of William Godwin and Mary Shelley* (London: Associated University Presses, 2001), pp.129–56.

145. See Cathy Caruth, *Unclaimed Experience: Trauma, Narrative, and History* (Baltimore and London: The Johns Hopkins University Press, 1996).

146. Crook quotes Sismondi on the 'Paterini, a sect of Manicheans known as the Albigensians or Cathars' who believed 'that the creator of the material universe is an evil spirit; that man is a fallen angel; that the individual is free to investigate religious questions' (V, p.234). Rajan gives Thomas Love Peacock's *Ahrimanes* as a source-text for Shelley's treatment of the sect, along with Asia's questioning of Demogorgon in the second act of *Prometheus Unbound* (Rajan, *Valperga*, pp.461–2). Although neither Crook nor Rajan state it, Paterinism is clearly an off-shoot of Gnosticism, for which see Hans Jonas, *The Gnostic Religion: The Message of*

the Alien God and the Beginnings of Christianity (1958) 2nd edn., revised (London: Routledge, 1992).

147. See Syndy McMillen Conger, 'Mary Shelley's Women in Prison', in *Iconoclastic*, pp.81–97.

148. See Rajan, *Valperga*, p.463. Shelley, *Poems*, II, p.692. *Julian and Maddalo* was dated 'Rome, May, 1819' by Mary Shelley when she first published it in the 1824 *Posthumous Poems*.

149. Bennett, *Mary Shelley: An Introduction*, p.59.

150. Lisa Hopkins, 'Death and the Castrated: The Complex Psyches of *Valperga*', in *Romanticism on the Net*, 40, November 2005.

151. Blumberg, *Mary Shelley's Early Novels*, p.91.

152. Castruccio here is figured as 'the evil genius of the scene', and as soon as he leaves '[t]he eternal spirit of the universe' descends once again upon her (V, p.320).

4. *THE LAST MAN*

153. See John Williams, *Mary Shelley*, pp.107–8; Walter Edwin Peck, 'The Biographical Element in the Novels of Mary Wollstonecraft Shelley', in *PMLA*, 38.1 (1923), pp.196–219; Noel Gerson, *Daughter of Earth and Water: A Biography of Mary Wollstonecraft Shelley* (New York: William Morrow & Co., 1973), p.234.

154. Bennett, *Mary Shelley*, p.73. See also, Bennett, 'Radical Imaginings: Mary Shelley's *The Last Man*', in *The Wordsworth Circle*, 26.3 (1995), pp.147–52.

155. See: Muriel Spark, *Mary Shelley*, p.188; Gregory O'Dea, 'Prophetic History and Textuality in Mary Shelley's *The Last Man*', in *Papers on Language and Literature*, 28.3 (1992), pp.283–304; Richard S. Allbright, '"In the mean time what did Perdita?": Rhythms and Reversals in Mary Shelley's *The Last Man*', in *Romanticism on the Net*, 13, February (1999); Clemit, *The Godwinian Novel*, pp.183–210.

156. For discussions of the largely negative reviews the novel received on first publication, see the following: Hugh J. Luke, Jnr., '*The Last Man*: Mary Shelley's Myth of the Solitary', in *The Prairie Schooner*, 39.4 (1965), pp.316–27; Robert Lance Synder, 'Apocalypse and Indeterminacy in Mary Shelley's *The Last Man*', in *Studies in Romanticism*, 17.4 (1978), pp.435–52; Steven Goldsmith, 'Apocalypse and Gender: Mary Shelley's *The Last Man*', in *Unbuilding Jerusalem: Apocalypse and Romantic Representation* (Ithaca and London: Cornell University Press, 1993), pp.261–313; Morton D. Paley, '*The*

Last Man: Apocalypse Without Millennium', in *Other*, pp.107–23; Lynn Wells, 'The Triumph of Death: Reading and Narrative in Mary Shelley's *The Last Man*', in *Iconoclastic*, pp.212–34.

157. Sophie Thomas, 'The End of the Fragment, the Problem of the Preface: Proliferation and Finality in *The Last Man*', in *Fictions*, pp.22–38 (p.22). The reference here is to 'The Last Book: with a Dissertation On Last Things in General', in *The Monthly Magazine*, n.s. II (1826), pp.137–43; see also Morton D. Paley, p.108.

158. Jean-Babtiste Cousin de Grainville, *The Last Man, or Omegarus and Syderia, A Romance in Futurity*, 2 Vols. (London: Dutton, 1806). For accounts of the 'last man' literature of the period, see: A. J. Sambrook, 'A Romantic Theme: The Last Man' in *Forum for Modern Language Studies*, 2.1. (1966), pp.25–33; Anne McWhir, ed, *The Last Man* (Peterborough, Ontario: Broadview, 1996), pp.xiii–xvi; Steven Goldsmith, pp.265–75. For a wider account of 'last man' and 'last of the race' literature, see Fiona Stafford, *The Last of the Race*. Oxford: Oxford University Press, 1994.

159. See Steven Goldsmith, pp.270–1. For the poems, see McWhir, *The Last Man*, pp.369–76.

160. See, Bennett, *Mary Shelley*, pp. 72–86; Gary Kelly, 'Last Men: Hemans and Mary Shelley in the 1820s', in *Romanticism*, 3.2 (1997), pp.198–208.

161. See Lee Sterrenburg, '*The Last Man*: Anatomy of Failed Revolutions', in *Nineteenth-Century Fiction*, 33.3 (1978), pp.324–47.

162. Blumberg, *Mary Shelley's Early Novels*, pp.134, 153.

163. Anonymous review of *The Last Man* in *The Literary Gazette and Journal of Belles Lettres, Arts, Sciences, &c*, 474 (18 February 1826), pp.102–3 (p.103).

164. Ibid, p.102.

165. See Jane Aaron, 'The Return of the Repressed: Reading Mary Shelley's *The Last Man*', in Susan Sellars, ed. *Feminist Criticism: Theory and Practice* (Hemel Hempstead: Harvester Wheatsheaf, 1991), pp.9–21.

166. See Sandra M. Gilbert and Susan Gubar, *The Madwoman in the Attic: The Woman Writer and the Nineteenth-Century Literary Imagination* (New Haven and London: Yale University Press, 1979), pp.93–104; Michael Eberle-Sinatra, 'Gender, Authorship and Male Domination: Mary Shelley's Limited Freedom in *Frankenstein* and *The Last Man*', in *Fictions*, pp.95–108; Maggie Kilgour, '"One Immortality": The Shaping of the Shelleys in *The Last Man*', in *European Romantic Review*, 16.5 (2005), pp.563–88.

167. See Julia M. Wright, '"Little England": Anxieties of Space in Mary Shelley's *The Last Man*', in *Fictions*, pp.129–49; Charlotte Sussman, '"Islanded in the World": Cultural Memory and Human Mobility', in *PMLA*, 118.2 (2003), pp.286–301.

168. Anne K. Mellor, 'Response to "The Last Man and the New History" (Greg Kucich)', in *Romantic Circles MOO Conference*, September 13, 1997.

169. See, for example, Alan Richardson, '*The Last Man* and the Plague of Empire', in *Romantic Circles MOO Conference*; Liz Rackley, 'The Last Man's Burden: A Response to Alan Richardson's "*The Last Man* and the Plague of Empire"', in *Romantic Circles MOO Conference*, September 13, 1997; Young-Ok An, '"Read Your Fall": The Signs of Plague in *The Last Man*', in *Studies in Romanticism*, 44.4 (2005), pp.581–604.

170. Paul A. Cantor, 'The Apocalypse of Empire: Mary Shelley's *The Last Man*', in *Iconoclastic*, pp.193–211 (p.202).

171. McWhir, *The Last Man*, p.xiii.

172. Nora Crook, 'Review of Mary Shelley, *The Last Man* (eds), Anne McWhir and Mary Shelley, *Lodore* (ed.) Lisa Vargo', in *Romanticism on the Net*, 11, August 1998.

173. Review of *The Last Man* in *Panoramic Miscellany; or, Monthly Magazine and Review of Literature, Science, Arts, Inventions, and Occurrences*, March 1826, pp.380–6, see Reiman, *The Romantics Reviewed*, C. II, pp.742–8 (p.744).

174. The journal entry is dated 14 May 1824. J, pp.476–7.

175. See Graham Allen, 'Mary Shelley as Elegiac Poet: The Return and 'The Choice' in *Romanticism*, 13.3 (2007), pp.219–32.

176. 'Albe' was the Shelleys' nickname for Byron.

177. For Shelley and the figure of Cassandra, see Barbara Jane O'Sullivan, 'Beatrice in *Valperga*: A New Cassandra', in *Other*, pp.140–58.

178. See Blumberg, *Mary Shelley's Early Novels*, p.114.

179. See also Blumberg, ibid, p.149.

180. See Gilbert and Gubar, pp.93–104 and Goldsmith, pp.275–83.

181. 'Preface' to *Posthumous Poems of Percy Bysshe Shelley* in Shelley, *Novels*, II, p.241.

182. Sophie Thomas, p.24.

183. For an extensive account of Jacobin fiction in England, see Gary Kelly, *The English Jacobin Novel: 1780–1805* (Oxford: Clarendon Press, 1976). Clemit's *The Godwinian Novel*, op. cit, is an invaluable guide to Godwin and Shelley's relations to this novel form.

184. See William Lomax, 'Epic Reversals in Mary Shelley's *The Last Man*: Romantic Irony and the Roots of Science Fiction', in Michael K. Langford, ed. *Contours of the Fantastic: Selected Essays from the Eighth International Conference on the Fantastic in the Arts* (New York: Greenwood Press, 1990), pp.7–17; Samantha Webb, 'Reading the End of the World: *The Last Man*, History, and the Agency of Romantic Authorship', in *Times*, pp.119–33; Kari E. Lokke, '*The Last Man*', in *Companion*, pp.116–34.

185. Lynn Wells, p.215.

186. The reading I am presenting here can be reinforced by reference to Chris Baldick's extended discussion of the relation between the body politic figure and modern figurations of monstrosity. See Baldick, *In Frankenstein's Shadow*, op. cit.

187. See Mellor, *Mary Shelley*, pp.148–69; Barbara Johnson, '*The Last Man*', in *Other*, pp.258–66; Audrey A. Fisch, 'Plaguing Politics: AIDS, Deconstruction, and *The Last Man*', in *Other*, pp.267–86; Mary Jacobus, 'Replacing the Race of Mothers: AIDS and *The Last Man*', in *First Things: The Maternal Imaginary in Literature, Art, and Psychoanalysis* (New York and London: Routledge, 1995), pp.105–25.

188. Mark Canuel, 'Acts, Rules, and *The Last Man*', in *Nineteenth-Century Literature*, 53.2 (1998), pp.147–70 (p.150).

189. Mellor, *Mary Shelley*, p.163.

190. Mellor, ibid, p.164.

191. See Jacques Derrida, 'Some Statements and Truisms about Neologisms, Newisms, Postisms, Parasitisms, and Other Small Seismisms.' Anne Tomiche (trans.) in *The States of 'Theory'*, David Carroll, ed. (New York: Columbia University Press, 1990), pp.63–94.

192. Mellor, *Mary Shelley*, p.169.

193. See Jacques Derrida, 'The Principle of Reason: The University in the Eyes of Its Pupils', Catherine Porter and Edward P. Morris (trans.), in *diacritics* 13.3 (1983), pp.3–20 (p.13).

194. Thomas Robert Malthus, *An Essay on the Principle of Population*, Philip Appleman, ed. (New York and London: W. W. Norton, 1976); William Godwin, *Of Population: An Enquiry Concerning the Power of Increase in the Numbers of Mankind, Being an Answer to Mr. Malthus's Essay on That Subject* (London: Longman, Hurst, Rees, Orme and Brown, 1820).

195. Allbright, p.8.

196. See Giovanni Franci, 'A Mirror of the Future: Vision and Apocalypse in Mary Shelley's *The Last Man*', in Harold Bloom, ed.

Mary Shelley, Modern Critical Views (New York: Chelsea House Pubs., 1985), pp.181–91.

197. Fisch, 'Plaguing Politics', p.279.

198. Shelley's use of the word comes before the invention of electric ('duplex') telegraphy and probably derives from established maritime technology in which, through a system of mirrors, ships communicated with each other. The maritime aspect of the figure sits well with the novel's most consistent and explicit figurative patterns. I owe these comments to conversations with Nora Crook.

199. *Metalepsis*, the metonymic substitution of one word for another word which is itself figurative (OED).

200. See Shelley's letter of 19 February 1825 to John Cam Hobhouse (L, I, p.466); LM, p.81; McWhir, *The Last Man*, p.79.

201. William's body, in fact, did not by this time lie under the small headstone near the grave of Keats: see L, I, p.257.

202. See Nigel Leask, *Curiosity and the Aesthetics of Travel Writing, 1770–1840* (Oxford and New York: Oxford University Press, 2002), pp.102–56. Jane (Webb) Loudon, *The Mummy! A Tale of the Twenty-Second Century*, ed. Alan Rauch (Ann Arbor: University of Michigan Press, 1994).

5. THE FORTUNES OF PERKIN WARBECK

203. See *The 'Perkin Warbeck' Project* http://www.radford.edu/~webpf-mind/pwp.htm. For the reviews of the novel see W. H. Lyles *Mary Shelley: An Annotated Bibliography* (New York and London: Garland Publishing, Inc, 1975), pp.177–9; de Palacio, pp.665–7.

204. Seymour, p.362.

205. Deidre Lynch, 'Historical Novelist', p.137; Charlene E. Bunnell, *'All the World's a Stage': Dramatic Sensibility in Mary Shelley's Novels* (New York and London: Routledge, 2002), p.133; Sunstein, p.300; Melissa Sites, 'Chivalry and Utopian Domesticity in Mary Shelley's *The Fortunes of Perkin Warbeck*', in *European Romantic Review* 15.5 (2005), pp.525–43.

206. See L, II, 64–5, 88. See also Gareth Dunleavy, 'Two New Mary Shelley Letters and the "Irish" Chapters of *Perkin Warbeck*', in *Keats-Shelley Journal* 13 (1964), pp.6–10.

207. John Ford, *The Chronicle History of Perkin Warbeck: A Strange Truth*, Peter Ure, ed. (London: Methuen, 1968).

208. Lidia Garbin, 'The Fortunes of Perkin Warbeck: Walter Scott in the Writings of Mary Shelley', in *Romanticism on the Net*, 6, May, 1997. For an extended version of this essay see 'Mary Shelley and Walter Scott: *The Fortunes of Perkin Warbeck* and the Historical Novel', in *Fictions*, pp.150–63.

209. Boyd Hilton, *A Mad, Bad, and Dangerous People?: England 1783–1846* (Oxford: Clarendon Press, 2006), pp.372–438 (p.372).

210. See Norman Gash, *Aristocracy and People: Britain 1815–1865* (London: Edward Arnold, 1979), p.142.

211. Linda Colley, *Britons: Forging the Nation, 1707–1837* (London: Pimlico, 1994), p.324.

212. Colley, p.336.

213. See de Palacio, pp.172–80.

214. Asa Briggs, *The Age of Improvement, 1783–1867* (Revised edn.) (London and New York: Longman, 1979), p.226.

215. For extracts from Canning's speech, see Timothy Morton, ed. *A Routledge Literary Sourcebook on Mary Shelley's 'Frankenstein'*, p.30. It is common in *Frankenstein* criticism to follow Chris Baldick's lead and to remark on the reactionary nature of Canning's speech: see Baldick, *In Frankenstein's Shadow*, p.60. As Shelley's remarks about his conduct as Foreign Secretary in her letter to Trelawny demonstrate, Canning was a complex political animal, once contributor to the *Anti-Jacobin Review* and founder of the *Quarterly Review*, and so associated with the reaction against 1790s radical politics in Britain. He was, by 1827, viewed as a figure who could bring greater liberalization and unification to British politics and society.

216. For further discussion of Canning in this period, see Bennett (L, I, p.570) and Hilton, pp.317–18.

217. See Melissa Sites; see also William D. Brewer, 'William Godwin, Chivalry, and Mary Shelley's *The Fortunes of Perkin Warbeck*', in *Papers on Language and Literature*, 35 (1999), pp.187–205.

218. Spark, pp.205–6.

219. Spark, p.206.

220. William A. Walling, *Mary Shelley* (New York: Twayne Publishers, 1972), pp.103–4.

221. Garbin, in *Fictions*, p.156.

222. See Smith, *Mary Shelley*, pp.81–91; Bennett, *Mary Shelley*, pp.86–91; Blumberg, pp.216–19; Lisa Hopkins, 'The Self and the Monstrous', in *Iconoclastic*, pp.260–74.

223. See Philip Tyree Wade, *Influence and Intent in the Prose Fiction of Percy and Mary Shelley*, Ph.D diss. (Chapel Hill: The University of North Carolina, 1966), pp.173–4.

224. Bennett, 'The Political Philosophy of Mary Shelley's Historical Novels', p.356.

225. Bennett, ibid.

226. See Jane Dunn, pp.296–7.

227. Shelley's portrait of Katherine's later life is a huge departure from the historical record. As Fischer reminds us: 'The suppressed acts of Katherine's "after life" .... included acceptance of a pension from Henry VII and three successive marriages (to James Strangeways, Sir Matthew Cradock and Christopher Ashton) contracted during the reign of Henry VIII' (PW, p.395).

228. Richard Holmes, 'Shelley Undrowned', in *Interrupted Lives*, ed. Andrew Motion (London: The National Portrait Gallery, 2004), p.31.

6. *LODORE*

229. Fiona Stafford has argued that the internal dates make the action of the novel 'coincide roughly with the period of composition between 1831 and 1833': '*Lodore*: a Tale of the Present Time', in *Fictions*, pp.181–93 (182). The proposed subtitle was eventually dropped before publication.

230. Poovey, *The Proper Lady*, p.143. Poovey's assessment is rather challenged, however, by the fact that various contemporary reviewers of *Lodore* felt that the literary strength of the novel had finally resolved any doubt about Mary Shelley's authorship of *Frankenstein*. See Vargo, *Lodore*, pp.535, 545.

231. Blumberg, *Mary Shelley's Early Novels*, p.186.

232. Richard Garnett, ed. *Tales and Stories by Mary Wollstonecraft Shelley* (London: William Patterson & Co., 1891). See Edward Dowden, *The Life of Percy Bysshe Shelley*. The 'fortunate discovery' is that Shelley's novels can be mined for biographical data about P. B. Shelley. For discussions of this biographist line, see Lisa Vargo, ed. *Lodore* (Peterborough, Ontario: Broadview Press, 1997), pp.9–40; Vargo, '*Lodore* and the "Novel of Society"' in *Women's Writing*, 6.3 (1999), pp.425–40; Vargo, 'Further Thoughts on the Education of Daughters: *Lodore* as an Imagined Conversation with Wollstonecraft', in *Mary Wollstonecraft and Mary Shelley: Writing Lives*, Helen M. Buss, D. L. Macdonald and Anne

McWhir (eds) (Waterloo, Ontario: Wilfred Laurier University Press, 2001), pp.177–87.

233. Kate Ferguson Ellis, 'Subversive Surfaces: The Limits of Domestic Affection in Mary Shelley's Later Fiction', in *Other*, pp. 220–34 (p.230).

234. See Jeanne Moskal, '"To speak in Sanchean phrase": Cervantes and the Politics of Mary Shelley's *History of a Six Weeks' Tour*', in *Times*, pp.18–37; Charlene E. Bunnell, '*All the World's a Stage*', pp.151–66; Erin L. Webster-Garrett, pp.161–84. See also Caroline Gonda, '*Lodore* and Fanny Derham's Story', in *Women's Writing*, 6.3 (1999), pp.329–44.

235. See Mellor, *Mary Shelley*, p.206; Barbara Jane O'Sullivan, p.154; Webster-Garrett, p.176.

236. Sunstein, p.329.

237. Gerson, p.254.

238. Vargo, *Lodore*, p.541.

239. Hunt, quoted in Vargo, *Lodore*, p.542.

240. See Vargo's various readings and the reading by Stafford already cited, plus Stafford's 'Introduction' to the Pickering edition (Lod, pp.ix–xiii), along with Richard Cronin's 'Mary Shelley and Edward Bulwer: *Lodore* as Hybrid Fiction', in *Fictions*, pp.39–54.

241. Gary Kelly, *English Fiction of the Romantic Period, 1789–1830* (London and New York: Longman, 1989), pp.220–7. See Vargo, 'Lodore and the "Novel of Society"', p.426.

242. Michael Wheeler, *English Fiction of the Victorian Period, 1830–1890* (London and New York: Longman, 1985), p.16.

243. See Stafford, '*Lodore*: a Tale of the Present Time?', pp.184–5.

244. Cronin, p.49.

245. I take this term from the Russian theorist and critic, M. M. Bakhtin.

246. See Stafford, '*Lodore*: a Tale of the Present Times', pp.182–4.

247. Stafford, '*Lodore*: a Tale of the Present Times', p.184.

248. Cronin, p.39.

249. Stafford, '*Lodore*: a Tale of the Present Times', p.189.

250. Williams, *Mary Shelley*, p.148.

251. See Stafford '*Lodore*: a Tale of the Present Times', pp.187–8.

252. Because of the structural importance of the 'desert' figure throughout the novel, I prefer the translation given by Vargo than the

'wildernesses' of Stafford: 'Deserts are made for lovers, but one doesn't make love in a desert' (*Lodore*, Vargo, p.69).

253. See L, I, p.245. See also Thomas Medwin, *The Life of Percy Shelley*, Intro. and Commentary by H. Buxton Forman (London: Oxford University Press, 1913), pp.404–5.

254. Claire Clairmont's negative response to *Lodore* was due to her frustration at her half-sister's insistence on portraying characters who resembled the 'vile spirit' of Byron. See Seymour, p.354.

255. Chiasmus, representable through the letter x, is in grammar 'A figure by which the order of words in one clause is inverted in a second clause' (OED). My use of the figure is, of course, highly metaphorical.

256. See Stafford, Lod, p.ix.

257. Bunnell, 'The Illusion of "Great Expectations": Manners and Morals in Mary Shelley's *Lodore* and *Falkner*', in *Iconoclastic*, pp.275–92 (p.277).

258. Mellor, *Mary Shelley*, p.190.

259. Hill-Miller, p.150.

260. Hill-Miller, p.142.

261. See Vargo, 'Further Thoughts', pp.183–4 and '*Lodore* and the "Novel of Society"', p.436.

262. Mellor, *Mary Shelley*, p.206.

263. Webster-Garrett, p.178.

7. *FALKNER, A NOVEL*

264. Smith, *Mary Shelley*, p.114.

265. Sir Boyville is Neville's father.

266. Mellor, *Mary Shelley*, p.203.

267. Mellor, *Mary Shelley*, p.204.

268. Poovey, *The Proper Lady*, p.163.

269. Hill-Miller, p.192.

270. Kate Ferguson Ellis, 'Subversive Surfaces', in *Other*, pp.220–34 and '*Falkner* and other fictions', in *Companion*, pp.151–62 (p.153).

271. Julia Saunders, 'Rehabilitating the Family in Mary Shelley's *Falkner*', in *Fictions*, pp.211–23 (pp.228, 230).

272. See Betty T. Bennett, '"Not this time, Victor": Mary Shelley's Reversioning of Elizabeth, from *Frakenstein* to *Falkner*', in *Times*, pp.1–17 (p.11); Webster-Garrett, pp.181–4.

273. For the semiotics of Elizabeth's needlework see Nora Crook, '"Work" in Mary Shelley's Journals', in *The Keats-Shelley Review*, 18 (2004), pp.123–37.

274. *Lives of the Great Romantics* 3, Vol. II, *Wollstonecraft*, ed. Harriet Jump (London: Pickering & Chatto, 1999), pp.157–67 (p.167). A selection from Godwin's *Memoir* is also contained in the above: for the full text see: Mary Wollstonecraft, *A Short Residence in Sweden* and William Godwin, *Memoirs of the Author of 'The Vindication of Woman'*, Richard Holmes, ed. (Harmondsworth: Penguin, 1987).

275. Saunders, p.215.

276. See Pamela Clemit, 'Mary Shelley and William Godwin: a literary-political partnership, 1823–1836', in *Women's Writing*, 6.3 (1999), pp.285–95; Ranita Chatterjee, 'Filial Ties: Godwin's *Deloraine* and Mary Shelley's Writings', in *European Romantic Review*, 18.1 (2007), pp.29–41.

277. See Florence Marshall, pp.241–2.

278. For a different account of Godwin's writer's block see: Peter H. Marshall, *William Godwin* (New Haven and London: Yale University Press, 1984), p.375.

279. See C. Kegan Paul, *William Godwin: His Friends and Contemporaries*, Vol. II pp.304–9. For a discussion of these contexts see Maurice Hindle's introduction to Godwin, *Novels*, VIII, pp.v–vii.

280. See Walling, pp.107–9; Nitchie, *Mary Shelley*, pp.123–6; Smith, *Mary Shelley*, pp.111–12; Williams, *Mary Shelley*, p.155.

281. Lynn Pykett, 'The Newgate Novel and sensational fiction, 1830–1868', in *The Cambridge Companion to Crime Fiction*, Martin Priestman, ed. (Cambridge: Cambridge University Press, 2003), pp.19–39 (p.21).

282. See Pykett, p.19.

283. C. Kegan Paul, p.305.

284. See William D. Brewer, 'Unnaturalized Englishmen in Mary Shelley's Fiction' in *Romanticism on the Net*, 11 August 1998; see also Brewer's *Mental Anatomies*, pp.78–82.

285. At this stage of the novel Mr. Neville has not yet gained the title of Sir Boyville.

286. Virgil, *The Aeneid of Virgil*, C. Day Lewis (trans.). London: The Hogarth Press, 1952, Book VIII, p.185.

287. See Bunnell, '*All the World's a Stage*', pp.175–7.

288. Bennett, 'Not this time, Victor', p.15.

289. See Graham Allen, 'Public and Private Fidelity: Mary Shelley's "Life of William Godwin" and *Falkner*', in *Fictions*, pp.224–42.

AFTERWORD: BEYOND THE NOVELS

290. See Clemit's notes to the 'Prefaces and Notes' section of Shelley *Novels*, II, pp.232–5.

291. See, Michael O'Neill, '"Trying to make it as good as I can": Mary Shelley's Editing of P. B. Shelley's Poetry and Prose', in *Times*, pp.185–97; Mary Favret, 'Mary Shelley's Sympathy and Irony: The Editor and Her Corpus' and Susan J. Wolfson, 'Editorial Privilege: Mary Shelley and Percy Shelley's Audiences', in *Other*, pp.17–38 and 39–72; Susan J. Wolfson, 'Mary Shelley, editor', in *Companion,* pp.193–210. See also Shelley, *Poems*, I, pp.xii–xxxii.

292. See the introductions and notes to the first three volumes of LL by Tilar J. Mazzeo, Lisa Vargo and Clarissa Campbell Orr; also see Greg Kucich, 'Mary Shelley's *Lives* and the Reengendering of History', in *Times*, pp.198–213; Greg Kucich, 'Biographer', in *Companion*, pp.226–41.

293. Moskal notes: 'The First Afghan War lasted from 1838 to 1842. In January 1842 British and Indian troops retreating from Kabul were massacred by Afghans. In September 1842 the British recaptured Kabul, executing hundreds of insurgents' (R, p.351).

Bibliography

Aaron, Jane, 'The Return of the Repressed: Reading Mary Shelley's *The Last Man*', in ed. Susan Sellars. *Feminist Criticism: Theory and Practice*. Hemel Hempstead: Harvester Wheatsheaf, 1991, pp.9–21.

Allbright, Richard S, '"In the mean time what did Perdita?": Rhythms and Reversals in Mary Shelley's *The Last Man*', in *Romanticism on the Net*, 13, February 1999.

Allen, Graham, 'Beyond Biographism: Mary Shelley's Mathilda, Inter-textuality, and the Wandering Subject', in *Romanticism* 3.2 (1997), pp.170–84.

—— 'Public and Private Fidelity: Mary Shelley's "Life of William Godwin" and *Falkner*', in *Fictions*, pp.224–42.

—— *Intertextuality*. London: Routledge, 2000.

—— 'Mary Shelley as Elegiac Poet: The Return and 'The Choice', in *Romanticism* 13.3 (2007), pp.219–32.

—— '"Unfashioned creatures, but half made up": Beginning with Mary Shelley's Spectre', in *Angelaki* 12:3 (2008), forthcoming.

Anonymous review of *The Last Man* in *The Literary Gazette and Journal of Belles Lettres, Arts, Sciences, &*, 474, 18 February 1826, pp.102–3.

Anonymous review. 'The Last Book: with a Dissertation On Last Things in General', in *The Monthly Magazine*, n.s., II, 1826, pp.137–43.

An, Young-Ok, '"Read Your Fall": The Signs of Plague in *The Last Man*', in *Studies in Romanticism*, 44.4 (2005), pp.581–604.

Baldick, Chris, *In Frankenstein's Shadow: Myth, Monstrosity and Nineteenth-Century Writing*. Oxford: The Clarendon Press, 1987.

Barbour, Judith, '"The Meaning of the tree": The Tale of Mirra in Mary Shelley's *Mathilda*', in *Iconoclastic*, pp.98–114.

Bennett, Betty, 'The Political Philosophy of Mary Shelley's Historical Novels: *Valperga* and *Perkin Warbeck*', in *The Evidence of the Imagination: Studies of Interactions between Life and Art in English Romantic Literature* (eds), Donald H. Reiman, Michael C. Joyce and Betty T. Bennett, with Doucet Devin Fischer and Ricji B. Herzfield. New York: New York University Press, 1978, pp.354–71.

—— and Charles E. Robinson (eds), 'Introduction' to *The Mary Shelley Reader*. New York and Oxford: Oxford University Press, 1990, pp.3–10.

—— *Mary Diana Dodds: A Gentleman and a Scholar*. Baltimore and London: The Johns Hopkins University Press, 1991.

—— 'Radical Imaginings: Mary Shelley's *The Last Man*', in *The Wordsworth Circle*, 26.3 (1995), pp.147–52.

—— 'Machiavelli's and Mary Shelley's Castruccio: Biography as Metaphor', in *Romanticism*, 3.2 (1997), pp.139–51.

—— *Mary Shelley: An Introduction*. Baltimore and London: The Johns Hopkins University Press, 1998.

—— ed., *Lives of the Great Romantics* 3. Gen. Ed. John Mullan. *Mary Shelley*. Vol. III. London: Pickering and Chatto, 1999.

—— and Stuart Curran (eds), *Mary Shelley in Her Times*. Baltimore and London: The Johns Hopkins University Press, 2000.

—— '"Not this time, Victor": Mary Shelley's Reversioning of Elizabeth, from *Frakenstein* to *Falkner*', in *Times*, pp.1–17.

Blumberg, Jane, *Mary Shelley's Early Novels: 'This Child of Imagination and Misery'*. London: Macmillan, 1993.

Botting, Fred, *Making Monstrous: 'Frankenstein', Criticism, Theory*. Manchester and New York: Manchester University Press, 1991.

—— ed. *Frankenstein: Mary Shelley*. New York: St. Martin's Press, 1995.

Brewer, William D., 'Unnaturalized Englishmen in Mary Shelley's Fiction', in *Romanticism on the Net*, 11, August 1998.

—— 'William Godwin, Chivalry, and Mary Shelley's *The Fortunes of Perkin Warbeck*', in *Papers on Language and Literature*, 35 (1999), pp.187–205.

—— *The Mental Anatomies of William Godwin and Mary Shelley*. London: Associated University Presses, 2001.

Briggs, Asa, *The Age of Improvement, 1783–1867*. Revised Ed. London and New York: Longman, 1979.

Bulwer, Edward, *The Novels of Sir Edward Bulwer Lytton*. 47 Vols. Edinburgh and London: W. Blackwood and Sons, 1859–74.

Bunnell, Charlene E., '*Mathilda*: Mary Shelley's Romantic Tragedy', in *The Keats-Shelley Journal*. XLVI (1997), pp.75–96.

—— 'The Illusion of "Great Expectations": Manners and Morals in Mary Shelley's *Lodore* and *Falkner*', in *Iconoclastic*, pp.275–92.

—— '*All the World's a Stage*': *Dramatic Sensibility in Mary Shelley's Novels*. New York and London: Routledge, 2002.

Butler, Marilyn, *Jane Austen and the War of Ideas*. 2nd edn. Oxford: Oxford University Press, 1987.

Byron, Lord, *The Complete Poetical Works* ed. Jerome J. McGann. 7 Vols. Oxford: Calrendon Press, 1980–93.

Cantor, Paul A., 'The Apocalypse of Empire: Mary Shelley's *The Last Man*', in *Iconoclastic*, pp.193–211.

Canuel, Mark, 'Acts, Rules, and *The Last Man*', in *Nineteenth-Century Literature*, 53.2 (1998), pp.147–70.

Caruth, Cathy, *Unclaimed Experience: Trauma, Narrative, and History*. Baltimore and London: The Johns Hopkins University Press, 1996.

Chatterjee, Ranita, '*Mathilda*: Mary Shelley, William Godwin, and the Ideologies of Incest', in *Iconoclastic*, pp.130–49.

—— 'Filial Ties: Godwin's *Deloraine* and Mary Shelley's Writings', in *European Romantic Review*. 18.1 (2007), pp.29–41.

Church, Richard, *Mary Shelley*. London: Gerald Howe, 1928.

Clemit, Pamela, *The Godwinian Novel: The Rational Fictions of Godwin, Brockden Brown, Mary Shelley*. Oxford: Clarendon Press, 1993.

—— 'From *The Fields of Fancy* to *Matilda*: Mary Shelley's Changing Conception of Her Novella', in *Romanticism*. 3.2 (1997), pp.152–69.

—— 'Mary Wollstonecract Shelley', in *Literature of the Romantic Period: A Bibliographical Guide* ed. Michael O'Neill. Oxford: Clarendon Press, 1998, pp.284–97.

—— 'Mary Shelley and William Godwin: a literary-political partnership, 1823–1836', in *Women's Writing*. 6.3 (1999), pp.285–95.

Colley, Linda, *Britons: Forging the Nation, 1707–1837*. London: Pimlico, 1994.

Conger, Syndy M., Frederick S. Frank and Gregory O'Dea (eds), *Iconoclastic Depatures: Mary Shelley after 'Frankenstein'*. Madison, Teaneck: Fairleigh Dickinson University Press, 1997.

Conger, Syndy M., 'Mary Shelley's Women in Prison', in *Iconoclastic*, pp.81–97.

Crisafulli, Lilla Maria and Giovanna Silvani (eds), *Mary Versus Mary*. Napoli: Liguori Editore, 2001.

Cronin, Richard, 'Mary Shelley and Edward Bulwer: *Lodore* as Hybrid Fiction', in *Fictions*, pp.39–54.

Crook, Nora, Review of Mary Shelley, *The Last Man*, eds Anne McWhir and Mary Shelley, *Lodore*, ed. Lisa Vargo, in *Romanticism on the Net*. 11, August 1998.

—— 'Sleuthing towards a Mary Shelley Canon', in *Women's Writing*. 6:3 (1999), pp.413–24.

—— '"Meek and Bold": Mary Shelley's Support for the Risorgimento', in *Mary Versus Mary* (eds), Lilla Maria Crisafulli and Giovanna Silvani. Napoli: Liguori Editore, 2001, pp.73–88.

—— '"Work" in Mary Shelley's Journals', in *The Keats-Shelley Review*. 18 (2004), pp.123–37.

Curran, Stuart, '*Valperga*', in *Companion*, pp.103–15.

Derrida, Jacques, *The Politics of Friendship*. Trans. George Collins. London and New York: Verso, 1997.

—— 'Some Statements and Truisms about Neologisms, Newisms, Postisms, Parasitisms, and Other Small Seismisms'. Trans. Anne Tomiche, in *The States of 'Theory'* ed. David Carroll. New York: Columbia University Press, 1990, pp.63–94.

—— The Principle of Reason: The University in the Eyes of Its Pupils'. Trans. Catherine Porter and Edward P. Morris. *diacritics*. 13.3 (1983), pp.3–20.

Dowden, Edward, *The Life of Percy Bysshe Shelley*. 2 Vols. London: Kegan Paul, Trench & Co, 1886.

Dunleavy, Gareth, 'Two New Mary Shelley Letters and the "Irish" Chapters of *Perkin Warbeck*', in *Keats-Shelley Journal*. 13 (1964), pp.6–10.

Dunn, Jane, *Moon in Eclipse: A Life of Mary Shelley*. London: Weidenfield and Nicolson, 1978.

Eberle-Sinatra, Michael, ed. (Intro.) Nora Crook. *Mary Shelley's Fictions: From 'Frankenstein' to 'Falkner'*. London: Macmillan, 2000.

—— 'Gender, Authorship and Male Domination: Mary Shelley's Limited Freedom in *Frankenstein* and *The Last Man*', in *Mary Shelley's Fictions*, pp.95–108.

Ellis, Kate Ferguson, 'Monsters in the Garden: Mary Shelley and the Bourgeois Family', in *Endurance*, pp.123–42.

—— 'Subversive Surfaces: The Limits of Domestic Affection in Mary Shelley's Later Fiction', in *Other*, pp.220–34.

—— '*Falkner* and other fictions', in *Companion*, pp.151–62.

Engelberg, Karsten Klejs, *The Making of the Shelley Myth: An Annotated Bibliography of Criticism of Percy Bysshe Shelley, 1822–1860*. Meckler: Mansell Pubs, 1988.

Favret, Mary, 'Mary Shelley's Sympathy and Irony: The Editor and Her Corpus', in *Other*, pp.17–38.

Fénelon, Francois, *Telemachus, Son of Ulysses* ed. Patrick Riley. Cambridge: Cambridge University Press, 1994.

Fisch, Audrey A., Anne K. Mellor and Esther H. Schor (eds). *The Other Mary Shelley: Beyond 'Frankenstein'*. New York and Oxford: Oxford University Press, 1993.

Fisch, Audrey A., 'Plaguing Politics: AIDS, Deconstruction, and *The Last Man*', in *Other*, pp.267–86.

Florescu, Radu, *In Search of Frankenstein: Exploring the Myths Behind Mary Shelley's Monster*. London: Robson Books, 1996.

Ford, John, *The Chronicle History of Perkin Warbeck: A Strange Truth* ed. Peter Ure. London: Methuen, 1968.

Ford, Susan Allen, '"A name more dear": Daughters, Fathers, and Desire in *A Simple Story, The False Friend*, and *Mathilda*', in *Re-visioning Romanticism: British Women Writers, 1776–1837* eds. Carol Shiner Wilson and Joel Haefner. Philadelphia: University of Pennsylvania Press, 1994, pp.51–71.

Forry, Steven Earl, *Hideous Progenies: Dramatizations of 'Frankenstein' from the Nineteenth-Century to the Present*. Philadelphia: University of Pennsylvania Press, 1990.

Franci, Giovanni, 'A Mirror of the Future: Vision and Apocalypse in Mary Shelley's *The Last Man*', in *Mary Shelley, Modern Critical Views* ed. Harold Bloom. New York: Chelsea House Pubs., 1985, pp.181–91.

Garbin, Lidia, '*The Fortunes of Perkin Warbeck*: Walter Scott in the Writings of Mary Shelley', in *Romanticism on the Net*, 6, May, 1997.

—— 'Mary Shelley and Walter Scott: *The Fortunes of Perkin Warbeck* and the Historical Novel', in *Fictions*, pp.150–63.

Garrett, Margaret Davenport, 'Writing and Re-writing Incest in Mary Shelley's *Mathilda*', in *The Keats-Shelley Journal*. XLV (1996), pp.44–60.

Gash, Norman, *Aristocracy and People: Britain 1815–1865*. London: Edward Arnold, 1979.

Gerson, Noel, *Daughter of Earth and Water: A Biography of Mary Wollstonecraft Shelley*. New York: William Morrow & Co., 1973.

Gilbert, Sandra M., and Susan Gubar, *The Madwoman in the Attic: The Woman Writer and the Nineteenth-Century Literary Imagination*. New Haven and London: Yale University Press, 1979.

Gillingham, Lauren, 'Romancing Experience: The Seduction of Mary Shelley's *Matilda*', in *Studies in Romanticism* 42.2 (2003), pp.251–69.

Gittings, Robert, and Jo Manton, *Claire Clairmont and the Shelleys, 1789–1879*. Oxford and New York: Oxford University Press, 1992.

Glut, Donald F., *The Frankenstein Legend: A Tribute to Mary Shelley and Boris Karloff*. Netuchen, N. J.: The Scarecrow Press, 1973.

Godwin, William, *Of Population: An Enquiry Concerning the Power of Increase in the Numbers of Mankind, Being an Answer to Mr. Malthus's Essay on That Subject*. London: Longman, Hurst, Rees, Orme and Brown, 1820.

—— *Collected Novels and Memoirs of William Godwin*. 8 Vols. Gen. Ed. Mark Philp. London: William Pickering, 1992.

—— *Political and Philosophical Writings of William Godwin*. 7 Vols. Gen. Ed. Mark Philp. London: William Pickering, 1993.

Goldsmith, Steven, 'Apocalypse and Gender: Mary Shelley's *The Last Man*', in *Unbuilding Jerusalem: Apocalypse and Romantic Representation*. Ithaca and London: Cornell University Press, 1993, pp.261–313.

Gonda, Caroline, *Reading Daughters' Fictions, 1709–1834: Novels and Society from Manley to Edgeworth*. Cambridge: Cambridge University Press, 1996.

—— '*Lodore* and Fanny Derham's Story', in *Women's Writing*. 6.3 (1999), pp.329–44.

Gordon, Lyndall, *Mary Wollstonecraft: A New Genus*. London: Little, Brown, 2005.

Grainville, Jean-Babtiste Cousin de, *The Last Man, or Omegarus and Syderia, A Romance in Futurity*. 2 Vols. London: Dutton, 1806.

Groseclose, Barbara, 'The Incest Motif in Shelley's *The Cenci*', in *Comparative Drama*. 19.3 (1985), pp.222–39.

Handwerk, Gary, 'History, trauma, and the limits of the liberal imagination: William Godwin's historical fiction', in eds. Tilottama Rajan and Julia M. Wright. *Romanticism, history, and the possibilities of genre*. Cambridge: Cambridge University Press, 1998, pp.64–85.

Harpold, Terence, '"Did you get *Mathilda* from Papa?": Seduction Fantasy and the Circulation of Mary Shelley's *Mathilda*', in *Studies in Romanticism*. 28 (1987), pp.49–67.

Hartman, Geoffrey H., 'Romanticism and Anti-Self-Consciousness', in *Beyond Formalism: Literary Essays, 1958–1970*. New Haven and London: Yale University Press, 1970, pp.298–310.

Hill-Miller, Katherine C., *'My Hideous Progeny': Mary Shelley, William Godwin, and the Father-Daughter Relationship*. Newark: University of Delaware Press, 1995.

Hilton, Boyd, *A Mad, Bad, and Dangerous People?: England 1783–1846*. Oxford: Clarendon Press, 2006.

Himes, Audra Dibert, '"Knew shame, and knew desire": Ambivalence as Structure in Mary Shelley's *Mathilda*', in *Iconoclastic*, pp.115–29.

Hoeveler, Diane Long, 'Screen-Memories and Fictionalized Autobiography: Mary Shelley's *Mathilda* and "The Mourner"', in *Nineteenth-Century Contexts*. 27.4 (2005), pp.365–81.

Hogg, Thomas Jefferson, *The Life of Percy Bysshe Shelley*. 2 Vols. London. Edward Moxon, 1858.

Holmes, Richard, *Shelley: The Pursuit*. London: Weidenfield & Nicolson, 1974.

—— 'Shelley Undrowned', in *Interrupted Lives* ed. Andrew Motion. London: The National Portrait Gallery, 2004, pp.22–35.

Hopkins, Lisa, 'The Self and the Monstrous: *The Fortunes of Perkin Warbeck*', in *Iconoclastic*, pp.260–74.

—— 'Death and the Castrated: The Complex Psyches of *Valperga*', in *Romanticism on the Net*. 40, November, 2005.

Jacobus, Mary, 'Replacing the Race of Mothers: AIDS and *The Last Man*', in *First Things: The Maternal Imaginary in Literature, Art, and Psychoanalysis*. New York and London: Routledge, 1995, pp.105–25.

Johnson, Barbara, '*The Last Man*', in *Other*, pp.258–66.

Jonas, Hans, *The Gnostic Religion: The Message of the Alien God and the Beginnings of Christianity* (1958). 2nd edn., revised. London: Routledge, 1992.

Jones, Frederick L., ed. *Maria Gisborne & Edward E. Williams, Shelley's Friends: Their Journals and Letters*. Norman: University of Oklahoma Press, 1951.

Jump, Harriet, ed. *Lives of the Great Romantics III: Godwin, Wollstonecraft & Mary Shelley By Their Contemporaries*. II. *Wollstonecraft*. London: Pickering & Chatto, 1999.

Kegan Paul, C., *William Godwin: His Friends and Contemporaries*. 2 Vols. London: Henry S. King & Co., 1876.

Kelly, Gary, *The English Jacobin Novel: 1780–1805*. Oxford: Clarendon Press, 1976.

—— *English Fiction of the Romantic Period, 1789–1830*. London and New York: Longman, 1989.

—— 'Last Men: Hemans and Mary Shelley in the 1820s', in *Romanticism*, 3.2 (1997), pp.198–208.

Ketterer, David, *Frankenstein's Creation: The Book, The Monster, and Human Reality*. Victoria, B. C.: Victoria University Press, 1979.

Kilgour, Maggie, '"One Immortality": The Shaping of the Shelleys in *The Last Man*', in *European Romantic Review*. 16.5 (2005), pp.563–88.

Klancher, Jon, 'Godwin and the genre reformers: on necessity and contingency in romantic narrative theory', in *Romanticism, history, and the possibilities of genre*, pp.21–38.

Knoepflmacher, U. C., 'Thoughts on the Aggression of Daughters', in *Endurance*, pp.88–119.

Kristeva, Julia, *Powers of Horror: An Essay on Abjection*. Trans. Leon S. Roudiez. New York: Columbia University Press, 1982.

Kucich, Greg, 'Mary Shelley's *Lives* and the Reengendering of History', in *Times*, pp.198–213.

—— 'Biographer', in *Companion*, pp.226–41.

Leader, Zacharay, *Revision and Romantic Authorship*. Oxford: Clarendon Press, 1996.

Leask, Nigel, *Curiosity and the Aesthetics of Travel Writing, 1770–1840*. Oxford and New York: Oxford University Press, 2002.

Levine, George, and U. C. Knoepflmacher (eds), *The Endurance of 'Frankenstein': Essays on Mary Shelley's Novel*. Berkeley and Los Angeles: University of California Press, 1979.

Levine, George, 'The Ambiguous Heritage of *Frankenstein*', in *Endurance*, pp.3–30.

Lew, Joseph, 'God's Sister: History and Ideology in *Valperga*', in *Other*, pp.159–81.

Locke, John, 'Some Thoughts Concerning Education', in *The Clarendon Edition of the Works of John Locke* (eds), John W. and Jean S. Yolton. Oxford: Clarendon Press, 1989.

Lokke, Kari E., '*The Last Man*', in *Companion*, pp.116–34.

Lomax, William, 'Epic Reversals in Mary Shelley's *The Last Man*: Romantic Irony and the Roots of Science Fiction', in *Contours of the Fantastic: Selected Essays from the Eighth International Conference on the Fantastic in the Arts* ed. Michael K. Langford. New York: Greenwood Press, 1990, pp.7–17.

Loudon (Webb), Jane, *The Mummy! A Tale of the Twenty-Second Century* ed. Alan Rauch. Ann Arbor: University of Michigan Press, 1994.

Luke, Jnr, Hugh, 'The Last Man: Mary Shelley's Myth of the Solitary', in *The Prairie Schooner*. 39.4 (1965), pp.316–27.

Lyles, W. H., *Mary Shelley: An Annotated Bibliography*. New York and London: Garland Publishing, Inc., 1975.

Lynch, Deidre, 'Historical Novelist', in *Companion*, pp.135–50.

Machiavelli, Niccolò di Bernardo, *The Portable Machiavelli* (eds), Trans. Peter Bondanella and Mark Musa. Harmondsworth: Penguin, 1979.

Malthus, Thomas Robert, *An Essay on the Principle of Population* ed. Philip Appleman. New York and London: W. W. Norton, 1976.

Marshall, David, *The Surprising Effects of Sympathy: Marivaux, Diderot, Rousseau, and Mary Shelley*. Chicago and London: University of Chicago Press, 1988.

Marshall, Mrs Julian (Florence), *The Life and Letters of Mary Wollstonecraft Shelley*. 2 Vols. London: Richard Bentley and Sons, 1889.

Marshall, Peter H., *William Godwin*. New Haven and London: Yale University Press, 1984.

McWhir, Anne, 'Teaching the Monster to Read: Mary Shelley's Education and *Frankenstein*', in *The Educational Legacy of Romanticism* ed. John Willinsky. Waterloo, Ontario: Wilfrid Laurier University Press, 1990, pp.73–92.

Medwin, Thomas, *The Life of Percy Shelley*. Intro. and Commentary by H. Buxton Forman. London: Oxford University Press, 1913.

Mellor, Anne K., ed. *Romanticism and Feminism*. Bloomington and Indianapolis: Indiana University Press, 1988.

—— *Mary Shelley: Her Life, Her Fiction, Her Monsters*. New York and London: Routledge, 1989.

—— *Romanticism and Gender*. New York and London: Routledge, 1993.

—— 'Response to "The Last Man and the New History" (Greg Kucich)', in *Romantic Circles MOO Conference*, September 13, 1997.

Moers, Ellen, *Literary Women*. Garden City: Doubleday, 1976.

—— 'Female Gothic', in *Endurance*, pp.77–87.

Morton, Timothy, ed. *A Routledge Literary Sourcebook on Mary Shelley's 'Frankenstein'*. London and New York: Routledge, 2002.

Moskal, Jeanne, '"To speak in Sanchean phrase": Cervantes and the Politics of Mary Shelley's *History of a Six Weeks' Tour*', in *Times*, pp.18–37.

Mulvey-Roberts, Marie and Janet Todd (eds), *Women's Writing*. 6:3 (1999), Special Number, *Mary Shelley*.

Myers, Mitzi, 'Mary Wollstonecraft Godwin Shelley: The Female Author between Public and Private Spheres', in *Times*, pp.160–72.

Nitchie, Eizabeth, *Mary Shelley: 'Author of Frankenstein'*. New Brunswick: Rutgers University Press, 1953.

—— 'Mary Shelley's *Mathilda*: An Unpublished Story and Its Biographical Significance', in *Studies in Philology*. XL.3 (1943), pp.447–62.

O'Dea, Gregory, 'Prophetic History and Textuality in Mary Shelley's *The Last Man*', in *Papers on Language and Literature*. 28.3 (1992), pp.283–304.

O'Neill, Michael, '"Trying to make it as good as I can": Mary Shelley's Editing of P. B. Shelley's Poetry and Prose', in *Times*, pp.185–97.

O'Sullivan, Barbara Jane, 'Beatrice in *Valperga*: A New Cassandra', in *Other*, pp.140–58.

Ovid, *Metamorphsis*. Trans. A. D. Melville. Oxford: Oxford University Press, 1986.

Palacio, Jean de, *Mary Shelley dans son oeuvre: Contributions aux etudes shelleyennes*. Paris: Editions Klincksieck, 1969.

Paley, Morton D., '*The Last Man*: Apocalypse Without Millennium', in *Other*, pp.107–23.

Peck, Walter Edwin, 'The Biographical Element in the Novels of Mary Wollstonecraft Shelley', in *PMLA*. 38.1 (1923), pp.196–219.

Plato, *The Complete Works* ed. John M. Cooper. Indianapolis and Cambridge: Hackett Publishing Co, 1997.

Poovey, Mary, *The Proper Lady and the Woman Writer – Ideology as Style in the Works of Mary Wollstonecraft, Mary Shelley and Jane Austen*. Chicago and London: University of Chicago Press, 1984.

Pykett, Lynn, 'The Newgate Novel and sensational fiction, 1830–1868', in *The Cambridge Companion to Crime Fiction* ed. Martin Priestman. Cambridge: Cambridge University Press, 2003, pp.19–39.

Rackley, Liz, 'The Last Man's Burden: A Response to Alan Richardson's "*The Last Man* and the Plague of Empire"', in *Romantic Circles MOO Conference*, September 13, 1997.

Rajan, Tilottama, *The Supplement of Reading: Figures of Understanding in Romantic Theory and Practice*. Ithaca and London: Cornell University Press, 1990.

—— 'Mary Shelley's *Mathilda*: Melancholy and the Political Economy of Romanticism', in *Studies in the Novel*. 26.2 (1994), pp.43–68.

—— 'Between Romance and History: Possibility and Contingency in Godwin, Leibniz, and *Valperga*', in *Times*, pp.88–102.

Ready, Robert, 'Dominion of Demeter: Mary Shelley's *Mathilda*', in *The Keats-Shelley Journal*. LII (2003), pp.94–110.

Reiman, Donald, ed. *The Romantics Reviewed: Contemporary Reviews of British Romantic Writers*. Part C, *Shelley, Keats, and London Radical Writers*. 2 Vols. New York and London: Garland Publishing, 1972.

Richardson, Alan, *Literature, Education and Romanticism: Reading as a Social Practice, 1780–1832*. Cambridge: Cambridge University Press, 1994.

—— '*The Last Man* and the Plague of Empire', in *Romantic Circles MOO Conference*, September 13, 1997.

Robinson, Charles E., 'Mathilda as Dramatic Actress', in *Times*, pp.76–87.

—— and Betty T. Bennett (eds), *The Bodleian Shelley Manuscripts*. X. New York and London: Garland Publishing, 1992.

Rossington, Michael, 'Future Uncertain: The Republican Tradition and Its Destiny in *Valperga*', in *Times*, pp.103–18.

Rousseau, Jean-Jacques, *Émile*. Trans. Barbara Foxley. London: Dent, 1993.

Sambrook, A. J., 'A Romantic Theme: The Last Man', in *Forum for Modern Language Studies*. 2.1 (1966), pp.25–33.

Saunders, Julia, 'Rehabilitating he Family in Mary Shelley's *Falkner*', in *Fictions*, pp.211–23.

Schoene-Harwood, Berthold, ed. *Mary Shelley. 'Frankenstein': A Reader's Guide to Essential Criticism*. Cambridge: Icon Books, 2000.

Schor, Esther, ed. *The Cambridge Companion to Mary Shelley*. Cambridge: Cambridge University Press, 2003.

Scott, Walter, *Ivanhoe*, ed Ian Duncan. Harmondsworth: Penguin, 1996.

Seymour, Miranda, *Mary Shelley*. London: John Murray, 2000.

Shelley, Mary, Bodleian Abinger Collection. MS Dep. d. 374/1.

—— Bodleian Abinger Shelley Collection. MS Dep. d. 1.

—— Bodleian Abinger Shelley Collection MS Dep. d. 374/2.

Tales and Stories by Mary Wollstonecraft Shelley ed. Richard Garnett. London: William Patterson & Co., 1891.

—— *Mathilda* ed. Elizabeth Nitchie. *Studies in Philology.* 3 October 1959. Chapel Hill, North Carolina: The University of North Carolina Press, 1959.

—— *Mary Shelley: Collected Tales and Stories* ed. Charles E. Robinson. Baltimore and London: The Johns Hopkins University Press, 1976.

—— *Frankenstein* ed. James Reiger. Chicago: The University of Chicago Press, 1982.

—— *The Letters of Mary Wollstonecraft Shelley* ed. Betty T. Bennett. 3 Vols. Baltimore and London: The Johns Hopkins University Press, 1980–88.

—— 'Relation of the Death of the Family of the Cenci', in *The Bodleian Shelley Manuscripts.* X (eds), Charles E. Robinson and Betty T. Bennett. New York and London: Garland Publishing, 1992, pp.161–272.

—— Mary Wollstonecraft, *Mary* and *Maria*, Mary Shelley, *Matilda* ed. Janet Todd. Harmondsworth: Penguin Books, 1992.

—— *Frankenstein* ed. Johanna M. Smith. Boston. Bedford Books of St. Martin's Press, 1992.

—— *The Journals of Mary Shelley* (eds), Paula R. Feldman and Diana Scott-Kilvert. Baltimore and London: The Johns Hopkins University Press, 1987 (reprinted 1995).

—— *Selected Letters of Mary Wollstonecraft Shelley* ed. Betty T. Bennett. Baltimore and London: The Johns Hopkins University Press, 1995.

—— *The Novels and Selected Works of Mary Shelley.* Gen. Eds. Nora Crook with Pamela Clemit. 8 Vols. London: Pickering and Chatto, 1996.

—— *The Frankenstein Notebooks. A Facsimile Edition of Mary Shelley's Manuscript Novel, 1816–17 (With Alterations in the Hand of Percy Bysshe Shelley) as it Survives in Draft and Fair Copy Deposited by Lord Abinger in the Bodleian Library, Oxford (Dep. c. 477/1 and Dep. c. 534/1–2).* 2 Vols. ed. Charles E. Robinson. *Manuscripts of the Younger Romantics.* Vol. IX. New York and London: Garland Publishing, Inc., 1996.

—— *Frankenstein* ed. J. Paul Hunter. New York: W. W. Norton, 1996.

—— *The Last Man* ed. Anne McWhir. Peteborough, Ontario: Broadview, 1996.

—— *Lodore* ed. Lisa Vargo. Peterborough, Ontario: Broadview Press, 1997.

—— *Valperga* ed. Tilottama Rajan. Peterborough, Ontario: Broadview Press, 1998.

—— *Frankenstein* (eds), D. L. Macdonald and Kathleen Scherf. 2nd edn. Peterborough, Ontario: Broadview Press, 1999.

—— *Mary Shelley's Literary Lives and Other Writings*. 4 Vols. Gen. Ed. Nora Crook. London: Pickering and Chatto, 2002.

Shelley, P. B., *The Letters of Percy Bysshe Shelley*. 2 Vols. ed. Frederick L. Jones. Oxford: Clarendon Press, 1964.

—— *Shelley's Poetry and Prose* (eds), Donald H. Reiman and Sharon B. Powers. New York and London: W. W. Norton, 1977.

—— *Shelley's Prose or The Trumpet of a Prophecy* ed. David Lee Clark. (Revised Ed.) London: Fourth Estate, 1988.

—— *The Poems of Shelley, Volume I: 1804–1817* (eds), Geoffrey Matthews and Kelvin Everest. London and New York: Longman, 1989.

—— *The Poems of Shelley, Volume II: 1817–1819* (eds), Kelvin Everest and Geoffrey Matthews. London and New York: Longman, 1989.

Sites, Melissa, 'Chilvalry and Utopian Domesticity in Mary Shelley's *The Fortunes of Perkin Warbeck*', in *European Romantic Review*. 15.5 (2005), pp.525–43.

Smith, Johanna M., *Frankenstein*. Boston: Bedford Books, 1992.

—— *Mary Shelley*. New York: Twayne Publishers, 1996.

Spark, Muriel, *Mary Shelley*. London: Constable, 1988.

Stafford, Fiona, *The Last of the Race*. Oxford: Oxford University Press, 1994.

—— '*Lodore*: a Tale of the Present Time', in *Fictions*, pp.181–93.

St Clair, William, *The Godwins and the Shelleys: The Biography of a Family*. London and Boston: Faber and Faber, 1989.

—— 'The Impact of *Frankenstein*', in *Times*, pp.38–63.

—— *The Reading Nation in the Romantic Period*. Cambridge: Cambridge University Press, 2004.

Stelzig, Eugene, '"Though It Were The Deadliest Sin To Love As We Have Loved": The Romantic Idealization of Incest', in *European Romantic Review*. 5.2 (1995), pp.230–51.

Sterrenburg, Lee, '*The Last Man*: Anatomy of Failed Revolutions', in *Nineteenth-Century Fiction*. 33.3 (1978), pp.324–47.

Sunstein, Emily W., *Mary Shelley: Romance and Reality*. Baltimore: The Johns Hopkins University Press, 1989.

Sussman, Charlotte, '"Islanded in the World": Cultural Memory and Human Mobility', in *PMLA*. 118.2 (2003), pp.286–301.

Synder, Robert Lance, 'Apocalypse and Indeterminacy in Mary Shelley's *The Last Man*', in *Studies in Romanticism*. 17.4 (1978), pp.435–52.

Thomas, Sophie, 'The End of the Fragment, the Problem of the Preface: Proliferation and Finality in *The Last Man*', in *Fictions*, pp.22–38.

Thorslev, Peter L., 'Incest as Romantic Symbol', in *Comparative Literature*. 2 (1965), pp.41–58.

Trelawny, Edward, *The Last Days of Shelley and Byron: Being the Complete Text of Trelawny's Recollections edited, with additions from contemporary sources* ed. J. E. Morpurgo. New York: Anchor Books, 1960.

—— *Records of Shelley, Byron, and the Author* ed. David Wright. Harmondsworth: Penguin, 1973.

—— *Adventures of a Younger Son* ed. William St Clair. London: Oxford University Press, 1974.

—— *Recollections of the Last Days of Shelley and Byron* ed. David Crane. London: Robinson, 2000.

Vargo, Lisa, '*Lodore* and the "Novel of Society"', in *Women's Writing* 6:3 (1999), pp.425–40.

—— 'Further Thoughts on the Education of Daughters: *Lodore* as an Imagined Conversation with Wollstonecraft', in *Mary Wollstonecraft and Mary Shelley: Writing Lives* (eds), Helen M. Buss, D. L. Macdonald and Anne McWhir. Waterloo, Ontario: Wilfred Laurier University Press, 2001, pp.177–87.

Virgil, *The Aeneid of Virgil*. Trans. C. Day Lewis. London: The Hogarth Press, 1952.

Volney, C. F. C., Comte de, *The Ruins: or A Survey of the Revolutions of Empires* (1791). London: J. Johnson, 1796.

Wade, Philip Tyree, *Influence and Intent in the Prose Fiction of Percy and Mary Shelley*. Ph.D diss. Chapel Hill: The University of North Carolina, 1966.

Walling, William A., *Mary Shelley*. New York: Twayne Publishers, 1972.

Webb, Samantha, 'Reading the End of the World: *The Last Man*, History, and the Agency of Romantic Authorship', in *Times*, pp.119–33.

Webb, Timothy, 'Religion of the Heart: Leigh Hunt's Tribute to Shelley', in *Keats-Shelley Review*. 7 (1992), pp.1–61.

Webster-Garrett, Erin L. *The Literary Career of Novelist Mary Shelley After 1822: Romance, Realism, and the Politics of Gender*. Lewiston, Queenston, Lampeter: The Edwin Mellon Press, 2006.

Wells, Lynn, 'The Triumph of Death: Reading and Narrative in Mary Shelley's *The Last Man*', in *Iconoclastic*, pp.212–34.

Wheeler, Michael, *English Fiction of the Victorian Period, 1830–1890*. London and New York: Longman, 1985.

White, Daniel E., 'Mary Shelley's *Valperga*: Italy and the Revision of Romantic Aestheticism', in *Fictions*, pp.75–94.

Williams, John, *Mary Shelley: A Literary Life*. London: Macmillan, 2000.

Wolfson, Susan J., 'Editorial Privilege: Mary Shelley and Percy Shelley's Audiences', in *Other*, pp.39–72.

—— 'Mary Shelley, editor', in *Companion*, pp.193–210.

Wollstonecraft, Mary, *The Works of Mary Wollstonecraft*. (Gen. Eds), Janet Todd and Marilyn Butler. 7 Vols. London: William Pickering, 1989.

—— *A Short Residence in Sweden* and William Godwin, *Memoirs of the Author of 'The Vindication of Woman'* ed. Richard Holmes. Harmondsworth: Penguin, 1987.

Wright, Julia M., '"Little England": Anxieties of Space in Mary Shelley's *The Last Man*', in *Fictions*, pp.129–49.

Zonana, Joyce, '"They Will Prove the Truth of My Tale": Safie's Letters as a Feminist Core of Mary Shelley's *Frankenstein*', *The Journal of Narrative Technique*. 21 (1991), pp.170–84.

Index

Aaron, Jane 194n
Agrippa, Cornelius 24, 25, 33
Allbright, Richard S. 110–11, 193n, 196n
Allen, Graham 182n, 185n, 186n, 188n, 190n, 195n, 203n
Alfieri, Vittorio 48–9, 53, 180, 190n
An, Young-Ok 195n

Bacon, Francis 118
Bakhtin, M. M. 200n
Baldick, Chris 17, 186n, 196n, 198n
Barbour, Judith 189n
Baxter, William 19, 20
Bennett, Betty T. 3, 4, 5–6, 10, 11, 13–15, 44, 65, 67, 85, 90, 118, 130–1, 135, 177, 182n, 183n, 184n, 189n, 191n, 193n, 194n, 198n, 199n, 202n, 203n
Bentley, Richard 8–9, 118
Blumberg, Jane 45, 46, 75, 76, 86, 91, 94, 113, 138, 189n, 192n, 193n, 194n, 195n, 198n, 199n
Botting, Fred 17, 185n
Bowring, John 118
Brewer, William D. 192n, 198n, 202n
Briggs, Asa 122, 198n
Bulwer, Edward 142–5, 169–70, 171
Bunnell, Charlene E. 117, 152, 190n, 197n, 200n, 201n, 203n
Burke, Edmund 101, 106
Butler, Marilyn 183n
Byron, Allegra 4
Byron, George Gordon 1, 4–5, 6, 7, 9, 44, 47–8, 90, 91, 94–5, 99, 100, 101, 103, 109, 124, 147, 148, 149, 159, 162, 163, 170, 177, 195n, 201n
  Cain 103
  Childe Harold's Pilgrimage 159
  Heaven and Earth 103
  Manfred 47

Calderón de la Barca, Pedro 48, 115
Campbell, Alexandra 122
Campbell, Thomas 91
Canning, George 122–3, 198n
Cantor, Paul A. 92, 195n
Canuel, Mark 105, 196n
Carlyle, Thomas 142
Caruth, Cathy 192n
Castruccio Castracani 65–74, 77–89, 96, 99, 103, 107, 118, 126, 131, 132, 170
Cenci, Beatrice 48–50, 54, 190n, 191n
Cenci, family 48–50, 190n
Chatterjee, Ranita 189n, 202n
Church, Richard 10, 184n
Clairmont, Jane (Claire) 3–5, 6, 44, 166, 201n
Clemit, Pamela 43–4, 70, 184n, 185n, 187n, 188n, 189n, 190n, 192n, 193n, 195n, 202n, 203n
Colburn, Henry 8, 118
Colley, Linda 121, 198n
Conger, Syndy McMillen 193n
Crane, David 183n
Crocker, Thomas Crofton 118
Croker, John Wilson 8, 9
Cronin, Richard 143–4, 147, 200n
Crook, Nora 11–12, 19, 64, 65, 66, 92–3, 113, 184n, 185n, 187n, 189n, 191n, 192n, 195n, 197n, 202n
Curran, Amelia 63, 114
Curran, Stuart 11, 184n, 192n
Cuvier, Georges 103

Dante Alighieri 51, 53, 54, 73, 88–9, 190n, 191n
Derrida, Jacques 106, 107, 186n, 196n
Dickens, Charles 142
Disraeli, Benjamin 142
Dowden, Edward 139, 182n, 199n
Dunleavy, Gareth 197n
Dunn, Jane 188n, 190n, 199n

Eberle-Sinatra, Michael   194n
Ellis, Kate Ferguson   139, 165, 184n,
   200n, 201n
Engelberg, Karsten Klejs   184n

Favret, Mary   203n
Feldman, Paula R.   185n
Fénelon, François   52, 85, 167,
   190n
Fisch, Audrey A.   7, 12, 105, 110,
   196n, 197n
Fischer, Doucet Devin   118, 199n
Florescu, Radu   185n
Ford, John   119, 197n
Ford, Susan Allen   188n
Forry, Steven Earl   185n
Franci, Giovanni   196–7n
Francis II (Emperor of Austria)   14

Garbin, Lidia   120, 126, 198n
Garnett, Richard   139, 199n
Garrett, Margaret Davenport   189n,
   190n
Gash, Norman   198n
Gatteschi, Ferdinando   180, 185n
George IV   122
Gerson, Noel   142, 193n, 200n
Gilbert, Sandra M.   194n, 195n
Gillingham, Lauren   188n
Gisborne, Maria   41, 44, 48, 63, 64,
   95, 103, 139, 141, 160, 163, 188n
Gisborne, John   48, 188n
Gittings, Robert   183n
Glut, Donald F.   185n
Godwin, William   2, 4, 5, 7, 8, 9, 13,
   18–23, 24, 25, 29–31, 32, 34, 35,
   41, 42, 43, 44, 45, 47, 48, 52,
   61–2, 69–70, 76, 84, 85, 87, 98,
   102, 105, 108, 112, 114, 119,
   126, 130, 131, 133, 137, 139,
   143, 144, 145, 146, 150, 154,
   160, 164, 166, 167, 168–70, 171,
   172, 174, 176, 186n, 187n, 188n,
   191n, 195n, 196n, 202n
   Deloraine   35, 164, 169–70, 171
   Caleb Williams   25, 44, 59, 61,
      143, 150, 159, 169, 170, 172,
      186n
   Cloudesley   145, 158, 167, 168
   Enquirer, The   20–1, 22, 22–3, 34

Fleetwood   35, 85
Mandeville   30, 35, 48, 70, 85,
   133, 174
*Memoirs of the Author of
   'Vindication of the Rights of
   Woman'*   4, 166, 202n
'Of History and Romance'   69–71
Political Justice   20–3, 29–30,
   34, 62, 63, 85, 87, 167,
   191n
St Leon   35
Goethe, J. W.   27
Goldsmith, Steven   193n, 194n,
   195n
Gonda, Caroline   188n, 200n
Gore, Catherine   142
Gordon, Katherine   128, 129–30,
   133–4, 135–7, 199n
Grainville, Jean-Babtiste, Cousin
   de   91, 194n
Groseclose, Barbara   189n
Gubar, Susan   194n, 195n
Guiccioli, Teresa   95, 123

Hall, Edward   118
Handwerk, Gary   192n
Harpold, Terence   44, 188n
Hartman, Geoffrey H.   187n
Hazlitt, William   142
Henry VII   119, 122, 123–5, 127,
   132, 133, 135, 199n
Hill-Miller, Katherine   52, 154–5,
   164, 186n, 188n, 189n, 190n,
   201n
Hilton, Boyd   120, 198n
Himes, Audra Dibert   189n
Hobhouse, John Cam   197n
Hoeveler, Diane Long   188n
Hogg, Thomas Jefferson   2, 3
Holcroft, Thomas   170
Holinshed, Raphaell   118
Holmes, Richard   137, 199n, 202n
Homer   52
Hood, Thomas   91
Hopkins, Lisa   86, 193n, 198n
Hume, David   118, 191n
Hunt, Leigh   3, 5, 7, 42, 97, 142, 150,
   161
Hunt, John   97
Hunter, J. Paul   185n

Imlay, Gilbert   4
Imlay, Fanny   4, 62, 157
Irving, Washington   15

Jacobus, Mary   196n
James IV   119, 128
Johnson, Barbara   105
Johnson, Samuel (Dr)   38
Jonas, Hans   192–3n

Keats, John   7, 114, 197n
Kegan Paul, C.   182n, 202n
Kelly, Gary   142, 194n, 195n, 200n
Ketterer, David   185–6n, 187n
Kilgour, Maggie   194n
Klancher, Jon   192n
Knoepflmacher, U. C.   11, 184n,
    188n
Kock, Charles Paul de   148
Kristeva, Julia   46, 189n
Kucich, Greg   203n

Lafayette, General   14, 122
Lardner, Dr Dionysius   179–80
La Rochefoucauld, François de   36
Leader, Zacharay   187n
Leask, Nigel   197n
Leibniz, G. W.   69
Levine, George   11–12
Lew, Joseph   191n
Lewis, Matthew (Monk)   48
Locke, John   22, 87, 186n
Lokke, Kari E.   196n
Lomax, William   196n
Loudon, Jane (Webb)   114, 197n
Luke, Jnr., Hugh J.   193n
Lyles, W. H.   197n
Lynch, Deidre   70, 117, 192n, 197n

Machiavelli, Niccolò   66, 67, 68, 69,
    81
Malthus, Thomas Robert   102, 108,
    196n
Manton, Jo   183n
Marshall, David   31–2, 187n
Marshall, Florence (Julian)   2–3, 5,
    182n, 186n, 188n, 190n, 202n
Marshall, Peter H.   202n
Macdonald, D. L.   185n, 199n
Mazzeo, Tilar J.   203n

McWhir, Anne   26, 92–3, 113, 187n,
    194n, 195n, 197n, 200n
Medwin, Thomas   3, 201n
Mellor, Anne K.   7, 12, 25, 92,
    105–6, 141, 152, 157, 161,
    163–4, 183n, 187n, 188n, 189n,
    191–2n, 195n, 196n, 200n, 201n
Mérimée, Propser   15
Milton, John   23, 28, 38, 98, 147
Moers, Ellen   184n
Morgan, Sydney, Lady   15
Morton, Timothy   185n, 198n
Moskal, Jeanne   200n, 203n
Murray, John   118
Myers, Mitzi   14, 185n

Napoleon, Bonaparte   67, 114, 124
Nitchie, Elizabeth   184n, 187n, 188n,
    190n, 202n

O'Dea, Gregory   193n
Ollier, Charles   139, 143, 152, 160
O'Neil, Michael   203n
Orr, Clarissa Campbell   203n
O'Sullivan, Barbara Jane   195n, 200n
Ovid   48–9, 51, 190n
Owen, Robert Dale   120–1

Palacio, Jean de   184n, 190n, 197n,
    198n
Paley, Morton D.   103, 193–4n
Paracelsus   33
Payne, John Howard   123
Peacock, Thomas Love   3, 66, 192n
Peck, Walter Edwin   193n
Plato   56, 57, 58, 61, 84
Plutarch   28
Polwhele, Richard   166
Poovey, Mary   3, 138, 164, 182n,
    199n, 201n
Pykett, Lynn   170, 202n

Rackley, Liz   195n
Rajan, Tilottama   46, 47, 61, 65, 66,
    68, 69–70, 189n, 190n, 191n,
    192n, 193n
Ready, Robert   190n
Reiger, James   187n
Reiman, Donald   183n, 184n, 195n
Reni, Guido   48

Richardson, Alan   186n, 195n
Robinson, Charles E.   7, 185n, 187n, 190n
Rosseau, Jean-Jacques   20–1, 24, 25, 32, 36, 37, 38, 186n, 187n
Rossington, Michael   67, 191n

Sambrook, A. J.   194n
Saunders and Otley   160
Saunders, Julia   165, 168, 201n, 202n
Schoene-Harwood, Berthold   185n
Scherf, Kathleen   185n
Schor, Esther   7, 12, 183n
Scott, Sir Walter   7, 9, 70, 118, 120, 123, 127, 130, 144, 183n
Scott-Kilvert, Diana   185n
Seymour, Miranda   62, 117, 190n
Shakespeare   19, 175
  Hamlet   175–7
  Macbeth   107–8
  Richard III   19
Shelley, Charles   4
Shelley, Clara Everina   42, 62
Shelley, Harriet   4, 5, 62
Shelley, Ianthe   4
Shelley, Jane, Lady   2
Shelley, Mary
  Falkner   138, 143, 160–78
  'Fields of Fancy, The'   42, 45, 48, 55–8, 60, 61, 62
  Frankenstein   1, 6–10, 11, 12, 13, 17–40, 41, 45, 61, 64, 65, 90, 95, 123, 126, 139, 140, 142, 143, 161, 186n, 187n, 198n
  History of a Six Weeks' Tour   116
  Last Man, The   64, 76, 90–116, 122, 161
  Lives   179–80
  Lodore   36, 138–59, 160, 161, 162, 164, 165, 166, 169
  Matilda   12, 41–63, 64, 65, 92, 161, 164, 177, 187n, 188n, 190n
  'Note on The Cenci'   48, 55
  'Note on Prometheus Unbound'   22, 75–6
  Perkin Warbeck   64, 86, 117–37, 158
  Poetical Works of P. B. Shelley (ed)   48, 75–6, 179

Posthumous Poems of P. B. Shelley (ed)   3, 97, 193n
  Proserpine   190n
  Rambles   14, 180–1
  'Relation of the Death of the Family of the Cenci'   49, 189n, 190n
  'Review of Cloudesley'   145, 158
  Valperga   10, 44, 57, 64–89, 96, 99, 107–8, 118, 130–1, 161, 180, 191n, 192n, 193n
  'Villani, Giovanni'   66
Shelley, P. B.   1–6, 7, 8, 9, 10, 15, 31, 33, 34, 35, 42, 44, 45, 47, 48–51, 52, 55, 56, 58, 60, 66, 67, 75–7, 82, 87–8, 89, 90, 91, 94, 95, 96, 97, 105, 106, 107, 111, 112, 114, 116, 122, 130, 134, 137, 179, 181, 189n, 190n, 199n
  Adonais   114
  Alastor   52, 54
  Cenci, The   48–51, 55
  Laon and Cythna   48
  'Mutability'   35
  'Philosophical View of Reform'   75–7
  Poetical Works   48, 75–6
  Posthumous Poems   3, 97, 193n
  Prometheus Unbound   22, 35, 57, 58, 67, 75–7, 82, 84, 111, 159, 190n, 192n
  Revolt of Islam   48
  Triumph of Life, The   97, 108, 111, 134
  Queen Mab   4, 82, 87–9
Shelley, Sir Percy Florence   2
Shelley, Sir Timothy   3, 5, 45, 158, 179, 180
Shelley, William   42
Sismondi, Simonde de   66–7, 192n
Sites, Melissa   117, 197n, 198n
Smith, Johanna M.   161, 185n, 192n
Socrates   56
Spark, Muriel   45, 46, 125, 131, 184n, 189n, 193n, 198n
Stafford, Fiona   144, 146, 199n, 200–1n
St Clair, William   7–9, 183n
Stelzig, Eugene   189n
Sterrenburg, Lee   194n

Sunstein, Emily W.   2, 117, 142, 182n, 183n, 189n, 197n
Sussman, Charlotte   195n
Synder, Robert Lance   193n

Tegrimi, Niccolò   66
Thackeray, William Makepeace   142
Thomas, Sophie   90, 97, 194n, 195n
Thorslev, Peter L.   189n
Trelawny, Edward John   3, 5, 6, 14, 120, 122, 161, 170, 183n, 198n
Todd, Janet   62, 63, 190n

Vargo, Lisa   140, 157, 195n, 199n, 200–1n, 203n
Villani, Giovanni   66
Virgil   174
Volney, Constantin François Chasseboeuf, Comte de   25, 27

Wade, Philip Tyree   199n
Walling, William A.   125–6, 131, 198n, 202n
Walpole, Horace   48
Webb, Samantha   196n
Webb, Timothy   182n

Webster-Garrett, Erin L.   158, 200n, 201n, 202n
Wells, Lynn   98, 194n, 196n
Wheeler, Michael   142, 200n
White, Daniel E.   192n
Wilhelmina of Bohemia   66, 77–8
Williams, Edward Ellerker   44
Williams, Jane   44, 158, 161
Williams, John   146, 191n, 193n, 200n, 202n
Wolfson, Susan J.   203n
Wollstonecraft, Mary   4, 6, 12, 36–40, 55, 61, 62, 84, 131, 139, 140, 141, 147, 157, 166, 168, 174, 186n
   'Cave of Fancy, The'   55
   The Wrongs of Woman; or, Maria   61, 159, 174
   A Vindication of the Rights of Woman   36–40
Wordsworth, William   102, 106
Wright, Francis   15, 120–1, 122, 125, 157
Wright, Julia M.   195n

Zonana, Joyce   37–8, 187n